CASH FOR HONOURS

CASH FOR HONOURS

THE STORY OF MAUNDY GREGORY

ANDREW COOK

THE HISTORY PRESS

First published 2008

The History Press
Cirencester Road, Chalford
Stroud, Gloucestershire, GL6 8PE

British Library Cataloguing in Publication Data.
A catalogue record for this book is available from the British Library.

ISBN 978 07509 4768 8

Typesetting and origination by The History Press Ltd
Printed and bound in Great Britain

Contents

Acknowledgements

I am greatly indebted to members of Maundy Gregory's family (Anna-May Gregory, Benjamin Gregory, Elizabeth Gregory, Gwen Gregory and Viola Gregory); William Lloyd George (3rd Viscount Tenby and grandson of David Lloyd George); Professor Derrick Pounder (Senior Home Office Forensic Pathologist and Head of Forensic Medicine, University of Dundee); Rosalind Rodway (granddaughter of Superintendent Arthur Askew); Julian Thomson (grandson of Sir Basil Thomson); Elaine Quigley (British Institute of Graphologists); and Norman Shaw (grandson of Harry Shaw). I would also like to thank the many heirs and descendents of those ennobled during the period 1917–1924, too numerous to mention here individually, whose generosity in making available family papers and records has been invaluable to my research.

I am also grateful to Bill Adams; Jordan Auslander; Dmitry Belanovsky; Dr Luca Carboni (Archivio Segreto Vaticano, Rome); Lord Clark of Windermere; Anne Clarke (Special Collections, Birmingham University Library); Brian Enstone; Lynda Fagan; Dr Nicholas Hiley; John Hodgson (Special Collections, John Rylands Library, University of Manchester); Helen Langley (Bodleian Library, University of Oxford); John Lidstone; the late Eileen McCormick; Lindsay Simitar; Bina Sudra (Parliamentary Archives); Phil Tomaselli; Graham Salt; Jane Walsh (British Library Newspapers); and John Wells (Department of Manuscripts, Cambridge University Library).

A special thank you also goes to Alison Clark; David Cook; Monica Finch; Ingrid Lock; Hannah Renier; Jill Thew; Chris Williamson and Daksha Chauhan. Finally, my gratitude must be expressed to Jacqueline Mitchell and Jane Entrican at Sutton Publishing for their help and support in this project.

Preface

Had it not been for his arrest and conviction under the 1925 Honours (Prevention of Abuses) Act in 1933, the name of John Arthur Maundy Gregory would today be unknown to history, rather than being a byword for political corruption and the sale of honours. This sullied reputation has been further blackened over the past four decades by suggestions that Gregory was a possible double murderer into the bargain.

Whenever the issue of cash for honours is discussed today, the names of Maundy Gregory and Lloyd George are held up almost as warning placards. History has not only overlooked Gregory's equally successful rival, Harry Shaw, but has failed to bring to book the other political leaders of the day who in reality eclipsed Lloyd George in terms of honours sales and political chicanery. Their reputations today remain spotless and polished.

Furthermore, it would now appear that contrary to the accepted version of Gregory's frequently told story, his arrest may not have been an accident of fate, the result of hubris or of ill luck on his part, but the result of a concerted and ruthless attempt by a group of highly placed individuals to monopolise and control the honours market.

Nearly a century of falsehood and fantasy has obscured the reality of Maundy Gregory's life. Like his one time acquaintance 'Ace of Spies' Sidney Reilly, Gregory was something of a Walter Mitty character, concocting a host of tall stories about himself that have only served to muddy the water still further. To piece together an accurate account of his mysterious life and to establish the reality behind the honours racket of the early twentieth century, it has been necessary to cast aside the myths and fantasies and to return to primary sources.

The ability to draw on a host of newly uncovered material has helped immeasurably in this task.

CHAPTER ONE

The Visitors

A wealthy provincial supplicant – an elderly, complacent, white-haired, wing-collared manufacturer, say, of socks or sewer pipes – visiting the tall, narrow, old house that was 38 Parliament Street in the 1920s, might find it a discomfiting experience. Power was implicit in the very location, within yards of the Houses of Parliament, Scotland Yard and the Home Office. Westminster Abbey, whose Archbishop still mattered, was across the Square. This was the political hub of an Empire which still covered a third of the world's inhabited land.[1]

Inside No. 38, respectful attendants wore uniform which identified them as messengers from the House of Commons.[2] The visitor was escorted up to the first floor, where he would sit in an ante-room, a sombre and claustrophobic chamber with a gothic stained-glass window, reading back numbers of the *Whitehall Gazette* and awaiting his audience with the great eminence.

A soft voice.

'Mr Maundy Gregory is ready to see you now.'

Maundy Gregory, whose name was so often whispered between very rich men, proved to be not particularly tall and rather chubby, with a beaming smile. He wore an expensive suit, a tie which signalled quiet affluence, and brilliantly polished shoes. He would take his place behind a large desk with three telephones and a bewildering bank of switches and tiny lights, and gaze benignly down upon his seated guest; there was something of the bishop in his demeanour, something that inspired respect, and wonder too, as the gold and pearl cufflinks flashed and Mr Maundy Gregory, his eyes knowing but sympathetic as the guest spoke, would remove a rose diamond the size of a pebble from his inner pocket and turn it thoughtfully between his plump, beringed fingers. He listened; he returned a few confidences, he hinted at social opportunities as yet undreamed of – perhaps an invitation to luncheon with a Lord, or a King – and the interview would be interrupted by a call from the Palace, or Number 10. The guest's uncomfortably intimidated feeling turned slowly to awe; then, to trust and growing confidence. At last he had found the captain who could navigate him through unfamiliar social waters. And when the visitor was visibly puffed up with his own good judgement, Mr Gregory would broach a proposition.

The *mise en scène* was everything. Long ago, before the Great War, Maundy Gregory had been a theatrical producer. He understood that first impressions mattered; that opulent packaging inspires confidence. The buyer must have faith that Maundy Gregory alone could deliver the goods.

Hence the telephone calls from Number 10. Few people knew Gregory well; one who did was Mr Pengelly, his accountant, and years later he would say that the Chief had looked all over London for a house called Number 10 so that he could dupe his clients into thinking that these calls came not from his home, but from the Prime Minister, across the road in Downing Street.

Maybe the house came first, and the number was a bonus. For Maundy Gregory would never look 'all over London' for a house; he was truly at ease only in Mayfair, St James's and Soho (and he certainly never wanted to see Southampton again). But 10 Hyde Park Terrace, which fell just a quarter of a mile north-west of his golden triangle, was Maundy Gregory's perfect bolt-hole. It was a pale stucco mansion on the Bayswater Road, set behind area railings, with bay windows overlooking Hyde Park. It stood just a few minutes' walk from Marble Arch. From a wide entrance hall, stairs ascended to a dog-leg turn at a half-landing, and upwards to grand reception rooms. Beyond the windows facing the park, a pretty iron balcony ran across the entire width of the first floor. More stairs rose to a second half-landing and a second floor, where Maundy Gregory had his private quarters. Above this were separate stairs to third and fourth floors, originally intended for children and servants but now unoccupied.[3]

On the ground floor, enjoying views across the road to the leafy Park at the front, and from another tall bay window giving onto the lawn at the back, lived Mrs Edith Marion Rosse, now in her fifties. She had been Gregory's closest friend since his days in the theatre.

Although it stood on the less fashionable north side of the Park, their neighbours at Hyde Park Terrace included a Member of Parliament, one of the Harmsworth dynasty, and several people of title. Snobbery and late-Georgian charm were not, however, the main attraction.

Maundy Gregory must have private access. He kept a personal taxi, with a driver who worked only for him. Secrecy befitted the man who was said to have run Britain's spy network during the Great War, who used black blotting paper lest his jottings should be read, who was said to own a West End club and to be a millionaire, and to have covert political interests which might yet change the course of European history. Later he would be accused of murder; later still, of two murders, and the framing of a man hanged for treason.

The house next door to the east was on the corner of Albion Street. A short walk up Albion Street, on the left, was Albion Mews West. The Mews extended behind 10 Hyde Park Terrace. Maundy Gregory could emerge from his cab in the Mews, quietly cross his own garden, and climb the back stairs of the two-storey extension and the last short flight to his private apartments without being noticed either inside or outside the building.

On a Friday evening early in February 1933, Chief Inspector Arthur Askew, of the detective branch at Scotland Yard, had almost certainly spotted Mr Gregory's taxi turning into the Mews. He and a police sergeant strolled around to the front portico.

The door-knocker boomed throughout the house. No-one inside would be in any doubt about the portent of this visit. Only policemen and bailiffs can convey their intentions so clearly from the other side of a door.

The summons that Askew intended to issue to Mr Maundy Gregory was even more significant than he knew. On the face of it, it was the result of a complaint to the police by a member of the public. Chief Inspector Askew had no reason to suspect that for MI5 and the Chairman of the Conservative Party, this knock on the door would represent the outcome of four years' work, a couple of aborted attempts to remove Maundy Gregory from his post as Purveyor of Honours to the rich, and the final defeat of high-level opposition. People in high places had been trying to get rid of Mr Gregory for a long time. They had tried, they had failed, and they had watched in frustration as Mr Gregory's activities became more dubious with every passing year.

For others in positions of power, though, Askew's rap on the door would represent a threat. If Maundy Gregory talked, and if Maundy Gregory came to grief, so would they. He had always, until now, received protection; but the system seemed about to fail them. Anything might happen.

Nearly eighty years later, a serving Prime Minister has been asked to help the police with their enquiries. At 10 Downing Street the repercussions of Maundy Gregory's predicament may seem only too familiar. For Maundy Gregory was an honours tout; and Tony Blair's Government is also suspected of having offered peerages in return for hard cash.

One cannot emphasise too much the huge cultural differences between 1933 and 2007. The British today are cynical. We are not surprised. We expect scandal; *and the protagonists survive*. In 1933 the pyramid of society was even more bottom-heavy than it is now, and circumstances and attitudes were very different. The powerful political, financial and social élite had been badly shaken by what could happen to élites, as in Russia in 1917. The economy depended on protecting capital, the generation of which depended in great measure on willing labour. The political system was protected by discretion, which was protected by mass deference, which depended on respect. Socially, that respect depended in large part on maintaining the ignorance of the masses.

Millions had gone to war because they believed what their 'betters' told them. When the soldiers came back, the social order did change – but slowly. The rich were not as rich as before, yet they were still rich enough to expect deference. Politicians were protected by a huge mandarin class. In all but a very few cases, their background and education set them apart from the man on the Clapham omnibus. Journalists did not snoop into their affairs; ordinary people would have been shocked. The growing middle class employed obedient servants just as the landed gentry did; and the peerage and the politicians and the mandarins were so distant as to seem almost superhuman. The millions at the bottom of the heap still stood up respectfully when the National Anthem was played at the end of every cinema performance. Children in the 1920s waved flags and had a holiday on Empire Day.

Scandal must not be allowed to approach the ruling class. And if it did, the rulers would find someone to sacrifice.

CHAPTER TWO

A False Start

Half a century before, Arthur John Maundy Gregory – this man of mystery and insidious power by 1933 – had possessed neither wealth nor influence. He was the second son of an impoverished High Anglican vicar and his well-born wife. Handsome but stern, old Reverend Gregory wore a biretta, a soutane and a heavy beard. When he first arrived at St Michael's, Southampton, the whiff of incense about the new vicar had been as the whiff of sulphur to the scandalised congregation. They never did become entirely reconciled to his theatrical, crypto-Catholic style.[1] But like his better-known son, the vicar proved thick-skinned, and stayed.

The family remained poor, by Mrs Ursula Gregory's standards: she had to manage with only a maid, a cook and a nurse when the boys were small. Michael arrived in 1873, Edward in 1875 and two more sons, Arthur and Stephen, followed at two-year intervals.[2] For a late-Victorian family, this was not a large brood, and there was enough money for their education.

Michael Gregory, his oldest brother, died in March, 1882 at the age of nine.[3] He had been attending a prep school at 9 Hereford Square, South Kensington, just around the corner from their uncle, Arthur Wynell-Mayow, who lived in the Cromwell Road. Their uncle was there when little Michael died of 'acute bronchitis' after a ten-day illness. Arthur would have been only seven and may have been at the same school. His feelings are unknown, although he was cruelly teased at his next school as a cry-baby.

When he was about ten, Arthur was sent to board at Banister Court, a school which had been installed in a mansion outside Southampton to educate the sons of officers on P&O ships. There he met a contemporary of his older brother Edward, a boy called Harold Davidson whose father was also a local parson.[4]

Gregory, the stronger of the two characters, loved to produce and write plays; Harold Davidson, the cleverer, loved to take part. Sadly, every other aspect of young Harold's time at Banister Court was unhappy. He was small (boys called him Jumbo) and weak, and too kind-hearted to endure what was quite a tough school, and was removed to the Whitgift School when he was thirteen. Arthur learned to survive. He and Harold would meet again later.

He left Banister Court at eighteen having passed Oxford Entrance,[5] and enrolled as a non-collegiate student at the university in order to study for Holy Orders. Extra-collegiate and studying theology, he was not in the vanguard of social or intellectual life. He boarded with a Mrs Johnson at 81 Iffley Road and passed unnoticed.[6]

Quite what he – or his father – thought he could do for religion was unclear. What religion could do for him would not become apparent until thirty-five years later. In the meantime, he developed his superstitious side. These were the late 1890s, when occultism, Spiritualism, table-tapping, Theosophy, Rosicrucianism and *The Order of the Golden Dawn* were in vogue and Aleister ('do what thou wilt shall be the whole of the law') Crowley was about to publish *Arcadia*. There was much whispering of shamanism, ancient truths hidden in long-forgotten languages, secret brotherhoods, and so on.

Uneducated in science, and haunting second-hand bookshops in search of mystery and conspiracy, Arthur came to reject his father's beliefs in the most public way possible. In 1898 back in Southampton he wrote and produced a successful play called *Self-Condemned* whose hero, a sometime priest, rejects High Anglican ways and all the Church stands for. He rejects the theatricality of the service and the hypocrisy of the vows, knowing that behind the religious façade humanity is forever fallible.

His father, by now a sick man, was hurt; the more so since at the first performance he saw priceless mediaeval artefacts from the parish church used as props, without so much as a by-your-leave.

Gregory ignored these protests. He was twenty-one and his play was much admired, for genteel Southampton audiences in those days cared about the issues it raised. He took *Self-Condemned* on tour. In the less rarefied atmosphere of the industrial north, it was a flop. It folded suddenly. Those who had depended on him for a living did not get paid; penniless actresses had to make their way home somehow.

There was nothing for it. A.J. Gregory must face reality. He was unqualified to make a living in the theatre and without even meagre parental support, he would be destitute. In despair, he returned to Oxford for his final year of theological study.

He was struggling through his penultimate term when the Reverend Gregory died, on 1 March 1899. The obstacle to Gregory's ambition was now removed. There was a little money as a buffer against rejection, but not enough to launch him or his two surviving brothers in life. Edward began work as a junior accountant. Stephen, two years younger than Arthur, left for the South African War.

Arthur Gregory did not return to the university. His pitch for stardom was reinstated and with it, the possibility of freedom. He could now aim at a career on the stage, with its atmosphere free of moral censure. At first he earned a paltry living as a drawing-room entertainer, playing the piano and relating amusing stories at gatherings in private homes, while he sought work in the theatre. By this time – it was around 1900 – he was friendly with a family called Loraine who lived in Lyndhurst, in the New Forest not far from Southampton. The young sisters were as stage-struck as Gregory was, perhaps because of a family connection to Harry and Richard Loraine. Harry Loraine was an actor-manager, and Richard, his son, had been a popular young leading man with Ben Greet's Woodland Players and a big West End hit before leaving to fight in the Boer War. He returned to the stage later before becoming even more famous as an aviator.

Gregory was twenty-three, smartly dressed, charming and baby-faced, with a strong sense of the effect he could make if he tried. The Loraines enjoyed his company and he theirs; he had the actor's gift for anecdote; and the Loraines eventually lost him to a Ben Greet touring company. [7]

Greet, then in his forties, had been running theatre companies for over twenty years and would go on to found the Shakespeare Company at the Old Vic. Gregory now knew that a solid training in repertory theatre was necessary for his credibility. He set out as a very junior touring actor, spear-carrying and understudying, sewing on buttons and taking the ticket money, and increasingly being given small parts to play in provincial towns.

Romantic leads were ten a penny, but young Gregory was well organised, determined, endlessly resourceful, good-humoured and didn't panic. He was ambitious and he could persuade temperamental people to carry out instructions. All these qualities got him a permanent job as manager of a burlesque theatre in Southampton. At the same time, he advertised himself as an agent for playwrights. Whether he discovered any new talent seems doubtful. In any case he was soon on the move again. He went to work for a cynical Irish-American showman called Kelly, who taught him to sell himself, rather than his professional talents; this is what people would buy.

After still more jobs for more impresarios, getting better parts all the time, he landed permanent work as a stage manager with a Frank Benson company in the north of England. His keenness and efficiency impressed everyone. He was earning £5 a week – a decent sum, in those days – and it was enough to bring out the showman in him. He *acted* the part of company manager, with a fresh flower in his buttonhole every day, a dapper suit and starched collar.

He had been in the job for about three years when it dawned on Benson, or his accountants, that Gregory's much-praised ingenuity and industriousness were devoted largely to his own ends. As the underlings in the company already knew, he was skimming off some of the profits for himself. He left Benson under a cloud.

It was now 1906; he was twenty-nine, knew his trade, and had landed in London for good. For several years he had taken rooms, when necessary, in Bayswater and Kensington. This time he was to find a small flat-cum-office at 18 Burleigh Mansions, at the south end of the Charing Cross Road between two theatres, Wyndham's and the Garrick. His aims were to make money and put on plays, in that order.

As for his image, he had not yet settled on the urbane and cultivated persona he would later adopt. He preferred to present himself as an American-style, fast-talking, fast-acting tycoon. *The Era* reported 'Mr Maundy-Gregory is a firm believer in the hustling principle, and thinks nothing of dictating in the train forty or fifty letters to his American manager, who types them all on the journey.' Who the American manager was, nobody knows. Gregory's business was a touring repertory theatre, and this he ran successfully – up to a point.

That point was arrived at with his ambitious pantomime, *Little Red Riding Hood*. After opening in Ipswich on Boxing Day, 1907, with a cast of sixty, it resulted in Gregory's appearance in the Magistrates' Court. Enthusiastic reviews in the local paper had given rise to a summons under the Prevention of Cruelty to Children Act. Little Red Riding Hood was an accomplished actress, but she was only seven, and to comply with the law she must be at least eleven.

Gregory gave not a fig for the magistrates. The following week in Peterborough the child appeared again, but not on the stage. Dressed in a Dutch girl's costume, she stood up and trilled *By the Side of the Zuyder Zee* from one of the boxes.

The typical con-man knows in his bones that world is full of suckers and that for every person who isn't taken in, a hundred will fall for anything. The Peterborough police were of the astute minority. They prosecuted, and the girl's mother took her out of the show once and for all.

For Little Barbara, this wasn't the end of it. She was determined to get back to work, and her mother was perfectly happy to let her. The following Christmas, under another name and claiming to be eleven, she had a great success on stage in a pantomime at Her Majesty's Theatre, Haymarket, with Ellen Terry in a starring role. When this came to the notice of Maundy Gregory he sent a woman to see the girl's mother. *He knew*, was the message. He knew she was eight and he knew she was using a false birth certificate. A sum was mentioned which might help him forget about it. The mother sent the woman packing. It is the first known instance of Maundy Gregory as a blackmailer.

He had two or three plays running at the time, but bookings were sporadic. Maundy Gregory was a young man about the West End; he was seen at the Café Royal and the Café de l'Europe; he didn't venture north to the Bohemian haunts of the Eiffel Tower in Fitzrovia or west to the gambling clubs of Mayfair, but frequented only the show folk in theatreland. Inevitably, therefore, he ran into an old friend from school.

Harold Davidson's time as a divinity student at Oxford had slightly overlapped with his, so it is possible that they had already renewed their acquaintance there. It is also true that before and during his studies Jumbo, like Arthur, had been a drawing-room entertainer and touring actor. But at 5ft 3, he was never going to be a leading man.

In the first decade of the twentieth century, they were working and living on the same patch – the colourful, slightly seedy strip of music shops and bookshops and theatrical agencies that occupied premises west of Covent Garden all the way from St Martin-in-the-Fields up to St Giles'.

Jumbo's devotion to the Church had proved more enduring than Arthur's. With twenty-seven churchmen in his family already, perhaps that was not surprising. In 1905 he had become a curate at St Martin-in-the-Fields. Inevitably he and Gregory would meet.

Jumbo was not yet the notorious figure he later became. Socially adept and quick-witted – he had been sponsored by the then Lord Wilberforce to study at Exeter College, and had been President of the Oxford Chess Club – he nevertheless had a boundless capacity for self-delusion. He recognised no scintilla of contradiction between his joyfully lubricious nature and his code of conduct as a parson. He had a passion for nubile young women, and since his post as curate was augmented by another as chaplain to the Actors' Church Union, he had every excuse to visit girlish actresses in their dressing rooms.

Unfortunately neither of his ecclesiastical posts brought in much money and in 1906 Jumbo had married an actress he first encountered at Oxford. A family would shortly begin to arrive. Through his acquaintance with Gladys, the Marchioness Townshend, who incidentally had married into the peerage under false pretences, he was offered the living of Stiffkey in Norfolk. It came with a huge country rectory with plenty of room for all the babies that would result from Jumbo's energetic visits home. And what visits they were; brief, and only on Sundays, for the Vicar of Stiffkey quickly discovered that country life was not for him. He caught the last train up from Liverpool Street after Saturday midnight – sometimes even the first train on Sunday morning – conducted services, and scampered back to London on Monday first thing. He lived and breathed the West End.

He was a small whirlwind, and an inspiration to Maundy Gregory exactly when one was needed. Up to now, Maundy Gregory had failed to distinguish his work in the theatre from his search for backers. Both had been part of the same thing: hard graft. Jumbo unwittingly introduced him to a new way of doing business, in which one's patron and one's profession were clearly distinct. Vicars in those days must have patrons. Livings were in the gift of people with land and property. It followed that if the right people with land and property knew and were charmed by you, sooner or later a good living would inevitably come your way. It was a question of targeting, and research. In the search for a living, a Vicar must be a salesman. Once he'd got the living, he could do as he pleased.

J. Rowland Sales, who as a boy of nineteen had begun work for Gregory in 1908, recalled a pertinent conversation between Davidson and Gregory around this time:

Davidson (after surveying Gregory's financial position): So you're broke, down on your luck, reduced to sending out pierrots to play at the end of the pier – very good, we'll soon put matters right. (He picks up the telephone, calls Wyndham's Theatre, asks that a box for that evening's performance be placed at the disposal of 'J. Maundy-Gregory, the well-known theatrical producer, who will be entertaining the Duchess of Somerset.')

Gregory (protesting): But I don't even know the Duchess of Somerset.

Davidson: You will, my boy, you will. Like all the aristocracy, she's
simply mad about the theatre.

Gregory: But why should I entertain a Duchess I don't know in
a box I can't pay for?

Davidson (pityingly): If you want to attract investors it's important
that you be seen in such company.[8]

When Maundy Gregory began to see life this new way, he realised
the implications at once. An influential, wealthy connection could
be used for anything. You didn't have to tie it to a particular play or
even to the theatre. The point was, to make the connection in the first
place. And not just *one* connection – lots.

At first, Jumbo was the more successful networker – he did after all
have more time, and the advantage of a clerical collar. He was able to
give Lord Howard de Walden and Baron Carl von Buch a gentle push
in the direction of Combine Attractions Syndicate Ltd[9], Gregory's
vehicle for putting on plays. Both became investors. Maundy also
inspired his older brother Edward, the accountant, to join him in the
business under his new hyphenated surname, Maundy-Gregory.

Maundy optioned a play called *Cleopatra*[10] and embarked upon
discussions with Ruby Miller. She was then at the height of her West
End stardom and would take the lead.

When development fell through he had already had a better idea.
Towards the end of 1908 Combine Attractions managed to get another
show into the New Theatre for an initial two-week run. This was
Dorothy, a musical comedy which had been a runaway success when it
first opened in 1886.[11] Its revival would feature, from the original show,
Hayden Coffin, a tenor renowned for his big hit *Queen of My Heart*;
a cast of sixty including other big names; and spectacular production
values.

It opened in December, 1908 to resounding acclaim from audience
and critics alike. At the New Theatre, it played to full houses. But at
the end of its initial fortnight, the show must of necessity transfer to
the Waldorf, at the wrong end of the Strand. And there was crippling

competition after Christmas from two dozen pantomimes in rival theatres. *Dorothy* now faced evening after evening when the houses were respectable but not full.

The Syndicate was losing money. Maundy Gregory was biting his nails. It was allegedly Jumbo Davidson who, casting about for words of comfort, saw a Messina Benefit as a way to revive the flagging production. It wasn't an original idea; every newspaper and department store was running some kind of appeal for the hapless victims of Messina. An earthquake estimated at 7.5 on the Richter scale had struck the Straits between Sicily and Calabria on 28 December, just after Christmas; a tidal wave engulfed the land; the death toll was estimated at 200,000.

But Jumbo was *connected*. In no time he had filled the auditorium for a full dress evening performance in late January, with tickets at £10 a head bought by several Ambassadors and a socially prominent Princess, the Lord Chancellor, the Lord Mayor of London, and Countesses and Duchesses in glamorous gowns and diamond tiaras. Actresses curtseyed low to the Prince of Teck.

Thus did Maundy Gregory's first experience of networking *en masse*, so to speak, emerge from the adversity of others. Presumably the Reverend Davidson had seen the Benefit as an opportunity to do good in the world while reaping welcome commission and boosting publicity. Maundy Gregory concurred about the publicity, but his plans for the income may have differed. The quantity of tents and blankets delivered to the Straits of Messina afterwards is not recorded. The £10 subscriptions rolled in; but nothing now could save *Dorothy*. After the matinée performance on the first Saturday in February, 1909, the musicians refused to play that evening unless they were paid. They would not be fobbed off with promises.

The foyer remained closed. From outside came an insistent, and rising, murmur of annoyance from evening theatregoers assembling in the cold. The musicians refused to enter the auditorium.

Gregory, for once, panicked. He rushed to the basement and threw the main switch. The entire building was plunged into darkness. As actors fumbled about backstage, cursing by candlelight, he appeared at the street doors of the theatre and regretfully informed the crowd that the evening performance was cancelled because of a power failure.

Nobody in the business was fooled. The stage papers reviled him. His brother dumped him. The actors and musicians were broke, hungry and out of work, the investors had lost money, and the electricity company angrily refuted any allegation that its service had failed.

Gregory disappeared. It was the end of his career in the theatre. Jumbo, the Vicar of Stiffkey, lost two thousand pounds; an amount equivalent to several years' salary, and far more than he could afford. He was devastated.

CHAPTER THREE

The Phoenix Rising

Maundy had hired *Dorothy's* unpaid orchestra, among the best in town, from the Gaiety Theatre. Its musical director was Frederick Rosse, well known as a composer of light music, who had recently married an actress called Vivienne Pierrepont. It was ironic that Maundy's downfall should have been provoked by the orchestra, because Maundy and Fred and Edith (Vivienne's real name) got on very well indeed.

Like him, they had already climbed a long way from their origins. Both were a little older than Maundy Gregory who was now thirty-one. They had married under Fred's real name of Lichtenstein. German names were already attracting suspicion and although Fred had been born in 1867 in London, he was careful to use his stage name unless a contract required his signature. Musical talent and personal charm had propelled him from an immigrant home in the East End to the well-appointed flat at 6a Hyde Park Mansions, between the Edgware Road and the Old Marylebone Road where he now lived with Edith.[1]

Edith had been born Edith Marion Davies in 1873 and married Harry Sheppard, the purser on a cruise liner, in 1896. So far as we know, the Davies family of Edmonton had offered the world nothing notable to date, although all the girls seem to have married well. The 1901 census records Mrs Edith Sheppard staying alone with relatives in the north of England. Her husband had died at sea the previous year. This was a tragic loss to her and a life-changing one; afterwards she took up – or returned to – her stage career.

For most of 1909 and 1910 Maundy Gregory was not to be found, and if the Rosses knew where he was, they were not telling. For him it was 'Goodbye, Piccadilly, Farewell Leicester Square', while he considered his next move. If he never wanted to show his face in a theatre again, he was deterred by more than mere humiliation. He owed a lot of people money and would be better off lying low for a while.

There is no clue to his whereabouts. The single intriguing hint that he may have left London is scarcely credible. Many years later, when Gregory was old and far from home, a young Frenchman called Jean-Jacques Grumbach knew him:

> Grumbach saw Gregory as a very kindly old gentleman, a little crotchety and set in his ways, a typical old bachelor, very fond of whisky. He spoke little of his past except to tell stories of his travels in the Far East.[2]

Either M. Grumbach was mistaken, which seems unlikely, or Gregory simply walked down to the Port of London and took the next boat to Shanghai, mentioned it to no-one for nearly thirty years; never showed any interest in travelling again; and never again left, willingly, his Mayfair/Soho/St James's patch . . .

Or Gregory was spinning extraordinary stories out of what he had read or heard from others. This tells us a little more about him, or possibly about tall tales he listened to later in life.

Perhaps the Rosses, of whom Edith in particular was to a great extent self-invented, and who had both done well despite a lowly start, gave him the courage to turn his back on the past. When he became successful he kept very quiet about his years in the theatre. And from now on for the next several years he, too, made a subtle alteration to his name.

When J.M. Gregory, journalist, resurfaced in 1910 he hadn't moved far. He may even have retained his Burleigh Mansions flat, because his new office was nearby at the north end of Charing Cross Road. It was at 9–15 Oxford Street, which is a late-Victorian office warren above an entrance to Tottenham Court Road tube station.

Somewhere, very probably in the course of raising money for the Messina disaster, he had come across the Keen-Hargreaves brothers. There were three of them, Baron Keen-Hargreaves and Harry being the only ones with whom he was concerned.

Baron John Clarke Keen-Hargreaves liked to relate the legend of his barony and how he had inherited it, and his story was strongly linked to Messina. In 1860 his father Jack Keen, as a young hot-head, had been inspired by Garibaldi's mission to conquer the Bourbon rulers of southern Italy and unite the whole country under the House of Savoy. He had been a leader of the English expedition that joined Garibaldi's thousand-strong band of Redshirts (*i Mille*) when they landed in Sicily to reinforce uprisings at Messina and Palermo. Garibaldi and his men gained great victories, roared on via Naples to Rome, threw out the Pope and proclaimed Victor Emmanuel II the King. In recognition of his valour in battle Jack Keen was made a Lieutenant Colonel and later a Baron. He later tacked on his wife's name. His oldest son, also Jack, in due course inherited the title.

Most of this was a pack of lies. In 1860 their father probably had been among the thousand Englishmen of whose urgent recruitment one of the organising Committee wrote that they 'soon had a gathering, a gathering of a strange crowd, earnest men, men with selfish ends, men of good repute and not so good, the sort of mixture in all such enterprises.'[3] The largest contingent, from London, was armed, equipped, and packed off by night train to Harwich to board a special steamer. Departure was delayed for the court-martial of one of their officers who, when forcibly turfed off the expedition, took out a warrant for assault and had his attacker hauled before the magistrate and fined five shillings. So they left in a shambles and got to Sicily too late to be any use.[4] They paraded through the streets and were shipped home at public expense. Jack Keen was never made a Lieutenant Colonel or a Baron. He died in the Sick Asylum at Poplar in 1905, and is recorded as a 65-year-old ship's clerk.

Whether Maundy Gregory knew that the second Baron Jack was bogus, we don't know either. If he did, he must have admired his nerve. For in 1911 – the fiftieth anniversary of Garibaldi's triumph – Baron Keen-Hargreaves would travel in style to Rome, leading a deputation of survivors of the English contingent, for an audience with King Victor Emmanuel himself.[5] As the two men faced one another, maybe neither the King nor Baron Jack believed the old story. Or maybe both were happy to delude themselves. If Maundy

Gregory had his doubts, another suspicion was now confirmed: you can be anything if you act the part.

And already he was an Editor. Jack and Harry – who by all accounts was both more charming and more amusing than his brother, though just as fond of actresses – provided both office space and backing for a weekly magazine called *Mayfair and Town Topics*. Baron Jack registered a company called Mayfair Ltd in October, 1910. J.M. Gregory is said to have pitched the original idea to the Keen-Hargreaves brothers, and this time he had a sure-fire proposition.

The costs and overheads of magazines are traditionally paid by advertising revenue and sales, in a ratio related to circulation, distribution and production costs. *Mayfair* by its nature would always have a limited circulation and rustling up advertising was time-consuming and difficult with so much competition from *Vanity Fair, Tatler* and other society periodicals. But Maundy had thought of a new way to rake money in. You might call it personal advertorial. He would write puffs about rich men in return for a fat fee.

It worked. The timing was perfect; provincial high achievers of the new middle class were frustrated by being cold-shouldered in London. They wanted to find their way around socially, but nobody knew them, far less invited them to join a Club. This way, Maundy told them, they could appear on the page next to a Duchess. (Duchesses, he didn't need to point out, would get into the magazine for nothing.) Everyone of substance read *Mayfair* when in Town, he assured them; it circulated in gentlemen's clubs and the best hotels.

Cash was handed over and the articles appeared. For a cover price of sixpence the one or two thousand eager consumers of *Mayfair* bought a magazine illustrated in colour with cartoons of 'Men of the Day' – some of whom really were of interest (like the Marquis de Soveral, GCMG, GCVO, amusing, well-connected and one of the founders of The Other Club, or Sir Fitzroy Maclean the traveller); some who were royal, like King Manuel of Portugal, the Duke of Orléans and the Maharajah of Cooch Behar; and many others of whom nobody had ever heard, like T. Frame Thomson, Reginald Blair and W.A. Vernon. Very, very occasionally there was a woman, such as F.E. Smith's great extra-marital love Miss Mona Dunn. But it was largely grateful nonentities from industry who came up with the cash.

There was more to this than initially appeared. It had been put to Maundy Gregory – by whom, we do not know, but the newspaper magnate and MP Horatio Bottomley, around 1910, is the likeliest person – that by ensnaring the vain and wealthy with free public relations in a magazine, he could put himself in a position to make them a further, and very special, offer.

Maundy was dazzled by moving in grand circles. He was politically ignorant but understood self-interest and had a weakness for anything as florid as a title. The very notion of royal patronage by title is mediaeval; a reminder of a gracious custom whereby the monarch rewarded outstanding conduct by bestowing a sign of respect. Maundy loved that kind of thing. What he had only recently discovered was that knighthoods and baronetcies may also be rewards for political favours, or for donations to political parties, for as we shall see, selling peerages was important to the Liberal Government at the time. Horatio Bottomley was a Unionist, but he was very thick with the young opportunist F.E. Smith, who had close Liberal friends like Winston Churchill.

Money did not cross Maundy's chubby palm without quite a lot of it sticking. On 29 July 1910 he took a long lease on a summer villa, a kind of little wooden dacha, on Thames Ditton Island. How did he know about it? It seems likely that he had originally gone to ground there in the immediate aftermath of *Dorothy*. The Rosses had a house of their own there in 1916, and probably knew the area before he did; they could well have alerted him to the place.[6]

It would be deeply depressing in winter; close to the water, icy cold and damp, and like all the houses on the little island, lacking mains water or drains. But when the summer came, it was charming, and inspired Maundy to call it *Vanity Fair*. The Rosses visited him there and the three of them spent many happy hours messing about in boats. In the September of 1910, he protected himself from predatory creditors by putting it in Edith Rosse's name.

He was happy; rejoicing in his new financial security, he tootled off to Lyndhurst one weekend in a taxi. All the way in a taxi! – exclaimed the Loraines. Good times were here again, he confided gleefully. 'Clean shirt every day now!' When times had been hard at Burleigh Mansions, he'd been reduced to pinning a cardboard collar over the frayed edges of his shirt.

In his *Mayfair* period Maundy Gregory made many useful acquaintances. These included: Robert P Houston MP, a shipping tycoon whose fortune would, in due course be generously disbursed to right-wing causes by his widow; Sir Francis Hopwood, who would become his great friend Lord Southborough; Sir George Lewis, solicitor to King Edward VII; Sir Joseph Robinson, Bart., a South African mining magnate and numerous members of the Victorian beerocracy.

Maundy also dignified Arthur Newton, solicitor, as Man of the Day no. 574. Irony is not a quality one associates with Maundy Gregory, but what else could have prompted him to effuse in 1911:

> Born three-and-thirty years ago to the actuary and manager of the Legal and General Life Association. . . he qualified for practice nine years ago; and in the last seven or eight years has made himself, by industry, and decent manners, till he has come to employ a considerable staff in Great Marlborough Street. . . He claims descent from that Sir Isaac Newton who was supposed to have been the only man to connect an apple with the fall –

The style, droopy with qualifiers and subordinate clauses, is all Gregory. It starts at the beginning (later, he would start before the beginning, preferably in times of antiquity) and goes on – and on, and on. The eulogy begins with a lie. Arthur Newton was not 'three-and-thirty'. In 1911 he was at least, as everyone knew, two score and ten.[7] It was true that his father was General Manager of the Legal and General and that he ran, until 1913, a successful legal practice in Soho. He was the solicitor of choice for almost every drunk and tart and gambler who appeared before the beak (coincidentally, another Mr Newton) at Great Marlborough Street Court from about 1885 onwards.

For Arthur Newton would do *anything* to get his client off, if his client paid him well enough. In 1889, in order to protect Lord Arthur Somerset from disgrace amid accusations about rent-boys, he put about a blatant lie that Prince Albert Victor, heir to the throne, had been involved.

In 1910, Arthur Newton colluded with Horatio Bottomley in a last-ditch attempt to lay a false trail to divert those who were about to hang Dr Crippen for murder. Crippen was Newton's client then, and *John Bull*, Bottomley's paper, printed a letter purporting to come from Crippen in his death cell at Pentonville, hinting that the condemned man was covering up for someone else. It was a fabrication. Just as Lord Arthur Somerset had been induced by Newton to imply that he was shielding Prince Albert Victor, so Crippen was painted as the heroic protector of an anonymous other – but Crippen's letter *must* be a fake, since the man had had no opportunity to write it. Not only this; there was also a bogus letter from Chicago, apparently from Clara Crippen the murder victim – long since dead – to Crippen awaiting execution, hinting at a faked murder and therefore, a vindication of Newton's client. It arrived at Pentonville before the hanging.[8]

Arthur Newton was suspended from the Rolls for a year from 13 July 1911 for the lying death-cell diversion 'by' Dr Crippen in *John Bull*. He went to ground. In July 1912 he resumed his practice.

In March 1913 he appeared at Bow Street charged with conspiracy to defraud a rich young Hungarian, was struck off and went down for three years' penal servitude.

He was in trouble throughout his life. In the late 1920s he resurfaced as a contact of the obsessively self-justifying Lord Alfred Douglas, who had once been the lover of Oscar Wilde. By that time, Newton was running a snoopery called The Confidential Agency, in Oxford Street. And in the 1930s, when he was seventy-three, he was embroiled in an acrimonious divorce – not, glamorously, as co-respondent, but as someone who had misled one of the parties and cost her money. 'Wherever Arthur Newton intervened, trouble followed.'[9]

Maundy Gregory appears to have got Newton's number. When he wrote that he was thirty-three years old, he can *surely* not have been serious. But the article was paid for – almost certainly by

Horatio Bottomley, who owed Newton a favour since the solicitor had effectively ruined his own career in taking all the blame for the Crippen Letter story.[10]

Horatio Bottomley, owner of the mass-circulation *John Bull* magazine, had been accused of conspiracy to defraud in 1893 and in 1908. He lived like a millionaire at the turn of the century and in 1911 was bankrupted (it was one of at least 211 petitions for bankruptcy 'all dismissed', he said airily, in his lifetime). He was a Member of Parliament, clever, articulate and amusing; he backed plays, musical comedies and revues at around the same time as Gregory; he successfully defended himself against allegations of swindling in 1901 and 1911. Colin Coote wrote 'His face was a slab with a slit of a mouth, which opened to imbibe great quantities of champagne.' Julian Symons perceptively noted that his popular appeal lay in his reputation as a womaniser, drinker and racing man – the sort of person poor men dreamed of being if ever they got rich.[11]

Gerald Hamilton, urbane, inveterate gossip and compulsive name-dropper who was allegedly the model for Mr Norris in Christopher Isherwood's *Mr Norris Changes Trains,* knew Maundy Gregory in the late 20s. He knew *everybody*, if he is to be believed (which is uncertain): Casement, the Maughams, the Somersets, Kate Meyrick, Gertie Millar, the Tsar and Tsarina, Anna Virubova, André Gide, Aleister Crowley, Gaby Deslys, Tallulah Bankhead, Christopher Millard and Robert Ross, Lord Alfred Douglas – the Pope – the list goes on. But he did know a lot of them and meet others, and although he moved in rather more louche and aristocratic circles than Gregory did, he had evidently heard gossip that Gregory owed a great deal to some newspaper magnate at the start of his career.[12] Gerald Macmillan, also, wrote about the mystery surrounding 'services [Gregory] claimed to have rendered to some press magnate, which released him from his previously persistent impecuniosity, and were the initial step in his rise to wealth.'[13]

Bottomley knew Newton very well, and he also knew the Keen-Hargreaves brothers – they had actress-chasing in common. He published some derisive copy about them in *John Bull*, pointing out that the Barony was a fake. But that is not to say that he hadn't backed them, and Gregory too, at some point. Maundy was making money somehow by the summer of 1910, and *Mayfair* did not commence publication until October of that year. He could have been contributing articles to *John Bull,* or – more likely, since his work shows no sign of journalistic discipline – he was running other errands for Bottomley, or Bottomley's friend F.E. Smith, after *Dorothy* and before *Mayfair.*

As to Baron Jack and suave Harry, they never had enough spare cash to make an enduring and reliable investment in anything. They were later said to be 'art dealers' but they ran a press agency. When they were in the money, they spent it, flashily and enjoyably. Mundanities such as rent were dealt with as an afterthought if at all. Inspector Herbert Fitch, investigating *Mayfair* in 1917, found that they had moved their United Press Agency, and *Mayfair* magazine, to 7 Albemarle Street in 1912. The landlords there told him they had little to do with the brothers or Gregory, 'and looked upon their mode of doing business with considerable suspicion, owing to the number of process servers and collectors calling for money.'[14]

The new address represented social progress. Gregory was now based half a mile west of his old theatrical stomping ground, but a world away in aspiration. Albemarle Street was on the dignified Mayfair side of Piccadilly Circus, close to the Royal Academy, the learned societies, the grand hotels and the antiquarian booksellers. It had *cachet*, which no-one would claim for Oxford Street or the Charing Cross Road.

Before the First War, the socially supreme were drawn from a more restricted pool than they are now; it was a time when journalists called people 'The richest man in London,' or 'The most beautiful woman in London' meaning the richest or most beautiful from a selection of about 1,000, most of whom were aristocrats. By 1912 and the move to Albemarle Street, Maundy Gregory had a passing acquaintance with many influential people, but he seems to have made very few enduring friendships with anyone who wouldn't be of use. He had always set himself apart in some way, as a big fish in a small pond: the manager of a theatre company, a producer, an editor. He was not, we would say, a team player. He operated best as a highwayman on life's road. He was good at spotting victims who would willingly hand over a bag of gold to clear the way to their destination.

As an annual routine, lists of honours to be awarded by the King or Queen are published at New Year and on the sovereign's official birthday in June. But this is part of the courtly myth, for in the past few hundred years almost everyone on the list has been recommended to the sovereign by the Prime Minister, who in turn is putting forward names recommended by Government aides and the leaders of the opposition.

In a different society an honour would not matter, but this was the last gasp of Edwardian England. Economic power shifted with changes in land ownership after the Great War, but the shift was socially imperceptible until long afterwards. In cash-for-honours theory, therefore, if a self-made man had the country house and the yacht, the only things lacking were education, style, respect and social connections. He could buy the style and education for his children; he could earn respect by good works; but an honour – a title – was a short-cut to a position in society. In return for a generous financial donation, a man could become a knight. 'Sir John Smith' would not be able to pass the title on to his son, but as a baronet 'Sir John Smith, Bart.' would hand it down through the male line in perpetuity. And in a cash-for-honours transaction, a baronetcy naturally cost more than a knighthood.

The difficulty, if you were a provincial industrialist, for instance, was to know how to meet people who could arrange this highly confidential deal. London society – people with great estates and seats in the House of Lords, people who knew one another from school or university or their regiment, people who gambled together and visited one another's country houses, whose cousins had married one's friends' cousins – was closed to a manufacturer from Cardiff or a railway king from Nottingham. To get past this obstacle, discreet agents – rudely known as honours touts – were employed by Chief Whips or party organisers from both the Liberal and the Unionist parties.

If a donation or a service were particularly valuable, a man might even be nominated for the Peerage; he might become a Baron or a Viscount. These higher hereditary titles allowed him to sit in the House of Lords with the landed Earls, Marquises and Dukes. It was whispered that the Press Barons had bought their titles either with money which passed, under the table, into party coffers, or by pouring out propaganda in successive elections; it was this latter possibility that made critics uneasy, since it enabled a manipulation of policy which was not all that different from the state of affairs in America. Northcliffe alone owned (not always at the same time) newspapers including *The Times, Daily Mail, Daily Mirror,* and the *Weekly Dispatch.*

Cash-for-honours went on tacitly, with little comment, until Asquith's Liberal government exploited it so blatantly that it threatened to bring the ruling class into disrepute. The Prime Minister must approve the list that goes forward to the King, and in 1911 Asquith threatened to manipulate it to give the ruling party a majority in the House of Lords.

The Liberals had been in office since December 1905. Lloyd George, Chancellor since 1908, introduced a budget to redistribute wealth by taxing the well-off and providing old age pensions for the poor. The House of Lords, led in those days by the great landowners, was a Tory stronghold and baulked at radical financial reform. Although passed by the Commons, Lloyd George's Finance Bill was voted down by the House of Lords on 30 November 1909 by 350 votes to 75. Asquith therefore announced the dissolution of the Commons and a General Election in January 1910. Following the precedent of 1832, he also asked King Edward what his response would be in the event of a request from himself for the creation of sufficient Liberal peers to ensure the passage of the Finance Bill through the House of Lords. Despite severe misgivings, the King indicated that he would only countenance such a radical step after the return of a Liberal majority in a further general election after that of January 1910.

While the Liberal cabinet were somewhat disappointed at having two hurdles to jump, they pinned their hopes on an electoral rally to Liberalism by the voters. While the turnout in January was a record 86.6 per cent compared to 83 per cent in 1906, this was not converted into Liberal strength. On the contrary, their majority was virtually wiped out by the Conservatives who gained over a hundred new seats. However, with the support of the Irish nationalists, Asquith's government was able to retain its dominance in the Commons. Three months later, in April 1910, the Government introduced the

Parliament Act providing for the exclusion of the House of Lords
from financial questions, restricting its veto on other matters to one
parliament, and shortening the life of a parliament to a maximum of
five years. At the same time, Asquith and his Chief Whip worked out
a strategy to be employed in the eventuality that the Lords ultimately
rejected the Bill. They therefore began preparing a list of men who
would be offered peerages if they were prepared to accept the Liberal
whip (see Appendix 3). It contained eminent and clever men from the
arts and sciences, as well as the merely rich or well-connected. While
all this was going on, King Edward died suddenly on 6 May. The new
King, George V, after much hand-ringing, finally agreed to honour
the men on the list with peerages if Asquith could demonstrate that
his government's policies had popular support via a second general
election. Parliament was therefore dissolved and an election was held
in December 1910. In a virtual re-run of the January election, the
Liberals and Conservatives ended up with 272 seats each and again,
the support of the Irish Nationalists gave Asquith the winning hand.

At the eleventh hour, the Lords gave in rather than see the mass
creation of the Liberal peers. 'I am spared any further humiliation,'
wrote the despairing King at last. The mere threat of the mass honours
list had been enough. The gentlemen's agreement that the Prime
Minister would not take advantage of his position remained unsullied
after all.

One general election is an expensive undertaking, let alone two in
the same year, and Alick Murray, Master of Elibank, as Liberal Party
Chief Whip, had to fund-raise as well as drumming up support. There
was nothing new, or illegal, in selling honours, although generations
of politicians had pretended it didn't happen. Kenneth Rose, in his
biography of George V, points out that:

> The sale of honours to replenish party funds or their bestowal
> in return for political support is as old as parliamentary
> government itself. Stanley Baldwin used to recall with delight
> an eighteenth-century document at Welbeck, the home of the
> Dukes of Portland: a list of persons who had to be squared
> by the Prime Minister. One was to be given an Irish peerage,

someone else a bishopric for his brother, a third a sinecure in the public service, and a fourth merely the gratification of a ducal handshake.[15]

At the dawn of the century, someone had asked Alfred Harmsworth why he wasn't a Lord yet. 'When I want an honour, I shall pay for one,' he had said dismissively. In 1905 he became a Baron.

Lloyd George, who despised titles, was comfortable with their sale in principle. In his view, an exchange of money for a title was less damaging to the democratic process than the American system, in which powerful lobby groups were able to dictate terms to the political parties.

Murray was a busy Chief Whip, and welcomed people who would act as intermediaries for a fee. In 1912 Lord Selborne, a Unionist, wrote to Lord Lansdowne:

> To my certain knowledge honours have been recently hawked about by agents . . . and the price of 'honours' has been paid by those agents into the radical treasury after the deduction of a handsome commission.

Unbeknown to Selborne, the new Unionist Leader, Andrew Bonar Law, had already adopted a similar approach and as a result had netted between £120,000 and £140,000 for party funds from the sale of honours during a two year period.[16]

Maundy Gregory was already among those 'agents', commonly known as touts. He had initially made the acquaintance of one of the Liberal Whips, Percy Illingworth[17] who had introduced him to Alick Murray. Later he would hint that although he first made money with the help of Bottomley, he learned everything he knew about the sale of honours from Alick Murray. At this stage in his career however, honours touting was merely a lucrative sideline. The *Mayfair* magazine was not only his staple income but was about to open the door to another money making opportunity.

By circulating complimentary copies of the magazine he obtained an *entrée* to concierges in hotels across London. He started a column called 'Around the Hotels'. The concept was not original to *Mayfair*, but it worked well. People learned who was in Town. 'Visitors at the Hotel Metropole include Lady von Bismarck, Sir James Long, Mr Senator Thompson, Senator Yeo'. You could read this and feel you were in touch with a more glamorous world. 'I hear the Countess of Mayo is at the Savoy this week.' You could imagine yourself dropping that into the conversation. But for Gregory, the morning ring-around of the hotels, restaurants and a few theatres was even more useful. He also learned who was who in the hotel trade. Hotel management was often a family affair and still more often, managers and staff were recent incomers from the Continent. The Italians, by contrast, were largely drawn from the Clerkenwell immigrant community of Calabria and Sicily. They had been in London for a generation, had intermarried and formed business partnerships. Among them, Gregory met someone who would prove significant in his life: Mrs Coletta of the Queen's Hotel in Leicester Square.

He learned that hotel-keeping was a seething ant-hill of gossip. He was told who had stayed at the Cecil with someone else's mistress and whose cheque to the Russell had bounced. He also learned that whatever Rosa Lewis knew about her guests at the Cavendish would not necessarily make its way to a German manager across town, and that the excellent Italian bush telegraph operated largely within the Italian community and news took a while to filter out. Noticing that he had become a kind of information hub, because he knew all of them, he decided to exploit his inside information. In return for a retainer, he would keep an informal credit check on prominent guests. He wrote a list, and it still exists, of all his hotel contacts (see Appendix I).

From here, it was a short step to answering queries about who was doing what, and with whom. In no time at all Maundy was not only an editor but a private investigator, and – given his previous form – almost certainly a small-time blackmailer. He no longer reacted to gossip at random; he actively hunted down information about specific individuals. The hotel network was proving its usefulness. Certainly the leverage afforded him by knowing people's secrets would come in useful in the honours trade later.

There is a suggestion that when war began in 1914, Maundy Gregory operated his investigation agency from a suite in the Queen's Hotel. There is a 1906 postcard of the hotel in the Westminster Archive: the sender, posting it from Leicester Square, wrote on the front *I hope you have never been here after ten*. The Queen's Hotel was next door to the Empire, a variety theatre famous for the nightly parade of prostitutes through its public spaces. The hotel was, and remains, a great wedding-cake of a building with a projecting iron porch to shelter those alighting from carriages in the rain.

Gerald Macmillan, in his book on Maundy Gregory published in 1954, quoted from an intriguing article in *Empire News* in 1950:

> During the First World War, while he was acting for the government in counter-espionage work, Maundy Gregory set up a suite of offices in an hotel in Leicester Square. His business was selling import permits and various other trading facilities. At the same time Gregory, unknown to his partners, was using a well-known solicitor as an intermediary for selling commissions in the services. Business prospered.

The 'well-known solicitor' does rather make Arthur Newton spring to mind. No good ever came of an association with him. Whether or not Gregory was in a position to obtain commissions (and later events would indicate decisively not) he must have been happy then. He was doing what he liked best: being mysterious. Also, he had met his partner in life.

Peter Mazzina was about fifteen, a very junior member of the Italian hotel clique. He seems to have been a page, or bus-boy at the Queen's Hotel. He was enrolled at Mercers' School, an institution of mediaeval foundation located, from 1894 to 1959, in Barnard's Inn on the South side of Holborn. (Barnard's Inn itself dates from the fourteenth century and part of the building is Roman.) Pupils at Mercers' School were taught by Professors of Astronomy, Divinity, Geometry, Law, Music, Physick and Rhetoric. Whether or not Maundy Gregory paid the fees is uncertain, but this kind of thing – with the emphasis on style over substance – was right up his street.

And he was a great believer in *background*, which an education at the Mercers' School would indicate.

Studies in Astronomy and Physick made an unusual grounding for a waiter at the Carlton Hotel, which Mazzina became. But one day, thanks to Maundy, he would become very prosperous indeed.

CHAPTER FOUR

Not a 'Sahib'

In the first half of August 1914, *Mayfair* wittered on about the Glorious Twelfth with barely a nod at the World War. Everyone else had heard the drumbeat of trouble advancing. They had seen the sandbags and recruiting offices and parades in the streets. Social advancement no longer attracted his readers, and to Maundy's astonishment *Mayfair's* sales dropped like a stone. He and Jack and Harry had to re-think their strategy.

This was the era of bucket shops and pyramid schemes offering insider advice to trusting punters who would 'invest' through dodgy companies in the belief that they would get huge percentage returns. A tiny proportion of the original investors often did, because their profits came directly from the funds deposited by others later. The role of these fortunate early investors was to encourage others.

Most of the money in such schemes went into the pockets of directors of the investment company. Horatio Bottomley had made a living that way for years. In 1914 Jack Keen-Hargreaves and Maundy Gregory set up Albemarle Investments Ltd at 174 New Bond Street. Perhaps neither of them had the nerve, or saw the necessity to perpetrate an outright swindle like this, because it remained entirely dormant and in 1917 it was wound up by the authorities.[1]

Maundy and the brothers were said to have fallen out by 1916.[2] This may not be strictly true. That summer, nearly every able-bodied man under forty had already joined up, or was taking refuge abroad. Jack Keen-Hargreaves joined the immensely courageous and glamorous Flying Corps. Harry, however, had arrived on 20 September, 1915, in New York City, and stayed at the St Regis. He found office accommodation at 347 Fifth Avenue, in the heart of the booming metropolis (the Empire State Building would go up next door later).

From there, his United Press Agency began public relations work; hanging around journalists, providing them with bits and pieces to the advantage of his clients, and picking up gossip.[3] He also supplied Maundy with information about suspects who were leaving New York Harbour for England. He sailed back at least once himself, before returning to New York on 24 February 1916.

Perhaps if the brothers and Maundy did quarrel, it was over Maundy's detective duties. He had become, if you set aside his usual blether about Loyalty to the Crown, a grass. Years later, Major Eric Holt-Wilson, the Deputy Director of MI5, pointed out that Gregory had been known to the security services since 1910.[4] He had 'had direct dealings with them since August, 1914.' In wartime he got very thick with the police, and probably failed to give fair shares of his rewards as an informer to the brothers. Not only that, but he saw informing as a way of keeping out of uniform. This it might be, so long as his assistance added gilt to the career of a sufficiently influential policeman.

The Metropolitan Police Sports Ground was not far from his little wooden hut at Thames Ditton. It was a link between Maundy and the Director of Intelligence, Basil Thomson.

Thomson, a son of a former Archbishop of York, educated at Eton and Oxford, had an overbearing personality and no scintilla of doubt about his own supremacy in all things to do with detection. Years of colonial service in Fiji, followed by work as a barrister, author, prison governor and Inspector of Prisons had brought him, in 1913, to Scotland Yard as Assistant Commissioner. The Commissioner, Sir Edward Henry, had been the subject of an assassination attempt the previous year, and undoubtedly this was taken into account when Thomson was appointed. There was a perceived need for a firm hand on the tiller; someone willing to take control if necessary.

Thomson was that, all right. When war was imminent he decided, in his capacity as Assistant Commissioner with responsibility for Special Branch, to be a clearing-house for all covert operations. Secret agencies were proliferating in the military and the navy, as well as the Metropolitan Police. Unless information about individuals and suspect networks were shared, then the bewildering plethora of units run by the War Office, the Admiralty, and Scotland Yard would duplicate work unnecessarily. Informal channels of communication already existed between these but as the new boy, ambitious and tidy-minded, Thomson was dissatisfied; he thought every agency should be duty bound to hand over all its news to a single Director of Intelligence and that Director of Intelligence should be himself.

Most empire-builders in his position would have suggested their immediate superior for such a post, but not Thomson. He was a forceful, persistent, voluble fellow and drove all before him. He retained his position as Assistant Commissioner and obtained, not merely the new post in addition to his regular duties, but a generous second salary, office facilities and a budget from Secret Service funds.[5] He dictated memo after self-important memo:

> Steps have been taken to secure the necessary rooms in Scotland House. They will be connected by private lines to the military intelligence, naval intelligence, MI5, the Secret Service and the Propaganda Office in Fleet Street.
>
> It is proposed to divide the Department into two branches, Home and Foreign, with a selected officer over each. Daily reports will be issued on labour unrest, and weekly digests of foreign intelligence. . . So far as possible, the expenses, including the pay and travelling expenses of Special Branch officers employed in the provinces, will be charged to the Metropolitan Police Fund and met from the Treasury Special Grant of £100,000. . . The contribution from S.S. [secret service] funds will be paid by the Treasury and the Home Secretary, and payments will be made by the Under-Secretary to Mr Thomson monthly or as occasion requires.[6]

Gregory was only too ready to help Thomson and the Special Branch. He had contacts at about forty important hotels from Anderson's in Fleet Street, via Claridge's and the Ritz to the Westminster Palace in Victoria. If Johnny Foreigner didn't at some stage stay in one of those, he wasn't worth investigating. For a regular retainer, Gregory could scan the guest list at any of them. He made a list of fifteen German suspects whose names he had passed to Thomson: Stoecker, Liebermann, Schonherr, Uhl, Blucher, Eberlain, Foerster, Gerhardt, Heinze, Hodel, Leuthold, Mohr, Schutz, Weiss, Voigt . . . How much he knew of these people when he reported them is unknown. Their names came from Harry Keen-Hargreaves in New York. Thomson was no liberal, and the popular mood was rabid, as expressed by Horatio Bottomley in *John Bull* on 15 May 1915:

> I call for a vendetta against every German in Britain, whether "naturalised" or not . . . You cannot naturalise an unnatural beast − a human abortion − a hellish freak. But you can exterminate it. And now the time has come. No German must be allowed to live in our land −

By being in England during the Great War, perfectly innocent strangers risked falling victim to xenophobic paranoia. So when every other able-bodied man felt he must fight or flee, Gregory was doing very nicely as a civilian. He had never liked joining things. He was temperamentally conservative, and certainly not averse to hunting down Socialists and Huns, Thomson style, but he had no affiliation to any political or religious body and belonged to no clubs and never had; he was an extrovert loner, truly happy with other people only when he was holding their attention. And if you had money in wartime, London was fun; soldiers and sailors crowded into town in search of the bright lights. As Frances Stevenson, Lloyd George's secretary and lover, noted in her diary in 1916:

> At the Savoy . . . things seem to be as gay as ever − you see the same crowds of showily-dressed, painted women, the same dancing, the same band − which still wears the costume of a Hungarian band![7]

Altogether, the Army did not appeal, and it was unlikely that the Army would be very keen on him, either. He was thirty-nine, five feet seven and a half, and had taken no exercise since Games at school.

On 4 February 1916 he attested, as required, his ability to serve, at the Recruiting Office at St James' Vestry Hall in Piccadilly. He then carried on with normal life.

On 22 June 1916, Basil Thomson began asking for a whip-round among the covert agencies with which to pay Maundy Gregory £150 for services rendered. He began with Vernon Kell, Head of MI5:

Dear Kell,

A Mr J M Gregory connected with the newspaper *Mayfair* has, at various times since the commencement of the war, given information, some of it useful, some not, and has now made a request for money to cover the expenses he has incurred.

I have discussed the matter with Sir Edward Henry and I think that a sum of £150 would be fair. Would you be disposed to allow £50 if D.I.D. and I do the same? . . . some of the information given covers matters in which the Admiralty was interested.[8]

D.I.D. was the powerful Director, Intelligence Division at the Admiralty, Captain Reginald 'Blinker' Hall. Kell, at MI5g, forwarded Thomson's letter appended to a shirty note cross-referenced to the files Campbell/Gregory, Gregory/Keen-Hargreaves, P Oppenheimer, Dr Heinrichs, Royal Hotel Bradford, Gunzberg, and Buell:

You may like to discuss with BT. I told him personally I was against anything of the sort on principle. People who give gratuitous information and then want payment lead one if paid to an expenditure which would have probaby been more profitably made in other directions – Here we are asked to pay for someone who merely goes over the same ground as we do, without any control from us. Some of the information is laughable and generally I should say it comes within the category of 'what's true is not new etc' [and what's new is not true].

If it's to help BT out of a hole that's another affair, but if it is so, let's have it stated frankly.[9]

Someone has scrawled an answer below:

> I have spoken to BT about this and told him I expected heavy
> weather to be made of his suggestion. He says D.I.D. has
> already paid up £50, so [?] we will stump up £50 and leave it
> at that. [10]

Now this is odd. Basil Thomson, as we have seen, had a perfectly
adequate supply of funds with which to pay the occasional informant.
What expensive work had Gregory completed in June of 1916?
Could it have had anything to do with the trial of Sir Roger
Casement? [11]

Sir Roger Casement was hanged in June, 1916, for treason. He
was a former British diplomat of Irish origin who had gained the
respect of his peers, and of liberal opinion generally, for his thorough,
compassionate reporting on the working conditions of indigenous
people in parts of South America and Africa between 1900 and 1910.
He was also a fierce supporter of the Irish republican cause. Since
the start of the war he had attempted (and when caught, he did not
dispute it) to gain German backing for a force of Irishmen who
would fight against the British in Ireland. However, fearing that the
Easter Rising of 1916 would be mis-timed, he had crossed to Ireland
in a German submarine and attempted to land in order to warn 'the
boys' not to shoot too soon.

The Germans were using codes they changed daily, which the
British deciphered. (Decoding staff were based in Room 40 at the
Admiralty and were under the command of Captain Hall at Naval
Intelligence.) Casement was arrested as soon as he got to the Irish
coast, taken to London, interviewed by Basil Thomson and charged
with treason, a hanging offence. As a traitor he was sent to the Tower.
It had been decided not to court-martial him but to put him before a
jury. Wyndham Childs, the War Office official responsible, decided that
a criminal trial 'would have more impact on the neutral countries.'

Casement's trial might have, but what about the sentence? The
man would become a martyr if he were hanged, but if he were not,
the Irish would roar that he had been working for the British secret

service all along. Were he condemned to death but reprieved under pressure, he might incite rescue attempts or retaliatory kidnaps. Whether he lived or died, there would be violence.

British counter-insurgency officers had been working against Irish republicans since about 1860. Now, in May 1916, the last thing the British wanted was further violence in Dublin diverting troops from the Great War, or morale-destroying explosions at armaments factories in England. If the court made a martyr out of Casement, anything could happen.

Supporters were promising to protest in favour of reprieve, should he be sentenced to die. Casement prepared himself for martyrdom.

There was one way to get these people to keep quiet: by repugnance against the man's character. In 1916 homosexuality was illegal, and almost unmentionable. The kindest opinion was that it was an illness, to be robustly treated with cold showers and hot women.

Before and during Casement's trial, Thomson and Hall circulated typed copies of his handwritten diaries describing in lurid note form his brief encounters with rent boys. They were said to have been brought from his pre-war lodgings in Ebury Street, and came later collectively to be known as the Black Diaries. They attracted prurient fascination from those in the know.

Casement's influential sympathisers, once convinced that the diaries existed and were genuine, melted away like snow in summer. By 22 June 1916 when Basil Thomson asked for the £150 for Gregory, calls for a reprieve were few. Casement was hanged exactly seven days later to murmurs, rather than howls, of protest. Had the special payment anything to do with the Casement affair?

Donald McCormick wrote that Maundy Gregory was the first to tell 'the authorities' that Casement was a homosexual (not the first to refer to the diaries).[12] Yet the mere fact of Casement's homosexuality was well known to the Foreign Office, at least, from 1914, if not sooner. In the first months of the war, Casement had picked up a seaman called Christensen in New York. This man immediately became his dearest companion and sailed with him to Oslo as his servant. Casement was travelling under an assumed name and American passport (supplied by Irish republicans in New York) en route to Germany, to recruit Irishmen from German prisoner of war camps.[13]

Casement was garrulous by nature and he trusted Christensen. According to Foreign Office files,[14] on 29 October, 1914, Christensen slipped away and visited the British Legation in Oslo. Over the next few days he spilled the beans on the German-Irish plot while refusing to identify Casement by name. A junior official, Francis Lindley, saw him on his first visit and noted:

> I understood that his relations with the Englishman were of an improper character.[15]

Mansfeldt Findlay, the British Minister, described Christensen as 'age twenty-four, about six feet, strongly made, clean shaven, fair hair, blue or grey eyes very small and close together, gap in front teeth... speaks English fluently, but with Norwegian-American accent... Has a fleshy, disippated appearance.' The police in New York, Findlay discovered, described him as 'a dangerous type of Norwegian-American criminal.'

Before leaving Norway for Germany, Christensen gave the British certain inflammatory articles, a pamphlet, and at least one letter from Christensen, apparently written to a third party. Findlay 'transmitted Christensen's information to Whitehall, enclosing the material Christensen had handed over'.

In November 1914 Casement's plans – written in clumsy doublespeak to sympathisers in America – were read by the Foreign Office. Immediately, action was taken.

Copies of Findlay's despatch, and the enclosures, were sent to Lord Kitchener at the War Office, and to Winston Churchill at the Admiralty; and with Kitchener's concurrence, Findlay was authorised to pay Christensen up to five thousand pounds – the sum he had demanded – for information leading to capture.[16] Thomson and Hall concocted a plot to trap Casement which involved borrowing a yacht and sending it to sail the Irish coast to pick up information about the man. This they put into action. Brian Inglis, in *Roger Casement*, thought 'it sounded like a parody of Erskine Childers' *The Riddle of the Sands* – except that Childers' plot was by contrast credible.'[17]

At Christmas 1914, Christensen left Casement, who still trusted him, in Germany and took incriminating documents to the British Legation in Oslo. He also gave them details of Casement's plan to land in Ireland, and tracings of some German minefield plans he had found in a drawer. 'The Foreign Office sent copies to Asquith, Kitchener, Churchill, the Irish Department, and the Intelligence Services.'[18] This was in the last week of December, 1914 and over the New Year. Basil Thomson was Assistant Commissioner, Scotland Yard, and Director of Intelligence. Whether or not Christensen was a trustworthy informant, enough information had – by early 1915 – come Thomson's way to make it *imperative* that he trace Casement's contacts in London and search places he had stayed in.

If Maundy Gregory had been the first to inform 'the authorities', military, civilian, or diplomatic, that Casement was a homosexual, then he must have done so before Christensen did. There is no known evidence to suggest this.

Were the diaries forged – by Maundy Gregory (as McCormick also alleged) or anyone else? Peter Singleton-Gates says:

> Gertrude Bannister, Casement's cousin, has made a statement, now preserved in the National Library of Ireland, which gives one version of how the diaries were discovered.

> "As a matter of fact, the trunks left behind by Roger in Ebury Street were handed over to the police by the landlady at the instigation of another lodger as soon as Roger went to Germany in 1914. Sir Basil Thomson had the diary in his possession at least 16 months before Roger's trial, and he had plenty of time to see that it was doctored to suit his purpose long before the time he needed it for propaganda purposes. It was shown to various people sometime during 1915, I think at the end of 1915, I am not sure."[19]

With beliefs like this, Casement's family, who loved him, wished uncomfortable facts away; but it depends whose facts you believe. A note in Metropolitan Police files from Inspector Parker lists Casement's London addresses over the years and states:

> During the month of May 1914 Casement deposited with Mr Germain of 50 Ebury Street, Pimlico, SW, some boxes containing books, etc. These books which included three diaries for the years 1903, 1910 and 1911, a ledger, an address book and a memorandum book were brought to New Scotland Yard by Mr Germain on the 25th April 1916.[20]

So if we believe the date and details of the Metropolitan Police file, Thomson had – not years, but just a few weeks, before the trial in which to read the diaries for the first time, edit and rewrite them in a way he would have found abhorrent, have them typed and organise a forgery that has since confounded investigators.

Hundreds of thousands of words have been written about the forgery theory and the overwhelming consensus is that the diaries were perfectly genuine and had not been tampered with before typed copies were circulated. Peter Singleton-Gates, who was shown the original Lett's and Dollard's diaries by Wyndham Childs (Basil Thomson's successor) in 1925, could compare them with other samples of Casement's handwriting, and could see how the notes on his sex life were mixed up with all the other entries. He was certain that they were genuine.

But Singleton-Gates nonetheless had reason to believe Gertrude Bannister that they had been taken as evidence much earlier. Artemus Jones, Casement's defence counsel, had received the diaries quite early in proceedings from the Attorney-General, F E Smith, who said the police had found them during a search of property where Casement had stayed in Pimlico. The search could have been undertaken at any time from Christmas, 1914 when the Foreign Office in Oslo alerted the British authorities to Casement as a danger.[21]

Gregory could have had something to do with the *retrieval* of the diaries. He had a contact at the Victoria end of Ebury Street – Mr Goring of the eponymous hotel. What did prompt 'Mr Germain' – if he ever existed – to turn up at the Yard? There is no record of this individual in street directories. One does not normally leave incriminating documents for years on end in the care of a person who often moves house. It has been alleged that Germain was Casement's ex-lover; the same thing applies. It is almost as though the diaries were in the possession of a blackmailer.

It is Thomson's own stories that incline one to think there was some mystery around the way the diaries got to Scotland Yard. He was a prolific and published writer and in later years, gave five separate accounts of how and where the diaries were discovered – in none of which were either he, or Captain Hall, present, and in none of which Inspector Parker or Mr Germain figure either. In every case the discovery happens so soon after the arrest that there is no time for forgery. Since the authenticity of the diaries is not in dispute, either this was to protect Germain, or it was to protect someone who had prompted Germain to act, or it was simply a pack of lies to conceal inferences that the British had been interested in Casement's activities quite early in the war.[22]

If Gregory had been prompted to snoop in Ebury Street by the police it seems unlikely that he would have missed the advantage to himself in taking the diaries into his personal custody. Would he have parted with them for £150? There are a lot of 'ifs'.

Gregory's least controversial involvement is with the *circulation* of the diaries. Thomson had them typed – no small task, but he had the resources – at once. Within weeks of Casement's capture, in May 1916 copies were circulating around London clubs. Generous luncheons spent entertaining opinion-formers with juicy extracts would account for some at least of the £150. Gossip about Casement's guilty secret spread so rapidly among men who mattered in London that if Gregory was involved, he was not the only one; Captain Reginald Hall and Sir Ernley Blackwell, the prosecuting solicitor, were among those mentioned later. Alfred Noyes, British propagandist in America, poet and lecturer at Princeton, was appalled. Copies 'were circulated behind the scenes of the trial, through London clubs, among Members of Parliament and others who might be thought to influence public opinion.'

The King saw them and showed them to a liberal, pro-Irish Bishop; the Archbishop of Canterbury decided not to look; and according to Brian Inglis:

Particular care was taken that influential Americans in Britain should see extracts. Captain Hall showed them to the Associated Press representative in London . . . They were shown to Walter Page, the Anglophile American Ambassador, who, even before he had seen them, had written to say that he had heard that much information about Casement 'of an unspeakably filthy character' was available, but had been withheld at his trial.

Casement's trial is of interest here in drawing attention to a charismatic individual who would remain friendly with Gregory for many years. This was F.E. Smith, leading the prosecution. He had handed the diary copies over to Artemus Jones, on Casement's legal team, suggesting that Jones's client might wish to plead 'guilty but insane'. As a fierce Unionist, he was perfectly well aware that this would hardly redeem Casement in the eyes of Irish nationalists: either he would be exposed as a man with unmentionable tendencies, or excused the death sentence on unknown grounds and therefore an undercover spy.

'F.E.' as people knew him was a wit and bon viveur, a one-time Oxford law lecturer and Liverpool lawyer with excellent connections who was also a good friend of Horatio Bottomley. Ironically, considering the allegations against the man whose execution he sought, F.E. himself was said to have been implicated with Edward Carson, his fellow Ulster Unionist, in running guns from Germany to fight the threat of Home Rule before the war.

F.E. won his case, Sir Roger Casement was hanged, the war went on, and the Irish stayed angry. Gregory, with £150 in his pocket, remained determined not to get drafted. People looked askance at men out of uniform, unless they were in a protected occupation. Basil Thomson, Director of Intelligence, was the only way Maundy's 'occupation' would ever be 'protected', so he clung to him. For his part, Basil Thomson came to depend on Maundy Gregory. The man impressed people.

In 1917 Gregory was asked to undertake surveillance in the office of Captain Craig, of the War Office Procurement Department. Craig worked out of an office at 11 Waterloo Place, using the cover of 'Craig & Co, Merchants'. Those who worked there were all arms experts of one kind or another.

Captain Craig had a secretary, Miss Phyllis Barnes. He told her in confidence that one of the men sharing the offices, an Australian scientist and inventor with connections to Germany, was suspected of being a spy:

> He said a very important member of the Secret Service was going to investigate and I was to carry out his instructions. It was Maundy Gregory who came to the office... He asked me to keep a list of all incoming and outgoing telephone calls from this man's room... and all names of visitors. He said he could not give me his address as it was strictly private.[23]

She took a phone number from Gregory, where he promised there was a 'trustworthy person who could take messages'; it was on the Gerrard (Soho) exchange. One thinks immediately of Peter Mazzina. Their relationship was as strong as ever, although Mazzina would soon marry, at eighteen, the daughter of Mrs Coletta of the Queen's Hotel, Leicester Square.

Maundy Gregory was very well dressed but wore too much jewellery. His hair was brown, he was not bald then, and he did not wear glasses, but used a monocle. He was always courteous although he had a pompous and grand manner. There was an air of mystery about him.[24]

What happened to the Australian arms expert is not recorded.

After the request for £150, the next set of documents in Gregory's MI5 file also reveals a direct connection with Thomson. Gregory's health – despite all the long lunches – when he was almost forty, was judged A1 by the Army medical board, so there was to be no exemption from service. In April 1917, Gregory was called up. On 19 April, Thomson wrote to Major Carter:

> I shall be glad if you will state what steps may be necessary to get Mr J M Gregory who appealed unsuccessfully at the

Westminster Tribunal put onto the 'not to be called up' list
for a short time as he is completing some enquiries on which
he is furnishing me with reports. He came to see me a day or
two ago and suggested that he might be made use of in some
branch of the Intelligence Service. He has from time to time
furnished useful information to this department.[25]

This plea surfaced at D.R.7, with a note from Carter at MI5g
appended, the following day:

Would it be possible to give him a small extension . . . ? I do
not suggest a period longer than a month.

Whoever got it stalled for time, writing back two days later:

Would you please supply Mr Gregory's registered address,
where we can look into his case?

The next day, the Tilinsky Case file began to re-circulate; a back
number from two years before. It was mentioned in a note from
Captain Merivale. Here was a photographed copy of 'an alleged bond
relating to a Russo-Japanese agreement dated 1904, supposed to have
been given to Tilinsky by Japanese Govt, shown to four officers by a
man who stated he was employed by British SS.'[26]

The Tilinsky case was a wild story of intrigue and the potential
release of 46 million yen, on 22 March 1915, to the bearer of the
bond; it had been passing from desk to desk in Scotland Yard and the
Foreign Office since October, 1914. A man in Brixton Prison had
said the bond belonged to him, and Captain Miller was to look into
it.

Westell wanted to know who the man was who had shown the copy
to the four officers. Someone else wrote 'Our old friend Gregory: see
note'. On 25 April Westell scrawled below 'I could not remember
yesterday who Gregory was: here he is.'

A scribbled note from Captain Cooke to Major Carter was
attached, ready to be typed. Gregory had turned up at Cooke's office

with a reference from Lord Athburney. As before he was trying to get out of the call-up and get work in Intelligence. Cooke wrote:

> I was very unfavourably impressed by him, but promised to let him know... He is not a 'Sahib', and he is evidently talkative, boastful etc., see attached reports. I think he had much better be called up, and I should put him on the gate with MI6c or he will get an intelligence job with the Home Forces... Note: I spoke to Mr Thomson about him. He said he could well do without him, though he is doing a particular job for S.Y. at the moment. He showed me the photos of the Tilinsky fake!!

On 1 May 1917 Major Carter wrote a letter to 6 Albion Street, where Maundy Gregory had a flat on the first floor:

> I have to inform you that there is no vacancy in this department in which suitable use could be made of your services, and in view of that fact I cannot see my way to make representations to the recruiting authorities with regard to your call-up.

The following day MI6c was duly minuted by Captain Cooke:

> – that if at any time this man applies for intelligence work, his application should be regarded with some suspicion, and that we can give full information about him.

He did not underestimate the thickness of 'this man's' hide. Maundy Gregory ignored Major Carter's rejection and wrote to the War Office again within weeks. His letter was not acknowledged, but it was circulated by Major Ritson with a note on which the relevant officers scrawled replies.

'Any use to you?'

MI1c – 'I fear we have nothing in the Intelligence Corps.'

MI5 – 'We cannot use him. Have you any vacancy?'

The letter came back via MI1a, MI5h and . . . Major Ritson.

'Thank you, but we have no vacancies at present.'

Once more it went the rounds. Pinned to the letter, handwritten notes succeeded one another.

'Passed to you for action. I don't want him, thanks.'

'This man seems to want [illegible]. If he would be willing to serve as a member of Port Police [perhaps] Major Spencer would like to have him [if] enlisted?'

'Major Haldane. . . Shall I apply for this man? If so shall I make a point of us wanting his services whatever his medical category may be? There appears no chance of his getting a commission as he is nearly forty years of age.'

'Spoke DIP who has seen this man and thinks it better not to employ him.'

Once a piece of paper was in the system, it was on a merry-go-round. Gregory's plea surfaced yet again in June.

'Any use to you?'

'No thanks.'

'See two red flags and considerable f.p. including recent correspondence. We cannot afford to waste good material, and it is important also to capture and discipline it. I should have said the best course was to see this man entered and at once drafted into one of the Port intelligence parties; unless G wants him here.'

'I agree. He is not a suitable person to be employed in the office.'

Vernon Kell decided to put a stop to this once and for all. He wrote on 1 July 1917, to Thomson asking him to make enquiries about J.M. Gregory. The result was a report by Scotland Yard Inspector Herbert Fitch, delivered on 16 July.[27]

Gregory, 'who is at present residing at 6 Albion Street, Hyde Park, W' had been 'originally associated with an individual styling himself Baron John Clark Keen-Hargreaves in the capacity of confidential clerk.' Fitch traced *Mayfair* from its foundation in October 1910 at 9 Oxford Street, to 7 Albemarle Street in October 1913, and thence to 174 New Bond Street (immediately behind the Albemarle Street office) in June, 1915. 'John Maundy Gregory joined the board as a director on 17 December 1914. Prior to this I am given to understand that he acted as editor of the paper.' *Mayfair* had appeared only spasmodically during the war. The company had 'never been strong financially'; there were several county court judgments against it.

Baron Jack and Maundy had also collected subscriptions for a magazine called *The Horseman* (with little knowledge of the field, in Gregory's case) but subscribers were understandably cheesed off when no issues appeared; one had lodged a complaint with the police that he had received no return for his money. Fitch noted the existence of Albemarle Investments, and its dormancy.

Whilst at 7 Albemarle Street, W. [*sic*] Keen-Hargreaves, and Gregory after the outbreak of war, started a private enquiry agency with a view to obtaining information relative to German propaganda in this country and the United States. To this end Harry Keen-Hargreaves went to New York to undertake this branch of the work. Certain information obtained from time to time was communicated to this office.

Fitch had blown the fake Barony out of the water, though. 'I have made a careful search in Ruvigny's *Nobilities of Europe*, and similar works. . . the 'Baron' is now a 2nd Lieutenant in the Royal Flying Corps, stationed at Reading, but according to the latest Army list his title is not shown.' He had also tracked down a disgruntled employee, who said that Baron Jack was 'overbearing' and that generally, the brothers and Gregory had done some pretty fancy footwork with charity collections and dud company promotions in their time. At the very end, Fitch – perhaps prompted by Thomson, who had to save face somehow – added a paragraph:

> It is, however, right to say that since the beginning of the War, Mr Gregory has been furnishing this office with a great deal of information at his own expense and that some of this information has been useful, though, naturally, much of it was already known to us.

Fitch's report was signed off by Superintendent Quinn, Head of Special Branch. On 19 July 1917 Thomson forwarded it to Kell. Maundy had been in the Army since 10 July.

Nothing daunted Number 3294 Trooper A.J.M. Gregory of Combermere Barracks, Windsor[28], and he kept on nagging about work in Intelligence and/or a commission. He completed Form Number MT393A, squeezing into the space available, in his characteristically florid black italics, with capitalisation to add *gravitas* –

> From Aug 1914 to July 1917 conducted a large organisation of informants and regularly supplied Intelligence Information to the Authorities & also received small Government Grants. May 16 1917 was advised to apply to War Office for Intelligence work.

This was signed off by a couple of referees. Gregory did not turn to the local vicar. Instead one signature was that of Lord Plymouth, Lord Lieutenant of Glamorgan (and Sub-Prior of the Order of St John of Jerusalem, although he did not consider this important enough to mention) who said he had known him since 1914. The other referee was Major-General Alfred E. Turner, of Carlyle House, Chelsea Embankment, who had known him since 1912. (Both had been profiled in *Mayfair* with accompanying picture.) A Doctor of Divinity at Oxford confirmed that Gregory had studied there.[29]

Gregory was interviewed by an officer deputising for the Brigadier-General. For a third time his application went the rounds of MI1c, MI6c, MI5, MI1a, and MI5h. It got short shrift.

> 'As this candidate is A1 but has had no active service overseas we have no opportunity of offering him a Commission.'

> 'Not required by MI1a, MI1c or MI5. So informed on 21/6/17.'

That was that, then.

Maundy Gregory's War Office record states that he spent 1918 in the Irish Guards, at the Caterham Guards' Depot. Assuming that by 1918 the Guards were desperate enough to accept a forty-year-old 5ft 8 Trooper from Combermere Barracks, and that Maundy Gregory survived a year of being bellowed at and drilled – he is not down as an orderly, storeman, driver or instructor – and that he was one of the few who remained clean-shaven, and that he didn't lose weight during training . . . and that he got plenty of leave – anything is possible. A batman to someone, perhaps an officer with one blind eye? Surely not. For years, some influential people thought that Basil Thomson had succeeded in keeping Maundy out of uniform. In 1926 Major Holt-Wilson at MI5 wrote:

> He succeeded in selling a good deal of rubbish during the war to BT, who responded by manipulating his exemption from military service in order to employ him further.[30]

The memo was wrong. Thomson's attempt to get him into the secret service had failed. A commission had also been turned down. He really did go into the army, and really was a Trooper. Ethel Davies, Edith's niece, later testified, unprompted, that during the war he was dressed in khaki and stationed at Caterham. She had been a schoolgirl at the time and remembered his flat at Albion Street and his constant visits to Edith and Frederick Rosse.[31]

MAUNDY WAS A SOLDIER; THE WAR OFFICE DOCUMENTS
ARE NOT MISLEADING. BUT HE RETAINED SOME RED HOT
IRONS IN THE FIRE, AND A FEW WERE CONNECTED WITH
THE 1918 ELECTION.

CHAPTER FIVE

Breakthrough

An unusual job had fallen vacant. The successful candidate would have the scruples of a mercenary, the morals of an alley-cat and the discretion of a sphinx. He must have a sufficiently solid background to pass as a gentleman, at least to the undiscerning. He must have a profession which permitted him to meet, and question, and shrewdly assess, people in all walks of life. He must be a salesman capable of inspiring trust.

Above all, he must take the risks a spy takes, for if his illicit role came to light, his employers would wash their hands of him. Until that happened, he would be well paid.

There is an irony in Maundy Gregory's lasting influence on British political life, because by nature he had no interest in the business of government or the democratic process. His eyes glazed as he scanned the long crowded columns of political news in *The Times*. He would repeat the opinions of people he knew, and he was interested so long as he was personally concerned with the actors in the drama, but the real political situation in 1918 was of little interest to him.

It had its origins at the start of the war, with the insistence by a few Liberals (led by Lloyd George and Winston Churchill), and nearly all Unionists and Labour Party members that Asquith's government was doing too little, too late, to prevent a bloodbath and defeat.

In May 1915 the government became a Coalition: still led by Asquith, but with Unionists in key positions. However, those who wanted strong decisive action in the cause of victory remained frustrated.

By the winter of 1916, matters were coming to a head. On the left, some influential people favoured a negotiated peace. On the right,

Beaverbrook supported Lloyd George in an attitude of 'We can win this war. We just need to get organised *now*.' Asquith's government – because it seemed supine – made frustrated observers suspect that peace talks had already begun.

The final crisis came on 1 December when Lloyd George, with the covert backing of key Unionists, wrote to Asquith proposing that the central direction of the war should henceforth be placed in the hands of a three man War Council of which he, Lloyd George, would be the chairman. Asquith knew full well that should he accept this poison chalice he would be Prime Minister in name only and cordially rejected the proposal. On receipt of Asquith's reply, Lloyd George promptly resigned from the Government. Asquith, over-estimating his support, resigned in retaliation.

On Bonar Law's recommendation the King therefore summoned the most dynamic Liberal force, Lloyd George. Lloyd George's hour had come. Many who thought at the time that he had had greatness thrust upon him recognised later that he had been steering a steady course towards it all along. By his own admission he was not by nature a party man.[1] He had strong views about the way the country should be run, but these views never included submission to majority opinion or even to the imperatives of a political philosophy.

Under his leadership, and with carefully-nurtured support from Beaverbrook and his *Daily Express* and *Evening Standard*, Bonar Law and the Unionists, and Henderson and the Labour party, the State took key economic sectors in hand. Men of action from business and industry galvanised the Departments. Every effort was made to stimulate supplies of raw materials, of arms, and of trained men. All civilian life was directed to one end only: winning the war. In these desperate circumstances, businesses conceded ultimate control to the demands of the state, and trade unions co-operated to increase production.

In 1917, Lloyd George focused on winning the war. The short Welshman with the leonine head had the country behind him, although *The Times*, not entirely convinced that leopards of any party could change their spots, drew the party-funds issue to the attention of its readers. Shortly after the controversially long Birthday Honours list of 1917 it printed a letter from Mr Walter Hazell, a Covent Garden printer and philanthropist who had produced the *Your Country Needs You* posters. He remembered revelations about the Liberal Party Fighting Fund after Marconi, and worried about accountability:

> That sums, evidently large but never defined, should be in the hands of an official who rendered no account to anyone and who received it from unknown sources, supposed to be donations in return for honours, and disposed of it in equally unknown ways without any kind of audit, seems in the last degree unsatisfactory. . . How many Honours are paid for in money, how many partly in money and partly in public service, and how many for public service of various kinds only, no man can tell, but we can all guess. The only definite statement I can make is that a well-known Liberal friend of mine told me some time ago that a Conservative peer informed him that his peerage cost him £80,000.[2]

Bonar Law was convinced of the need to maintain the Coalition in power should an election be called, and get the job done. The need to raise money for the Coalition, rather than for the Diehard Unionists or the disgruntled Independent Liberals, was justified as the only way to make sure the war was won.

In 1918, fund-raising was more important than ever, because the Coalition's need to gain popular support by election had become imminent. The War was going badly. Russian opposition in the East had collapsed. There was mounting animosity between British High Command and Coalition politicians. In February, the Coalition sacked the Chief of the Imperial General Staff, General Robertson. In March, Ludendorff made a big push at Amiens. That spring America at last declared war on the Axis but only slowly began sending troops to Europe, and the British were suffering.

In May, General Frederick Maurice, former Director of Military Intelligence, alleged that Lloyd George and Bonar Law had held back arms and equipment due to Haig in France since the previous September. Asquith demanded a vote of no confidence.

The Army wanted victory by attrition – which meant getting the Americans in. The Government wanted peace, though not at any price. In their turn, some people in Government suspected that Maurice and other Generals were determined to prolong the war and get rid of Lloyd George; maybe even to replace him with General Robertson, if not with Asquith. Lloyd George – being a bit slippery about the relevant figures – won resoundingly in the debate Asquith had initiated over munitions for the Western Front. American troops were now pouring into France and armistice talks quietly started.

The Maurice uproar, resulting as it did in an albeit unsuccessful vote of censure against the Coalition, concentrated their minds. Just how fragile was their position? As 1918 progressed and an end to the war at last seemed in reach, Lloyd George had to consider renewing democratic endorsement of his leadership. A general election would be necessary at some point. Where did he stand?

The Diehard Tories seemed a spent force. In a three-cornered fight – a ruling Coalition dominated by Unionists and led by Lloyd George; Labour; and the Asquithian 'Independent' Liberals – the latter would try to regain power from the Coalition. And they had the party funds to back them. Could he seduce the Independents? He did not represent what they stood for any more than they represented his position.

Could he, perhaps, switch his allegiance to become leader of the Unionist party? It was true that the few anti-Coalition Diehard Tories had neither numbers nor influence on their side. The vast majority of Tories supported Lloyd George as Prime Minister. At least, they did in wartime, when his persuasiveness, political ruthlessness, and rat-like cunning meant he could do the job. As for their reservations about him – leaving aside the Irish question and his anti-drink campaign – he was not *one of us*. He suspected that if ruling-class disdain counted against him even with Liberal opponents (and it did),[3] it would prove insuperable in peacetime to Tories.

Could he, then, found a party of his own? It was too soon to think of this; he lacked the necessary funds, personal following and reliably positive press.

No; Lloyd George must maintain the Coalition as it stood, and strengthen his own position within it. At the end of 1917, foreseeing that such a decision might be necessary, he had consulted advisors from inside and outside the House. Captain Freddy Guest and Sir William Sutherland would be key to any plan they hatched. Guest, a dashing cousin of Winston Churchill, wounded in combat and still recuperating, was the Coalition Liberal Chief Whip (Lloyd George's preferred candidate had been Neil Primrose, but he had been killed). Sir William Sutherland, a bombastic fellow and old friend, was Patronage Secretary. They began to formulate a three-point plan.

First, they must get the Unionists to stick with them in the Coalition through an election.

Second, they must get hold of a newspaper.

Third, they must raise funds to promote a new party that would continue the Coalition's ideals long after the wartime emergency was over.

In July 1918, after the attack by Maurice and the vote of censure, they began to move forward with the first part of this plan. Bonar Law didn't take a lot of persuading to maintain the status quo,[4] for Lloyd George's personal stock had never been higher. Dr Addison, the Coalition Liberal Minister for Reconstruction, chaired a group of Coalition politicians from all three parties who worked out what future policies would be.

Next they worked out their electoral tactics. The Labour party took a back seat while Freddy Guest and the Unionist Chief Whip hammered out a deal. The constituencies would be carved up between them. In some, Coalition Unionists would oppose Independent Liberals and Labour candidates, and in others a 'Coaly Lib' would stand. The final list contained over 400 Coalition Unionists and only 150 Coalition Liberals. This was not a bad deal at all for Lloyd George. He could neither find, nor financially support, any more candidates. In order to get Coalition Unionists to vote for Coalition Liberals in certain constituencies, and vice versa in others, the parliamentary party would provide candidates with a letter of endorsement from HQ. This proved awkward to compose and rather long, so it was scrapped in favour of something short and to the point on one page. As smirking candidates turned up with their passport to nomination, Asquith made a sour remark about its resemblance to a ration coupon. The election of December, 1918 became known as the coupon election.

In many cases, the endorsement was paid for. Years later, J. C. C. Davidson – Bonar Law's secretary at the time – told an interviewer that Sir George Younger, the Unionist Chairman,

> ...told me that in 1918 Lloyd George had sold coupons to some disreputable Tories who would not, in normal circumstances, have been adopted in a village constituency. George Younger disliked this method of raising money, and thought that Lloyd George was getting most of it from Conservatives. [5]

His impression was reinforced by the Duke of Northumberland in his evidence to an enquiry in 1922. [6]

The second necessity, a voice in the press, had been under discussion for over a year. Again it was Captain Freddy Guest, the Chief Whip, who had been negotiating on Lloyd George's behalf, this time to buy a newspaper. He had received a rebuff from the *Westminster Gazette,* but after much politicking and argument had reached agreement with Frank Lloyd, owner of the *Daily Chronicle.*

The *Daily Chronicle*'s editor, Robert Donald, was dismayed. He kept saying that the owner was unwilling to sell. Privately he disliked the idea of being employed to write puffs for Lloyd George. He had met the Prime Minister to talk this over in March of 1918, but Lloyd George – just possibly distracted by the German offensive at Amiens, which had begun that very morning – was not particularly attentive. Provoked, Donald hired Lloyd George's enemy General Maurice as his military correspondent, and tried to raise a counter-bid elsewhere. Some time after this Sir James Dalziel intervened on Lloyd George's behalf with the asking price, and the owner was persuaded to sell. [7]

In the autumn of 1918, the matter was settled: Lloyd George would have his newspaper. 'The *Daily Chronicle* purchase has been completed. LG is to have full control of the editorial policy through Sir James Dalziel who will in effect be his agent,' noted Sir George Riddell, owner of the *News of the World*, who had just heard the gossip from Winston Churchill and Lord Rothermere. (Riddell, a friend of Lloyd George, had given him a house at Walton Heath, in Surrey.)[8] Silent newsreels showing politicians getting off liners or emerging from No. 10 served only to convey an image. Printed media – books, pamphlets and newspapers – were the only means of communicating ideas. Parties set out their stalls in the constituencies at election time with posters, public meetings and speeches at the hustings. Every day of the year, persuasion relied on print.

Lloyd George took over the *Chronicle* in October. One of his first moves was to sack its editor and with him, General Maurice. How had he raised the money to buy it? Beaverbrook had at one time been ready to put up the money, and possibly the Berry brothers. A likely donor was Lord Leverhulme (although he denied it, not very convincingly. He was deaf, and favoured short negative answers). Lord Inverforth was believed to be a significant contributor.

The purchase price was £1.6 million, which indicates that if Lloyd George's own war-chest contributed very much of it, either he had been accepting huge sums for honours since becoming Prime Minister just eighteen months before, or he had extraordinarily generous benefactors, or the Lloyd George Fund would be in hock for a while yet.

Suddenly, on 11 November, the Armistice was upon them. The Coalitionists were ready for it: the newspaper was in place.

> Mr Lloyd George had a most enthusiastic reception at Wolverhampton on Saturday . . . said the task of the new Parliament would be 'to make Britain a land fit for heroes to live in' . . . comprehensive housing scheme and improved transport. . .[9]

The *Chronicle* opened the election campaign with whole speeches by Lloyd George reprinted in full – Slums Must Go; How our Mineral Riches May be Utilised; What the Coalition Ministry has achieved; Prime Minister's Profound Belief in Great Britain. . . Lloyd George, Churchill, the entire Cabinet were buoyant, positive, allowing for no vision but that of a golden future under the Coalition.

The coupons were issued, the homecoming troops and new women voters were urged to cast their votes, the opposition was in disarray – and weeks later, the election was won. By Christmas, the Coalition had a vice-like grip on power, with a majority of 526 of whom all but fifty had been 'coupon' candidates. The Independent Liberals were almost all gone. The fifty-seven strong opposition were mostly Labour men, whose support outside parliament was greater than that number would indicate.

In Cabinet, there were eleven Unionists, including Austen Chamberlain, Arthur Balfour, F.E. Smith who was now Lord Birkenhead the Lord Chancellor, and Bonar Law, Lloyd George's Deputy. There were eight Liberals, including Lloyd George, Winston Churchill and Sir Eric Geddes who had been in charge of shipping during the war. There was one Labour member and a couple more Lords, including Lord French as Viceroy of Ireland, and Lord Inverforth.

For Lloyd George, the golden fruits of triumph had a worm at the centre. He was now even more vulnerable to the Unionist majority in his own government. The Coalition could fracture at any time along party lines.

Without delay, Freddy Guest acted on part three of the master plan. He must raise funds to promote a new party to replace this fragile edifice. He would step up contributions to the Lloyd George Fund. The *Daily Chronicle* would show a profit in due course; but most of the ready money would be raised, as Asquith's election fund had been raised in 1910, by selling honours.

It wasn't going to be difficult to dispose of a few baronies. All sorts of people had made their pile in the War, and were queueing up for a seat in the Lords. But a new party would need a *lot* of money: the outrageous figure of £4 million was mentioned. Guest and Sutherland agreed that it would be a full-time job just to vet the candidates, not to mention haggling over commissions and vetting the touts. And the more people you approached, the more likely it was that the straight cash-for-honours deal would be gossiped about. It was not illegal; but it must remain confidential. A note on 10 Downing Street headed paper reads:

> You will have noticed that Mr Marple postdated his cheque – Jan 7 1919 – in order to get his honour on Jan 1, and to enable him and his sponsors to say that when he received his knighthood he had paid nothing for it. The first thing is surely to return his cheque and the second not to give the knighthood. Otherwise if these stories get out – and presumably I am not the only person to whom he has told it – it will be a bad hour for us.[10]

Freddy Guest talked to Alick Murray about putting a reliable intermediary between himself and the touts. Lord Murray had resigned – indeed, had temporarily fled to South America 'on business' – as a result of the Marconi Scandal of 1912. This had revealed among other things the Liberal Party's dependence on honours sales for its funds.[11] Murray carried the can for that. Lloyd George survived Marconi and so did Lord Reading, who would become Viceroy of India; but Murray never quite recovered. So he was out of the honours game, but still the undisputed expert on how to do it. The Independent Liberals were still flush with the money he had raised for the Party.

It was messy, Murray admitted. You got the party faithful who'd drop heavy hints and reel people in for nothing, but they could be indiscreet; at the other end of the scale there were crooks who'd accept money from fools with no intention of passing it on to the Party. You had to make yourself available to the people who were willing to pay, and explain to the ones who'd been duped that you had no idea what they were talking about.

Freddy Guest and Sir William Sutherland came to a decision. The job was too time-consuming and potentially politically disastrous if they were to be involved only once removed from the candidates.

They must deputise. As Murray advised, they would turn the messy business over to a single intermediary who would farm out the work, get the trussing and plucking done elsewhere, so to speak, and bring them a reliable list of names. He would be rewarded by a retainer plus commission. The retainer could be paid in kind – rent, maybe, on some office accommodation. The commission would be a percentage of the purchase price; an excellent incentive to maximising returns.

They thought of the existing touts – a seedy lot. Men in brown hats, Freddy called them. An exception was Harry Shaw,[12] a horse breeder and property developer who had three town houses in Belgravia and farmed 2,000 acres in Leicestershire. He was discreet, and would approach rich punters fearlessly and effectively – the only problem was that he worked for Bonar Law.[13]

There must be somebody . . . Maybe Murray could come up with a name. Someone he had used before, perhaps? There was one chap, he said. Fellah who ran a magazine before the war. Friend of Thomson, so no difficulties there. . . He'd done well in this line before. . .

Maundy Gregory was delighted to receive an invitation to join Lord and Lady Murray at their Scottish castle, where the other guests would include Captain Frederick Guest.

Freddy had found a man who fitted the job description. A man with the scruples of a mercenary, the morals of an alley-cat and the discretion of a sphinx.

CHAPTER SIX

A Vanishing

As the post-war era dawned, Maundy Gregory emerged like a butterfly from the khaki. Significant resources were devoted to Mr Gregory, so recently blackballed by the secret service. On 4 February he had been demobbed, and had given his address in peacetime *c/o* Frederick Rosse, at 24a, Hinde Street, off Manchester Square. (Edith had begun to buy property).[1] In the summer of 1919, he was installed in a suite of offices at 45 Parliament Street on the corner of Derby Gate. There he would set himself up as editor of the *Whitehall Gazette and St James' Review*. Number 45, like number 38 which became his office later, is part of the Parliamentary Estate. The houses have been re-numbered, but as they are Parliament's property they are the responsibility of either the Lords, or the Lords and Commons jointly. In 2007, they are *maintained* by:

> the Parliamentary Estates Directorate and the Parliamentary Works Services Directorate within the Serjeant at Arms Department in the House of Commons... Security costs are arranged and monitored jointly but are billed separately to the two Houses by the Metropolitan Police on a pre determined ratio. Additionally, the two Houses incur administration costs on each other's behalf.[2]

In 1919, so far as we can tell, they were similarly owned and administered, and anyone occupying space in them was doing so under the stewardship of the Parliamentary Estate as then constituted. In other words, it was within the power of individuals in Government to provide, or deny, accommodation in the terrace of houses between numbers 38 (close to the Bridge Street end) and 45.

Maundy Gregory was provided with a suite of rooms, and funds with which to set up his establishment and employ a modest staff. He commissioned the uniforms of the attendants – who, give or take a detail here and there, looked just as though they worked at the House of Commons, fifty yards away. He chose an important-looking desk and a chair, its back to the window, that raised him an inch or two above the one where his visitor would sit.

He would need a secretary. He had been impressed by Captain Craig's young lady, Miss Barnes. He invited her to attend an interview.

'His manner was as impressive as usual,' she remembers. 'He said he was going to publish an important periodical and he wanted to engage a confidential secretary and receptionist who was capable of receiving well-known and influential people, including royalty. This last I thought rather amusing.' Miss Barnes politely turned the offer down.[3]

He found an alternative (so discreet that we still do not know who she was, although eventually he would be joined by a Mr George Pratley). Then the publisher of the 'important periodical' set about summoning, one by one, certain gentlemen, whose names he had been given, to discuss their future with him. They were not journalists. They were the men in brown hats so despised by Freddy Guest, who were already dismayed that their hotline to power had been cut. Recent approaches had been turned down out of hand by the Coalition Liberal Whips' Office and the Patronage Secretary. The touts had been told that further dealings of that nature would be arranged by other means: *wait and see*. So they were intrigued, and relieved, to hear that from now on, business would be handled by Mr J. Maundy Gregory in person. He told them that as accredited agent, he was willing to consider employing these gentlemen as consultants on an *ad hoc* basis for a small commission.

Number 45, he quickly recognised, was not ideal for this business. It was laid out in such a way that there might be embarrassing encounters between touts and hopefuls, and its entrance was within yards of the front door of the Red Lion. Therefore within his first year of operation, he moved the office of the *Whitehall Gazette* to Number 38, where he took over what had been barristers' chambers. He then instructed his network of furtive gentlemen that should they wish to see him on business, he would indicate a time when they might visit his office for discussions after dark. Before arriving, they must stroll to a point on the corner of Parliament Square from which they could see his office window. A system of lights, operated by a switch on his desk, would confirm whether or not they were welcome.

Personally, he avoided running into anyone he knew as he entered and left. The tall old terrace along Parliament Street backed onto Cannon Row, a short parallel lane – still cobbled – leading from Bridge Street to Scotland Yard, and back to Parliament Street via Derby Gate. Every morning Maundy Gregory took a taxi to Cannon Row and alighted, unnoticed, at the back of the building. This taxi was not available for public hire as he employed its driver full-time. In this way he could move swiftly from home to office, from office to the Carlton Hotel for lunch or to the office of a client.

He had an impressive consulting room, a monthly magazine to run and honours touting to do; but he had been onto another good thing before the war, and saw no reason to let it drop. On the first day of August, 1919, Colonel Sir Vernon Kell, of Military Intelligence, received a letter. Spookily, it dropped onto the mat at 34 Argyle Road, Kensington, his home address.

Dear Sir Vernon,

I am sending you under separate cover a copy of the *Whitehall Gazette*, of which I am the proprietor and editor.

I am much occupied with various matters of propaganda and investigation, and if I can be of any service to you through the columns of my paper or otherwise, I shall only be too delighted.

Yours sincerely,
J Maundy-Gregory

It was enough to make a man move house. Grimly, between forefinger and thumb, Colonel Kell took it to his office, showed it around as a warning, and added it to the file.

Lloyd George was not concerned with the minutiae of how money was raised for his funds. Early in 1919 he bustled off to Paris with an entourage that included his wife and his secretary/mistress to negotiate the peace. In Parliament, Bonar Law, as Deputy Prime Minister, presided over the huge Coalition majority and Freddy Guest, the Liberal Chief Whip, with the help of Sir William Sutherland, got busy fund-raising for Lloyd George's coffers.

> Freddy was a mixed character – he had a streak of the playboy in him, but also a strong sense of duty and a sincere devotion to the public service. I used to write many of his speeches. . .[4]

Colin Coote, who is quoted above, is describing Freddy Guest as a fellow-member of The Other Club (in fact Guest had put him up for membership). Once again, with Guest and later Coote himself, Maundy Gregory had latched onto somebody who knew everybody. The Other Club was one of many Maundy Gregory was never invited to join, although in years to come he would be introduced to many of those who belonged to it; and it is a useful reminder of the limits and, conversely, the reach, of his acquaintance. He was one of those people whom everybody knows, but nobody wants to.

The Other Club was an exclusive dining club set up by F.E. Smith, a Unionist, and Winston Churchill, a Liberal who was about to become First Lord of the Admiralty, after the 1911 election. Its members were the men who made history for the next thirty years. Membership was limited to fifty, of whom only twenty-four could be Members of Parliament. They met on alternate Thursday evenings when the House was sitting, at 8.15pm.

Among Unionists on the original executive committee were Bonar Law, F.E. Smith, and Lord Castlereagh; among Liberals, Rufus Isaacs (Lord Reading), Lloyd George, Winston Churchill, Alick Murray 'the Master of Elibank', and Freddy Guest. Lord Knollys was an august connection to the Palace. Others at the inaugural dinner included the grandest and most amusing Edwardians such as Viscount Esher and Lord Charles Beresford; Herbert Beerbohm Tree, W. Dudley Ward, MP for Southampton and son-in-law of Viscount Esher; Lord Riddell, who owned the News of World; and the popular Marquis de Soveral. After the War, Rothermere and his son, Esmond Harmsworth, would become frequent attenders and Trenchard was prominent.

The only candidate I recall being repulsed was Sir Samuel Hoare, who shared with Sir John Simon an extraordinary capacity for getting himself disliked, coupled with a fervent desire to get himself beloved. Of the other original members, why were so many in such close touch with the Court? Of those already mentioned, Sir Francis Hopwood, afterwards Lord Southborough, was fresh from attending the Duke of Connaught on a visit to South Africa for the opening of the Union Parliament, and had similarly accompanied the Prince of Wales to Canada in 1908. But he was by profession a high-ranking civil servant rather than a Court official.[5]

This account of an élite close to the centre of power reminds us that influential Unionists and Liberals knew each other well, outside Parliament. They belonged to a social stratum that Maundy Gregory desperately wanted to join, some of whose members he knew slightly from his days at *Mayfair.*

In 1919, Colin Coote was a young man, just back from the War, and had been re-elected on the 'coupon' as Liberal member for Ely. He was sharing a house with another MP and working hard to do his best for his constituents. There was a strong post-war empathy among those of all classes who had fought alongside one another. He was also fortunate enough to be taken on by the brilliant Edwin Montagu, 'a great, gaunt, craggy creature with the soul of an Old Testament prophet and the look of an Assyrian bas-relief'[6] at the India Office. Coote, as his Parliamentary Private Secretary, resisted attempts at head-hunting, although:

> ... I received one day a letter on imposing notepaper headed The *Whitehall Gazette* asking me to call on the editor and signed 'J Maundy Gregory.' It must be recalled that I had, including my parliamentary salary of £400 a year, about

£1,100 a year out of which I had to pay a constituency agent and keep up a house in London. My best chance seemed to be free-lancing in journalism...

It will thus be understood that the word 'editor' had an irresistible attraction. I called on the *Whitehall Gazette* and was ushered into the presence of an impeccably dressed personage who could not by any possibility live up to his trousers, but who possessed a kind of ingratiating flamboyance. He laid it on with a trowel. 'It was always useful for brilliant young politicians to get publicity. He had the best cartoonist in the world; and if I paid him fifty guineas, he would produce a cartoon of me which would be the sensation of Westminster!'

...I said that I hadn't got fifty guineas, but that if he would pay *me* that sum I would produce an article that would be the sensation of the periodicals. This tickled him; to my astonishment he agreed; and to my even greater astonishment, he paid. I soon saw that the magazine was a cover for something. Nobody could flaunt so many appurtenances of wealth, including a fountain-pen with a twenty-two carat nib half an inch broad, a taxi perpetually engaged, and an infinite capacity for champagne, on the profits of a rag like that.

Where an experienced journalist makes the story fit the page, the one unfailing characteristic of the *Whitehall Gazette* was its slackness. The editor seemed able to slop about as many words as he liked, and get the paper to fit whatever was contributed. Since it was distributed, rather than sold, to a carefully selected list of hotels, clubs in St James's and government offices, and Maundy didn't sell advertising in it, it wasn't hard to see that he must have to bring in lots of fifty-guinea donations to make it pay. Colin Coote worked out what was going on in the end, and decided not to have anything to do with the honours trade, but relations with Maundy remained amiable and the *Whitehall Gazette* provided him with a useful income stream for several years.

The August 1919 edition established the format: no advertising except for the occasional (free) half-page trumpeting National Savings certificates or some other Government issue; no news photography, although there were excellent tinted portraits of men in suits and uniforms; and no attempt to attract attention with short, snappy copy. In an era when popular dailies, and Sunday papers like the *News of the World,* could count their circulation in the millions, this was journalism for the unhurried.

The name, the coat of arms, the lack of advertising and the two-column pages gave it a vague resemblance to the *London Gazette,* the official newspaper of record published by successive governments. But the content was different. The *London Gazette*, produced to inform and not to entertain, carried notices of bankruptcies, significant land registrations, changes of name and so on; it also published supplements about honours recently awarded, including those such as DSOs won for valour in the field. The *Whitehall Gazette* was a lot more like *Mayfair*. It specialised in opinion pieces and eulogies of contemporary figures (who would have paid, of course). Sometimes people paid to put their opinions in, anonymously. In a pompous, Victorian sort of way, some of the articles were bye-lined with Latin pseudonyms like *Vigilate, Carfax,* or *Gellius.* In due course Maundy would buy a couple of motor launches on the proceeds of *Vigilate* and *Carfax.* He named them as such, and kept them at Hart's Boat House, Surbiton.[7]

The August 1919 launch issue sent to Vernon Kell 'under separate cover' carried one of an occasional series: 'Officials I Have Met, By the Editor'. The Official he felt inspired to describe that month was an Official he had met rather a lot – since they now worked in buildings that stood about thirty yards apart – Assistant Commissioner of Police, Sir Basil Thomson, KCB (Thomson had just got his gong). It was a full-page piece – no details, of course, for reasons of security – painting a positively feline picture of one who smiled only 'when the real motive in some situation is suddenly revealed to him. . .This smile has been the sign of the undoing of many an enemy agent.'

There were also 'think' pieces, many thousands of words long, many of which peddled right-wing paranoia. Not all, though: the first issue carried under the 'The Investigator' banner a well-informed history from Marx onwards of 'the Revolutionary movement in England' by someone called Rigby Hallam. At least, it was well-informed if you assumed, as the *Whitehall Gazette* did, that revolution was going to come from the left. Many movements that threatened democracy from the right, including the British Empire Union and the British Fascists, were either in existence or soon would be. Rigby Hallam's history was progressive among *Gazette* articles in that it recognised gradations of opinion and ignored national or racial stereotypes. The far-right pieces in the magazine would be full of phlegmatic Britishers, clever untrustworthy Jews, agitators as 'outsiders', all socialists as violent revolutionaries, and so on.

Under 'British Enterprise' in this early issue Phillip Jackson wrote enthusiastically about the commercial future of the motor trade, which at the time compared unfavourably with that in America. This was not blamed on the war, but on the comparative accessibility of the family runabout pioneered thanks to mass production across the Atlantic. It was a call to British management, exhausted from providing millions of shells and uniforms, to catch up with the consumer society.

Later editions would typically carry some foreign news, an insider's political view from the right or far right, a compilation of contrasting *bons mots* mostly from politicians, and at least one laudatory piece about an industrialist, entrepreneur or public servant – or someone who was simply rich, powerful and a jolly good sport, like the twenty-four year old Rajah, Sir Hari Singh, aide de camp to Lord Reading, the new Viceroy of India:

> He is shrewd, gifted with sound business acumen, and is keenly interested in the development of Jammu and Kashmir, which, with its annual revenue of over one million, under the Maharajah's autocratic rule – dealing through a council – has constructed not only canals but great electric stations.

Waiting for Maundy and idly skimming the *Gazette*, a maker of tubing from Birmingham or track from Crewe might well make a note. Contracts up for grabs in Kashmir, then . . . a magazine worth looking at.

Coote contributed reasoned, un-hysterical articles in the early years on Unemployment, The Case for the Coalition and The Coal Problem. But long essays by Gellius set the more usual tone. 'A Jewish

Conspiracy: The Hidden Hand of Bolshevism'. That kind of thing. Today the material by 'Gellius' and 'Vigilate' would place its authors to the right of the far right and probably in prison. We do not know who they were, but they had time on their hands, made clear by the thousands of words contributed over the years.

One of them could have been Basil Thomson, although the style is more unreasonably vicious about minorities than is usual for him. Or Major G.R. Hennessy (a contributor from the secret service who was later Treasurer of the Royal Household); Colonel Gretton or Oliver Locker-Lampson who also knew Maundy.

It is difficult to believe, looking at the articles published under his own name, that Hennessy would be so rabid, but Locker-Lampson and Gretton were allegedly among the founders of an anti-Red campaign in the early 1920s which was sufficiently unprincipled to ask for assistance from the British Fascists.[8]

Some have suggested Vernon Kell might just have been Gellius – except that when asked about Maundy Gregory, his view would be reported as 'knows him well and likes him not at all.'[9] Captain (later Admiral) Reginald 'Blinker' Hall of Naval Intelligence is another candidate. He ran an outfit called National Propaganda which was closely allied to the Economic League and sundry other well-funded anti-Bolshevik organisations. Maundy was the key agent for the Liberal Chief Whip, but he remained useful to some Diehard Tories.

All this has a bearing on questions arising from David Clark's biography of Victor Grayson, which appeared in 1985. Did Maundy Gregory employ Victor Grayson, a political animal, to write for him? And was he responsible for Grayson's disappearance, which has remained a mystery since 1920?

In 1907, Victor Grayson was a young Socialist orator from Liverpool, who was elected to parliament with a wafer-thin majority of 153 in the Colne Valley by-election. From there until 1918, his career tumbled painfully downhill.[10]

He had a deeply troubled personality. In 1907 he was young, probably shy and over-awed, and in the House of Commons made a fool of himself by telling the truth as he saw it – from a socialist, rather than a Labour, point of view. His private life was also difficult since he was bisexual.[11] He was also a hopeless, chronic, self-destructive drunk.

Any of the other weaknesses may have become part of the Victor Grayson legend; the alcoholism destroyed it. He married a pretty and talented actress, whose loyalty and hard work probably kept him alive.

Grayson did nothing much in parliament once he was there. Within a couple of years he had lost his seat. He became editor of an influential Labour paper, Robert Blatchford's *Clarion*, although his writing lacked the outstanding vibrancy and power of his speeches. In 1911 he began to have epileptic fits with blackouts. He tried to re-enter parliament but inevitably, people lost faith, and he did nothing to restore their confidence. Meetings would be organised at other people's trouble and expense; he would be dead drunk, unable to speak, or he would excuse himself on grounds of unspecified illness. He was endlessly self-indulgent and always left other people to clear up the mess.

One humiliation followed another. He tried his luck in Kennington and the voters rejected him. He split with the mass of the Labour party as he was certain that war was inevitable and necessary. He had always been impatient with trade unionism, and its wide-eyed faith that workers would hold hands across the sea. He took Ruth to New York, where they nearly starved during her first pregnancy while he continued to drink; they came back and in 1914 he was sued for bankruptcy.

In 1915 he took Ruth and their little daughter to New Zealand. Here too he staggered about, drunk, at public meetings. His wife generally mended matters with her charm and talent. The more willing she was to play the parental protector, the more often he played the wilful child. He began to 'borrow' small sums of money, never to be repaid, from people who had little to spare. He was lying, self-pitying and abusive. It was alleged in a New Zealand paper that he had promised to guarantee a small loan by showing someone a cable to 'an alleged banker in England'. This was almost certainly his wife's father, a Manchester bank director, who was endlessly called upon to relieve them from debt.

At last, late in 1916, he enlisted in the army, stopped drinking of necessity, and expected to be sent to Europe. His wife and child returned to England in June, 1917 and stayed with her parents in

Bolton. He arrived by troopship from New Zealand in July and was despatched to fight in France with the British Expeditionary Force in September. In October he became a casualty of war and was finally evacuated to Brockenhurst Hospital, in the New Forest, where fellow soldiers remembered him as 'quiet, reserved' and 'brooding.' This person was so different from the sober, but lively, man they had known in France that severe shell-shock was suspected. Nowadays it would be called post-traumatic stress disorder.

In December 1917, a medical board recommended Grayson be discharged unfit with a 30 per cent pension. He was given leave pending his discharge. This eventually took place in March 1918. He began to accept speaking engagements and to write articles about his experiences in the trenches. In January 1918 he appears to have been planning a new life for all of them. Ruth was about 8 months pregnant and staying, presumably with him, at 42 Belgrave Road in Pimlico. He approached the manageress of a block of flats called Vernon Court, half a mile away opposite the stables of Buckingham Palace. In about 1984, when she was ninety, Miss Hilda Porter told David Clark that:

> . . . early in 1918 a soldier in a New Zealand Army uniform called in to her office and booked a suite of rooms. He explained these were for his wife who was expecting a baby in a nearby nursing home. A few days later, however, Grayson arrived in a very distraught state and explained that his wife had died.

His wife, and the baby who also died, were buried at Kensal Green. Hilda Porter did not see him again for some months, by which time she had been promoted to a most prestigious block of flats, Georgian House in Bury Street . . .

Georgian House is a large corner block with shops below, close to the Jermyn Street end of Bury Street. One side abuts Christie's north building on Ryder Street. The flats – they are still flats, not offices – are conveniently located for Chatham House in St James's Square.

It was to these apartments that Victor Grayson went in the latter months of 1918 and found accommodation in suite forty-two on the fourth floor. His apartment comprised a medium-sized bedroom, a sitting-room and a bathroom, for which Grayson paid five guineas a week – a considerable sum in those days. In addition he had to buy his own food, for none was provided.

Where was this money coming from? He was no longer a public figure. He never claimed his army pension. His old acquaintances had no funds. His patient in-laws in Bolton appear to have been supporting his daughter and his dog. He was not mentioned on his wife's headstone, which could indicate her family's refusal to shell out on his behalf. He had published very few articles that year, and those for the most part in obscure journals.

Yet from Georgian House, he was able to travel by train most weekends – at a fare of £2 12*s* – to Bolton, where he had his own room (his daughter, interviewed by David Clark, remembered his visits). Hilda Porter, who was only twenty-four at the time, saw a good deal of him in London. He spent most of every day writing, drank too much whisky, and liked to dress in a dinner suit and take her to the theatre. David Clark reports:

> He also had a regular set of callers, the principals of whom were Robert Blatchford, J Havelock Wilson, Horatio Bottomley and Maundy Gregory. This was an unlikely set of visitors with patriotism, assumed or genuine, being the only obvious link.

Blatchford, he had known before the war; like Grayson, Blatchford had rejected pacifism. But had Grayson been writing for the *Clarion* his articles would have been signed.

J. Havelock Wilson was a Trade Union Coalitionist, pro-war, with a reputation for rough tactics in his pre-parliamentary days of two decades before, when he was a seamen's union leader. According to Mike Hughes in his book *Spies at Work,* Havelock Wilson in 1919 was running the Merchant Seamen's League out of 76 Victoria Street and had 'close links with the British Commonwealth Union and the British Empire Union and Makgill's Anti German Union'.[12]

Bottomley, who lived close by in King Street, was now back in Parliament after wrathful creditors had kept him out for six years. He was in the money again and sponsoring a new party called the People's League. *The Times,* 17 December 1920, informs us that the forthcoming election in East Leyton will be fought on behalf of the People's League by Sir George Makgill. Here is an idea: could Victor Grayson have been writing not articles, but speeches? These were traditionally his forte.

However, *John Bull* was still going strong and Bottomley:

> . . . was a very successful journalist and commanded high fees.
> For example the *Sunday Pictorial* engaged him in 1915 at £100
> an article. Later this was increased and he began the practice
> of employing others to write articles for him at one quarter of
> his fee. It is possible that Grayson wrote some articles on his
> behalf . . .

And Maundy Gregory? It is possible that he wrote some on his behalf, too.

At no time during this period of his life did Victor feel any financial pinch. His rent was automatically paid for him but by whom Hilda did not know. Such matters were handled by her secretary, although she felt sure she would have known if the cheques had been signed by a well-known personage. However she did recall that every two weeks a package for Grayson was delivered to the apartments by two men in uniform or livery. She was under the impression that they were government employees but this is unlikely.

It is; but it was typical of Gregory to pay cash. He kept, by all accounts, a huge stash of ready money in a safe in his office, and liked people to catch a glimpse of it. It was part of the *mise en scène*, like the whopping great diamond he toyed with. And cash was delightfully untraceable.

The rent cheques are less easy to pin down, although anyone relying on Grayson would have good reason to make sure of the roof over his head. He was, after all, an extravagant alcoholic who had been bankrupt at least once.

So commissions as speechwriter or ghostwriter, however unlikely in view of the political tone of *John Bull* and The *Whitehall Gazette,* may explain why Grayson saw Bottomley and Maundy Gregory. How he got to know them is unknown, although Bottomley had been in Parliament when Grayson was and there is an intriguing possibility that he may have been in contact with him during the First World War. A reliable witness is said to have been told that Grayson once went on a recruiting drive with Bottomley. This witness was shown a photograph of the orators in action, perched on top of a tank in the street with megaphones; the tank, however, would put this pretty late in the war, when Grayson had already gone to New Zealand.[13] Coincidentally J Rowland Sales, Maundy Gregory's former secretary, organised one of Bottomley's recruitment tours during the war.

Hilda Porter remembered Grayson's only female friend other than herself being a platonic one: a Dr Von Sawyer from Hampstead:

> . . . a German in her late fifties. According to Miss Porter, she
> was also a Socialist who on occasions treated Victor and they
> became close friends.[14]

For most of the twentieth century, the Royal Free Hospital was located in the Gray's Inn Road. Its archives, like the hospital itself, are now in Hampstead and so are the case notes, 1914–1919, of Ethel M. Vaughan (later Vaughan-Sawyer), a surgeon in obstetrics and gynaecology who was professionally active between 1902 and 1924. It seems highly unlikely that she was German and not particularly likely that an obstetric surgeon would volunteer to treat Grayson, either. She may have helped his late wife.

In September, 1920, nearly two years after coming to Georgian House, Grayson disappeared.

Hilda Porter recalls that one mid-morning in late September 1920 – she does not remember the precise date and of course had no reason to do so – two strangers came and asked for Grayson. They sent up a visiting card and he invited them to his rooms. They stayed there most of the day, sending out for some drinks. Towards evening, the two men descended in the rickety lift and called a taxi. A few minutes later, Victor appeared carrying two very large suitcases. When he came out of the lift, he put down the cases, ascended the few stairs adjacent to the lift and went into the manageress's office. He told her 'I am having to go away for a little while. I'll be in touch shortly.' With those few words he rejoined the two men and went out to the taxi. That was the last she saw of Victor Grayson.

It was seven years before the newspapers began to run articles about his mysterious vanishing. As soon as they did, sightings were reported. Some were from people who had known him and reported having seen him in the early 1920s, some from people who had talked to a stranger who said he was Victor Grayson and who made remarks, in conversation, that indicated (in retrospect) that he really was; searches were made, books were written, a sister came from Canada to hunt for him.

The mystery was never solved. Donald McCormick, in *Murder By Perfection,* was the writer who linked Gregory and Grayson as murderer and victim. His version of the disappearance began with Grayson drinking at the bar of a place called the 'Georgian Hotel', popping out for a minute into the night to collect luggage from the Queen's Hotel (link to Gregory there) and never returning to his pals. There appears to be no substance in any of it. Another part of this story has been called the Flemwell Fabrication ever since.

George Flemwell was an English artist who spent much of his working life in Switzerland. McCormick claimed to have a letter in which Flemwell said that on 28 September 1920, he had been sketching on the riverside at Thames Ditton when two men passed in an electric canoe; that he had recognised one of the men as Victor Grayson; and that they had moored the boat and gone ashore into a little house, 'Vanity Fair'. When he visited the house later, the door was opened by a 'handsome woman of bohemian appearance' who denied any knowledge of the incident, or of Grayson.

Hilda Porter existed and David Clark is still with us and remembers meeting her. Flemwell also existed, although he died in 1928, forty-two years before his alleged sighting of Grayson was revealed to a startled public. David Clark rang Donald McCormick, who claimed that he had disposed of the letter, with others, by auction at Maples some years before. The firm has no record of this and soon after, he died. [15]

I interviewed McCormick's widow Eileen in November 2000, at her retirement home in Bexhill-on-Sea, and asked about her husband. 'I was deeply involved in his work and ideas,' she wrote sadly to me soon afterwards.[16] The Grayson story was one I had been intrigued about for many years, and I asked Eileen McCormick about the Flemwell incident. In particular, I pondered on how Flemwell, from his claimed vantage point on the opposite side of the river, could have been so sure it was Grayson in the boat. She immediately responded that it had been an Indian summer, sunny with clear blue sky, and that Flemwell had a perfect view of the river. However, while researching this book I approached the Met Office Archive to see if this could be confirmed.[17] The weather report for that date, 28 September 1919, was however cloudy, overcast sky with poor visibility. While reading the report, I noticed that 28 September 1919 was in fact a Sunday, which prompted me to check Hampton Court Palace records. I discovered that Barge Walk, the north bank of the Thames on which Flemwell was allegedly sitting while painting, is owned and controlled by the Palace, and was in fact closed to the public on Sundays – how then could Flemwell have been there? The balance of evidence not only suggests he was not, but points to the whole scenario being fabricated by McCormick in order to knit together two unrelated stories (the death of Edith Rosse and the disappearance of Victor Grayson) to create his 'Murder by Perfection' book.

Eileen McCormick also said that all her late husband's papers had been sold, although she had no record of the purchaser either. She did rather intimate that other alleged testimony I asked her about, such as that of a 'Private Adams' which appears in 'Murder by Perfection' was equally unsubstantiated. 'He often used his imagination to flesh things out a little,' she told me sheepishly.[18]

CHAPTER SEVEN

Ups and Downs

No doubt Maundy still saw Peter Mazzina, if only when the young man smilingly discussed the menu at his table at the Carlton Hotel. But Mazzina's private life included a young wife who was to bear him three children and it would be some time before circumstances allowed him and Maundy to become close associates.

So Maundy Gregory often consoled himself with evenings at the theatre in the company of Edith Rosse. He and the Rosses had become great friends over many a long summer day on the river at *Vanity Fair* and at Henley. Now Edith and Maundy were seen about together all the time, for Fred had a two-year contract with the orchestra at the Palace Theatre which kept him out until after midnight. Edith had 'dabbled' in property for some time and around 1921, she confided that she was in a state over the accounts. He had recently engaged an accountant to work at the *Whitehall Gazette* – a disabled man called Pengelly. He liked Pengelly, though how much he knew about him is uncertain; Pengelly had been an adventurer once, until a gunfight in Buenos Aires left him partly paralysed and he spent a year in an Argentinian prison for manslaughter. Anyway, Maundy suggested to Edith that this fellow could do her accounts, too. She willingly agreed so he introduced them, saying that Edith was his half-sister.

Frederick Rosse saw that Maundy was never going to cause jealousy. Both he and Edith probably welcomed a third presence as a diversion from the fact that their marriage was crumbling.

In the summer of 1922 Edith and Maundy (Frederick Rosse would follow; he was on tour) moved into a roomy, double-fronted early-Victorian villa called Abbey Lodge, at 3 Abbey Road in St John's Wood. When, over forty years later, the Beatles stepped through the front door,

it had been chopped up and added to and turned into EMI's Abbey
Road recording studios; but in 1922, it was just a pleasant detached
house with a garden. Maundy had taken it on a lease, while Fred and
Edith rented out their old flat in Hyde Park Mansions.[1] Maundy had
the upper rooms and the Rosses the lower. They had many mutual
friends by now, including a young man, barely out of school, called
Hugh Donaldson who lived close to the flat that Edith Rosse owned
in Hinde Street. They had seen a lot of him during the war. At Abbey
Road they invited friends to evening parties where there would
be dancing to ragtime on the wind-up gramophone and in winter,
fireworks in the garden for local children. Maundy would shake
cocktails and sometimes play his baby grand piano and sing popular
songs.[2] He was genial and extremely generous. The MacKinlays,
a couple they knew from the theatre, went everywhere with them,
although regretfully they had to back out of the friendship in the end.
Maundy's beneficence was overwhelming and they simply couldn't
keep up with the clothes and time required for dinners at the Savoy
and days on the river at Henley.

There was now a young girl in the household. In 1916, Edith had
unofficially adopted her twelve year old niece *Ethel* Marion Davies.[3]
Ethel had had a difficult start in life. Her father Fred, Edith's brother, was
a carpenter in modest circumstances in Islington. Her mother, Harriet,
had died shortly after the birth of Ethel's younger brother, Reginald,
in 1906. Fred also fell ill for about two years and was in hospital so the
two children were farmed out. In 1908 (when little Ethel was four) he
remarried, set up house with his new wife Harriet, and retrieved his
children.

Aunt Edith Marion Rosse probably stepped in because in 1916 Fred
was called up, leaving his wife with Ethel, Reginald and three younger
half-siblings to look after. Ethel seems to have been a difficult girl. Edith
sent her to a school in Burlington Gardens for three years and later to
a convent in Finchley. In 1921 she was seventeen and rebellious. When
the Rosses moved to Abbey Road she was occupied with a two-year
secretarial course. She then embarked upon another two-year course
at St John's Wood Art School. As an art student she became even less
manageable, so Edith and Maundy ('Uncle Jim') had a serious talk.

Edith happened to know that her sister Clara was visiting England from Canada; and Maundy told her just what needed to be done.

One day, Ethel was ordered home urgently from college. At 3 Abbey Road, she found her younger brother Reginald and a woman she had never set eyes on before. This, she learned, was Aunt Clara, who had kindly offered to accompany Reginald and herself – Ethel – back across the Atlantic. They were booked to leave from Liverpool. The boat would leave in about six hours.

Ethel was given her expenses for the journey and must keep in touch. That night, she was on a liner sailing down the Mersey. She had begun a journey to Saskatchewan, where, Edith told her, she must find work. An allowance would be sent regularly.

The way this departure was managed has Maundy Gregory written all over it, and shows how much influence he had over Edith. Alone again with him, Edith was ambitious and did not let Fred's money lie idle. She added to her small portfolio of rental properties on Thames Ditton island and flats in the West End, and employed a voice coach. Whether she felt in need of a Professor Higgins to her Eliza Doolittle, or whether she was planning a return to the stage, is unclear. She was a sociable woman, especially with a few drinks inside her. As for Maundy, he was slightly plump, and already, in his early forties, cultivating the smiling, benevolent, favourite-uncle persona that would lead F. E Smith (by 1919, Lord Birkenhead) to call him, with barely a *soupçon* of irony, The Cheerful Giver.

Post-war Paris, and a delightfully lively social life, gave Lloyd George time to think, and not only about punishing the Germans with the cost of reparations. He was distracted by the obvious admiration of rich Albert Stern for his constant companion, Frances Stevenson. About 'Bertie' Stern she confided to her diary on Friday 16 May:

> He is a most generous and thoughtful person and the best host I have ever met. One of his friends asked me the other day why I did not marry him. 'One excellent reason,' I replied 'is that he has never asked me.' But all the same I think he might ask me if he did not know perfectly well that I would not leave D. [David Lloyd George]

On the same day, across the Channel at 12 Downing Street, Freddy Guest sat down to write a difficult letter to the Prime Minister. His role, in the PM's absence, was to send him weekly summaries of key debates in the House, of election issues – and, of course, honours. There were complications with the forthcoming bye-election in Ashton-under-Lyne; Sir George Younger, Chairman of the Coalition Unionists, had consented to let Freddy choose a Liberal, but he knew perfectly well that:

> At such very short notice, and with the knowledge that the official Liberals are on the move in that Division, I cannot but feel anxious as to the result. I am however taking immediate steps to try and secure the adoption of the better of the two Liberal names supplied to me by Beaverbrook.
>
> I must here state that it is due to his advice that the nomination has been handed over to us. Max has undertaken to obtain Hulton's full support with one of his papers which circulates very widely in that Division, in return for which we are to exceed his ration of K.B.Es for services rendered to the old Ministry of Information. This is very unprincipled of our friend Max, but not an excessive price to pay for his full support.
>
> RE: HONOURS LIST.
>
> I am proposing to submit to you in a few days a short list, and am hoping that you will rely to a certain extent upon my discretion. I think that I should be able to come over to you, if you so desire, on Friday next, returning on Sunday, as it is almost impossible to communicate the details of my recommendations over the telephone ... [4]

Freddy Guest was making every endeavour to keep the list short. Working in England, he was much more sensitive to public opinion than his master.

The following Friday, 23 May, he duly paid a flying visit to Paris, where Lloyd George saw him on the Saturday. The Prime Minister's meeting with Guest was sandwiched between two others of a more personal and private nature with Frances Stevenson.

Colonel, now Sir Albert, Stern had been useful for the past three years. If Lloyd George wished to have Frances' company, Stern was his cover, the sort of person who might appear, to an uninformed observer, to be her 'intended'. But he was beginning to suspect it had not been such a good idea. He did not know, but six months before after a visit to a night-club she had written girlishly in her diary of the kind of people who go there:

> They are very entertaining, & I like the glitter and light and laughing, but I'm glad I don't go *home* to it! However, Col Stern is one of the least frivolous of them, though he seems to have a considerable reputation! He is not quite sure how much I know about him!

And now Freddy Guest was expected, and would occupy David's Saturday while she and the younger, more entertaining Bertie Stern were left flirtatiously unsupervised yet again.

> D & I had a long talk. I know Stern would marry me if I gave him the slightest encouragement. . . It is a great temptation in a way for although I don't love him we are good friends and I know he would be very kind to me. It would mean title and wealth, whereas now I may find myself old and friendless and having to earn my own living. . . People will not be so anxious to marry me in 10 years' time.[5]

She sighed and promised not to leave 'D', or his fast-diminishing head of hair.

The next day, it is clear that Lloyd George got his own way as usual in discussions with Freddy Guest. On the Sunday, when the Chief Whip, heavy-hearted, was on his way home, and they had a picnic planned, he was in a particularly good mood:

D told me this morning that he had definitely made up his mind that he could not let me leave him. So that is final, and I am very glad. I need not worry about it any more. It would be very foolish to spoil for material prospects the most wonderful love which ever happened.

The following Friday, with the Birthday Honours list due to be announced the week after, Freddy wrote a stronger letter to Lloyd George:

> . . . there is still considerable restlessness in the public mind on this subject, more particularly on the grounds that soldiers and sailors have, so far, failed to receive recognition. . . I have consulted Bonar Law, Younger, Talbot and F.E. separately, and we are all of opinion that the ordinary political list should be deferred and the soldiers and sailors recognised. I therefore strongly urge that the only List which should appear on the King's birthday should be the Departmental List of civil servants.

OBEs (for non-combatants) were ten a penny – so much so that the French jeered that they stood for *l'Ordre Britannique Embusqué*, which is not neatly translatable, but conveys an image of an Order for a man who cowered behind his desk while others fought. Guest was aware, as those in Parliament could not fail to be, of the economic distress and anger of returning soldiers and sailors and the dangers of complacency. In his weekly report he pointed out, obliquely, the situation that many of these men were facing. Writing about a Coalition Unionist he noted:

> Horne's speech was rather thin and he dwelt more upon the percentage of re-employed workers than upon any practical solution of the difficulties of the 20% or 30% who are still unemployed.[6]

Lloyd George took the hint. There was a compromise over the Honours list. There had been a debate in the Commons on a Private Member's motion to force publication of party subscription details, and reveal their alleged relationship to honours; and there were demands for a Privy Council committee of enquiry. Guest got his way, and only the Civil Service list was issued in June, followed by a suitably short August supplement of one Earl, two Barons, sixteen Baronets, and twenty-four Knights.

In Lloyd George's absence the triumvirate next to the top of the tree, after himself and Bonar Law, were Churchill, 'F.E' and Austen Chamberlain. In his 30 May 1919 letter, Guest also reported back on Unionist efforts to corral their MPs into supporting Lloyd George's initiative to create a new centre party (F.E. Smith, Lord Birkenhead was a key mover). It would be a new entity, essentially the Coalition Liberals and Unionists with their deeper fissures filled in, and Lloyd George hoped that if all went well, he would win the next election as its leader.

> They are planning to hold a full meeting towards the end of July and intend to invite you and Bonar Law to be their guests. I think the movement is firmly on its legs and will deserve some guarded encouragement before the end of the summer. I am trying to train our Coalition Liberals to regard the group with favour.

'Their membership is now 130', he added next to this, in his small, neat writing.

Lloyd George came back from his Parisian expedition in July 1919. He was personally unpopular with the few remaining Independent Liberals. They disliked some of his foreign policies and they didn't much like the Lloyd George Fund, either. Maundy Gregory, behind the scenes, was busy building it up. A look at the New Year's Honours list of 1920, as reported in the *Whitehall Gazette*, might suggest that he had circulated a mailshot to Town Halls. There were knighthoods for the Mayors of Windsor, Preston, Dover, Newcastle, Newcastle-under-Lyme, Salisbury, Tenby, Stoke Newington, Wrexham, Greenwich, Deptford, and the Sheriff of York. It was as if the howls of protest at the 1918 list – packed with nonentities, when millions had fought for their country – had never been raised. In the same issue there appeared reasoned articles on the economy and one of Maundy's 'British Enterprise' puffs, headed in underlined capitals:

WOOD FIREPROOFING: A TRIUMPH OF MODERN SCIENCE

It began (and why not?) with Thales of Miletus (*c.* 500 BC) and after about a thousand words reached the crescendo of 1905 and Mr A. W. Baxter and the 'Oxylene' process, where the story bounced along for several thousand more:

> Many other foreign Governments are, we hear, testing this process with more than gratifying results. The Admiralties of the United States of America and Japan are greatly interested in the process, and are taking steps to avail themselves of its use for warship and other constructions.

So get on the blower to your stockbroker now. Almost every issue contained something similar, along with a eulogy on a royal 'personage' or a congratulatory piece on someone who had made his pile in mining or shipping. The motor trade was another rich seam.

A few puffs came under 'The Services'. A description of an ancient Assyrian tablet about 'serpents of fire, smiting unto utter destruction the enemies of the land' opened a triumphant biography of Mr F. M. Hale, one-time General Manager of the New Explosives Company and since provider of Hale's Patent Illuminating Grenade and the Hale Bomb. These terrifying weapons, of genuine importance to winning the war, both took life and saved it; but there was something about Gregory's unctuous style that made every encomium sound shifty, as though he were selling patent socks.

He was getting on terribly well socially. In May 1920 he attended Westminster Abbey for an installation of Knights of the Order of the Bath by the King. Sir Basil Thomson was there. Maundy's great friend Lord Southborough, one of the Knights Grand Cross, was 'overcome by faintness towards the close of the service, and was unable to take his place in the final procession through the Abbey.'[7]

Sir Basil was writing in *The Times* on Tonga and Nuei in the Cook Islands. He knew the South Pacific, having been a colonial servant in Fiji. Colin Coote contributed again to the *Whitehall Gazette*. His 'Case for the Coalition' piece in June 1920 ended comfortably:

> Peace on earth cannot be achieved without goodwill among men, and because the Coalition stands for goodwill, therefore it stands for peace.

The early summer of 1920 was the height of the Coalition's effectiveness and the point at which a centre party would be discussed in earnest. 'Fusion' was the idea—fusion of all the coalitionist politicians in a single, effective party to fight socialism under Lloyd George. That would be the brand identity. Now, how to name it? A list drawn up at the time read:

SUGGESTIONS

Constitutional Reform Party

United Reform Party

United Constitutional Party

National Reform Party

Reformed Unionist Party

Reformed Constitutional Party

United Constitutionalists

British Constitutional Party

Liberal-Constitutionalist Party.[8]

The moment was missed. The Coalition Unionists insisted that the new party, to exist at all, must control the Lloyd George Fund. Sir George Younger called it 'Gate money.' Freddy Guest was scrabbling to build it up, and not at all anxious that anyone should know where it was coming from. At 17 Park Lane on 17 May 1920 he addressed a letter to the Prime Minister, sealed with wax and treble-underlined SECRET, pleading for those who should definitely be rewarded in this honours list. His last page, marked BURN AS SOON AS READ, mentioned three people; one, Vaughan Davies, whom Lloyd George was looking after; and two others who should wait for their peerages;

> . . .and – <u>on another subject altogether</u> – the financial calls upon me to keep pace with expanding publicity and agents departments are becoming increasingly heavy and I am making a tremendous effort to stimulate our friends to subscribe. Of course some of them figure in these lists.[9]

Lloyd George took the hint and did not enquire too closely into the names. The Lloyd George Fund was there to be enlarged. He did not reconsider his refusal to hand it over and the Unionists dug in their heels. They thought he would give in, for without them, he was the leader of a minority party. There was no doubt that he did not have full Liberal support. Late in June he met a group of Liberal colleagues to try to get them to support Fusion in principle. Ministers, Under-Secretaries and colleagues, under the leadership of T. J Macnamara, Ian Macpherson and Alfred Mond, were opposed to the plan as they were not prepared to sacrifice their Liberal affiliations. Following the meeting, Lloyd George journeyed to Beaverbrook's home at Cherkley, Surrey, dejected and despondent.[10] He could choose: exchange his control of the Fund for leadership of an uneasy centrist party; or stay in office and accumulate a still bigger Fund. This he chose to do.

Pressure to grow the Fund was huge. The New Year's Honours List of 1921 rewarded some unlikely men and upset King George V. Lord Stamfordham, his Private Secretary, wrote to Davies, his opposite number at 10 Downing Street

Communications are being addressed to the King about Mr Rowland Hodge's baronetcy – and Col. Wigram has had a letter from a friend in Northumberland which contains the following: 'The person who overshadows the Honours list up here is Rowland Hodge who after a notorious career was convicted about two years ago in a most disgraceful case of food hoarding – made the North too hot for him and is now the laughing stock of Kent.'

Lord Stamfordham had been told that the King, when he visited shipyards in the north-east, had inspected one of Hodge's ships. When he told him this, His Majesty recalled the man as:

> . . . the only individual of a personally unattractive (to say the least of it) character whom he met on that tour. His appearance, dress and manner left an indelible mark on His Majesty's mind . . . the King has expressed to me his feelings of annoyance and indeed disgust that this man should have received any honour, let alone a Baronetcy.[11]

The Coalition Unionists must have wondered what Hodge had paid. Winston Churchill was getting very thick with them, and he knew where the bodies were buried. A note from Churchill's Private Secretary just weeks before the 1918 election had informed Davies, Lloyd George's secretary, that:

> Mr Churchill thinks he ought to let you know that he was approached on Saturday, to his great surprise, by an acquaintance who should have known better, with a suggestion that he should procure a baronetcy for a certain Hodge, a Newcastle shipowner, and receive £5,000 on delivery of the goods.

Naturally the intermediary received short shrift – and Mr
Churchill thinks you may wish to make a note, to be borne
in mind if the idea of any honour for Mr Hodge is mooted
again.[12]

Nothing daunted, Lloyd George still thought Fusion would work; he
had high hopes of F.E, who at the time seemed to have Beaverbrook's
support should he wish to make a move towards leadership of the
Tories. Beaverbrook, according to F.E.'s biographer, supplied his friends
with money, drink and sex:

> . . . plying each with whichever he could least resist. F.E.
> unhesitatingly accepted all three, in the same way as he
> cheerfully took hospitality and gifts from Maundy Gregory and
> other open-handed millionaires. . .[13]

Beaverbrook gave a 'haven for infidelity' to F.E. and Mona Dunn at
his house. Frances Stevenson had no idea of the competition Lloyd
George was up against. On 1 June 1921, she noted 'D said he is going
to detach F.E. from Winston' and seventeen days later:

> D said last night that he thinks we shall very soon have to do
> what Smuts has done – take our courage in our hands – commit
> suicide as a Coalition and like the phoenix rise from Coalition
> ashes as a new party.

As pillow-talk goes, this was worthless. Many Liberals baulked at uniting
with the Conservatives. Now that the war was over and the common
enemy vanquished, the old differences were revived; there were similar
reservations on the Tory side. But the deal-breaker in the end was Lloyd
George's refusal to hand over his Fund. 'Share the money' had been Sir
George Younger's condition for fusion, and he wouldn't.

After that, fragmentation – always cracking gently beneath the
surface – took on a frightening momentum. Also, in these years
Lloyd George and the Coalition's policies were immensely
vulnerable to the Press Lords. Viscount Northcliffe, whose ruthless

commercial mind he despised, would live until 1922 and although Lloyd George had told Frances Stevenson that he was 'playing him off' against his brother Viscount Rothermere, to the man in the street, Northcliffe appeared to have official sanction for the *Daily Mail's* ongoing anti-Bolshevik campaign and general alarmism. *The Times* and the *Mail* led the move to the right, drum-banging against Jews and Germans and for an aliens' restriction bill, fulminating about white slaves, public expenditure as 'waste', gambling hells, vice and drugs. The die-hard Unionists reflected all this in Parliament. It emerged in paranoia about socialism and a dismissiveness – not shared by all in Parliament, or by any means all in the Unionist party – of the rights of organised labour. The results were visible as urban unrest and a stronger commitment to Labour in many parts of the country. Lloyd George himself was convinced that Bolshevik cells were operating, or would be if Mr Thomson were not vigilant enough.

And Mr Thomson was not. In May 1921, one Sunday at Chequers, Lloyd George and a party including Frances Stevenson went for an evening walk in the grounds. The weather was glorious. The Prime Minister and Seebohm Rowntree walked on ahead, and the others lost sight of them – but ran into four strangers close to a wood. Later, Lloyd George and Rowntree ran into the very same four, and shortly afterwards found UP THE REBELS – UP SINN FEIN – I.R.A! written inside a summerhouse on the wall.

The protection squad – the 'detectives' – thought nothing of it, but when forced to stir their stumps, found the four men. They were all Irish and one of them was the editor of a left-leaning journal. Frances Stevenson reported to her diary that after a night in Aylesbury Jail:

> . . . today they were brought up to London and examined and three of them let off. We found later that they had only been very scantily questioned and that Sir Basil Thomson admitted that he had forgotten to make any mention to them of the writing in the summer-house! Also he'd not sent to Ireland for information. . . D. very annoyed about the

way the whole thing has been managed and had Thomson, Shortt [Home Secretary] and Gen. Horwood [Commissioner, Metropolitan Police] up this afternoon for a talk. . . It transpires that a very detailed plan of Chequers which Randall [PM's detective] had made when the PM first went there, and which he had handed in at Scotland Yard, is missing!

Whether or not Lloyd George had any reason to feel jittery in this instance, assassination was a chronic and omnipresent danger. He had other private anxieties, not life-threatening but constant: a suspicious wife and a rebellious daughter. And in Parliament there were disagreements on every front. Labour relations, unemployment, India, Ireland, Greece, Palestine, Russia, everyone had their own axe to grind. Bonar Law was drifting away. There was dissension in the ranks.

Thomson felt the full force of his pent-up anger.

The Assistant Commissioner/Director of Intelligence lasted six months after this. On Tuesday 1 November 1921, *The Times* reported that he would no longer be Director of the Special Branch. *The Times* would be publishing his reminiscences. He would take a month's holiday, and by January would have officially retired.[14]

There were questions in the House, and on the Friday, a full report: did he go or was he pushed? Joynson-Hicks, the far-right Mancunian MP, along with Admiral Hall thought he was pushed. There had been rows between Basil Thomson and General Horwood. Since the War began, Thomson had insisted on behaving as an equal of the Commissioner, and received the same salary. Horwood, a career policeman and head of the York force before the war, had been appointed Met Commissioner in 1920. In his view, the war was over and any reason Thomson may once have had, as Director of Intelligence, for going over his head direct to the Cabinet had now evaporated.

Shortt, the Home Secretary, was 'sphinx-like'.

Thomson insisted that he did not necessarily have to pass on all information, even if it came from the police, to the Commissioner;

Horwood remained unconvinced. But this had been the case since Horwood came to Scotland Yard, and the Unionists thought that the Labour Party, and/or the *Daily Herald,* and/or Lloyd George, were behind Thomson's precipitate departure. J. C. C. Davidson was among forty-odd Thomson supporters who voted for an adjournment in which to quiz Mr Shortt; others included Colonel Gretton, Sir Reginald Hall and Sir Frederick Banbury.

Exactly a week after Thomson left the Yard a *Times* reporter was granted 'an audience' with the great man himself. It was unctuous in the extreme, and appeared headed REPLY TO THE HOME SECRETARY – CHARGES DISPROVED.[15]

'Denied' would have been more accurate. Sir Basil insisted that he had always provided Horwood with all available information, although he had never been his subordinate. He, like the Commissioner, reported directly to Cabinet. His successor would report to the Commissioner. He was allowed two columns in which to make his case and said that Horwood had been talking to 'a committee' behind his back. He thought Horwood was aggrieved because they got the same pay.

The row rumbled on in Parliament and died down. From December, Basil Thomson would be getting a police pension of £1,120 a year. His memoirs were serialised in *The Times.* He wrote about the 'octopus' of revolution, and how the strikes of 1919 and 1920 had been supported by money from Russia. The strikes were an 'epidemic', the revolutionaries as if 'intoxicated' with 'pupils dilated as if by fire'. Their activities took place at a 'storm-centre'. However, 'the great body of Labour opinion is not and never has been in favour of revolutionary methods' which was a good thing otherwise his readers would have been afraid to walk the streets. But you had to be careful, for after the War:

For the first time in history the revolutionary agitator need not be a fanatic at all, for his profession had now become lucrative and a loud voice and a glib tongue now became worth anything from £6 to £10 a week.[16]

Sir Borlase Wyndham Childs, the War Office official who had recommended that Casement have a criminal trial, would take over from Thomson as Assistant Commissioner. He had time to write a great many articles for *The Times*, *English Life* and other, less dignified publications (such as the *Whitehall Gazette*)[17] in the following year or two, and in 1922 paid a short visit to New York, for the first of several foreign assignments as a private detective.

CHAPTER EIGHT

Gathering Storm

'A main reason for the decline in the cohesion of the Coalition,' wrote Colin Coote:

> ... was Lloyd George's neglect of the House of Commons. He took no trouble at all with the back-benchers. The famous charm was exhaled on foreigners – incidentally, without much effect – but not on us...[1]

Lloyd George's relationship with Prime Minister Venizelos, of Greece, was particularly controversial. Sir Basil Zaharoff, who had cultivated Lloyd George's acquaintance in Paris, had been friendly with Venizelos for years. Zaharoff was the international arms salesman for Vickers. He had backed Greek newspapers in promoting Venizelos and his Government when they sent King Constantine into exile in 1916. The King had had been an obstacle to the Allies as he wanted Greece to remain neutral (or, as reliable intelligence suggested, join the enemy camp). Zaharoff certainly wanted them in the War, on the Allied side, and armed to the teeth by Vickers. His support promoted Greece's attack on Bulgaria in 1918, which kept the Central Powers occupied well away from France.

In 1919, Greece looked like being able to benefit from the break-up of the Ottoman Empire, and Venizelos' army invaded Turkey. France protested about Greek aggression but ignored Zaharoff's involvement. He lived in Paris and was very cosy with the French Ministry of War too; their President had already made him a member of the *Légion d'Honneur*.

Zaharoff benefited from Greek warmongering. It helped Vickers' share price and Lloyd George was entirely supportive. Venizelos and his supporters were unexpectedly ousted in an election in 1920, and King Constantine was recalled. He continued the attack on Turkey with Lloyd George defending him against protests on all sides but the Greek advance collapsed and refugees fled in their thousands from the fighting.

Edwin Montagu, Secretary of State for India was implacably opposed to Lloyd George's support for the Greeks, as in fact was the Indian Government and the Viceroy who believed that support for an attack on the Muslims in Turkey would upset the Muslims in India. When it was agreed to hold a Peace Conference in San Reno, Montagu wrote to the Prime Minister, insisting on his right as plenipotentiary for India to send a memorandum in favour of Turkey to the conference. Lloyd George was outraged and rejected the proposal out of hand. Montagu's resignation was made inevitable after Unionist Central Office wrote to Downing Street reporting that he and his wife had not only failed to support the Coalition candidate at the South Norfolk by-election but had actually voted for the opposition. [2]

Montagu made a rousing speech before his Cambridge constituents soon after his resignation. In this, he denounced the one-man band which the government had become, under which collective responsibility by the Cabinet had been supplanted by quasi-presidential dictatorship. [3]

As 1922 ploughed on, the far right learned to exploit every failure. Landowners were outraged; redistributive taxes meant that the great estates were being broken up and sold, the palaces of Park Lane knocked down and replaced by hotels. The 'new poor' were mortified. Some of their more distant female relations had to open little shops in Bruton Street, or take flats in places like Victoria or Shepherd Market. The young thought it was all too thrilling, but the old saw the decline of civilisation as they knew it. From the Russian Revolution onwards, the conservative right was in a regular state about Socialism and in particular the tiny British Communist Party.

Hostility to the left was spread by the right-wing papers and attracted some unpleasant elements. All sorts of extra-parliamentary organizations, from the merely opinionated to the thuggish, sprang up: the Economic League, the British Commonwealth Union, the National Citizens' Union, and the Anti-Socialist Union were among them. The most extreme had begun by attacking Germans, pacifists and so on during the War, and went on to disrupt strikes and meetings, usually using hired muscle recently discharged from the services. It seems that, as John Hope has written, 'to combat the Bolshevik danger the Security Service collaborated with those right-wing groups actively engaged in fighting 'the anti-Christ of Communism.'[4]

There is an interesting twist to all this. In many issues of the *Whitehall Gazette* Maundy Gregory published articles which would have gained the heartfelt approval of all those who loathed Lloyd George and everything he stood for, while – as every insider knew – its editor was selling honours for the benefit of the Lloyd George Fund. The Unionists didn't mind honours sales, for they were old hands themselves. What rankled was the fact that Freddy Guest's man was poaching on their territory. In 1921 Sir George Younger, the Unionist Chairman, wrote a memo to Bonar Law.

> There must be a stop to Freddy poaching our men. I haven't a doubt that if I had got Mills [a baronet in the 1921 list] a seat, and got him into the House he would have proved a generous annual subscriber, and it was for us and not for Freddy to give him something more later on.[5]

J. C. C. Davidson, who would later become responsible for Tory party funds, recorded his recollections of Younger's pique.

He had done a great deal behind the scenes to maintain the unity of the Party in the country even though the great majority of the rank and file were prepared to support the Coalition. What he had resented most was the fact that Guest, who did the sort of job which he, Younger, was expected to do at the time of the 1918 election, approached very strong Conservatives for subscriptions to the Party, but the money did not go to the Conservative Party but to the Coalition in the first place, and eventually into Lloyd George's Fund. Younger always referred to it as 'poaching'... I suppose Lloyd George must have raised something in the neighbourhood of two or even three million pounds out of the businessmen who were prepared to pay for honours they received.[6]

The Duke of Northumberland, who disliked the trade, liked it a lot less because the Unionists were not getting their dues. Giving evidence to the Royal Commission about a couple of cases he protested:

> ...it is noteworthy that both Mr Sale and Mr Clarence Smith are Conservatives. Why, therefore, should they be approached by persons purporting to be acting on behalf of Lloyd George?[7]

Maundy Gregory had no political allegiance but a lot of Diehard Tory friends, and here he was, working all out for Freddy Guest. Maybe Guest paid better commission for Liberal catches. If Maundy's Unionist clients insisted that their fund must go into Unionist coffers, he could reassure them that their money would make its way to the Coaly Unionist account. So it may have done, but this was eventually to be swallowed up by the Lloyd George Fund for a Coalition victory – and the Unionist party, when it eventually re-united, would never get it back. In March 1921 Bonar Law's declining health had finally led to his resignation as Unionist Leader. Austen Chamberlain then took over Law's post as party leader and Lloyd George's de facto deputy. If anything, Chamberlain was keener on fusion and the creation of a new centre party than Bonar Law. On the sale of honours he seems to have steered a similar course to his predecessor.

A note from 'Bal' – David Lindsay, the 27th Earl of Crawford and Balcarres, to Chamberlain on 24 November 1921 shows that Freddy Guest wasn't the only greedy one. A Mr Murray (no relation of Alick) was on their list but had never looked promising. But now, skies cleared:

. . . apart from general respectability there has been no particular title to distinction except that which is now projected . . . but anyhow Kintore writes to say that Mr Murray would be glad to contribute £10,000 to the Coalition Party funds (Unionist side thereof) if this would assist matters. The contribution is of course comfortable, but I have not yet said anything to our Whips on the subject, as I should desire you to know how the matter stands before approaching Wilson.[8]

Leslie Wilson was the Coalition Unionist Chief Whip. Chamberlain replied that he'd already been told. 'The less I know about offers of that kind the better. They should be made only to the Whips!'[9] But what he had been told about was 'Murray's additional offer' so evidently Mr Murray had misjudged his contribution the first time around.

The new annual edition of *Debrett* appeared in December, 1921 and *The Times* reviewer noted:

Mr Lloyd George's administration has, in its five years of office, made the largest number of peerages created by any Government in modern times, beating the previous 'record' of 82, conferred during Mr Asquith's first administration in 1908–1915. The baronetcies, too. . . number 210. It is pointed out, however, that the period covers the war honours. . .

Resentment was coming to a head. Lloyd George was increasingly annoyed by personal attacks, overt and covert. Chamberlain was terrified of allowing the Die-hard Unionists to know that he was taking advice on whether or not to go for an election, and continuing with the Coalition. Sutherland advised Lloyd George that the Government was unpopular and Labour in the ascendant.

Lloyd George, typically, got away. In the New Year he was at Cannes and writing light-heartedly, on 10 January, to Chamberlain:

As to the Election, although I have had several talks. . . the greater preoccupations of golf (!) and the conference have left me no time for really thinking out the problem . . .[10]

By May, 1922 Chamberlain was overwhelmed with approaches from would-be honours recipients which he rebuffed, telling people to ask the Whips. McCurdy, who had replaced Freddy Guest as Chief Whip in the Coaly Lib camp, was also extremely busy, the less welcome fruits of his labour arriving in July 1922 with a letter to Lloyd George above the King's signature:

I cannot conceal from you my profound concern at the very disagreeable situation which has arisen on the question of honours.

The Peerages which I was advised to confer upon Sir J B Robinson and Sir William Vestey have brought things rather to a climax; though for some time there have been evident signs of growing public dissatisfaction on account of the excessive number of honours conferred, the personality of some of the recipients, and the questionable circumstances under which the honours in certain instances have been granted . . . The case of Sir J B Robinson and all that it has evoked in the debates of the House of Lords and in the newspaper reports of interviews given by him to press representatives must be regarded as little less than an insult to the Crown and to the House of Lords and may, I fear, work injury to the Prerogative in the public mind at home and even more in South Africa.[11]

What the King did not say was that matters were even worse. The courtier Colonel Clive Wigram wrote to Lloyd George's die-hard Unionist opponent Sir Samuel Hoare on 1 July:

You will remember telling me yesterday that Taft had said he thought the King made something out of the sale of honours

– Would it be possible to trace this statement to its source and find out the man to whom Taft made the remark?[12]

Howard Taft had been the President of the United States before the war and was now Chief Justice; he was a frequent, and well-connected, visitor to London. Wigram wrote again on 4 July thanking Hoare and saying that another source had reported the same remark. Taft was soon to have lunch with their Majesties, 'and without doubt the honours question will crop up in conversation.' The King and Queen would presumably put an end to these damaging stories.

Lloyd George, knowing nothing of this, responded to the King's letter immediately with a long letter that expressed vindication and half-truth, rather than apology.

Rumours about large bribes were rippling out across England and some Unionists were convinced that Lloyd George was pocketing some of the proceeds himself. The King was right; the result would be a loss of respect for the Crown. By blatantly dealing in benefits that were supposed to be the King's to bestow, Lloyd George destroyed any fiction about the Head of State having supreme power. In 1922, that fiction lay at the heart of all the British Empire stood for.

Sir J. B. Robinson was a South African millionaire who had swindled his own shareholders. The Privy Council had dismissed his appeal only last year.

Vestey, the other man whose name appalled the King, was a meatpacking tycoon, one of two brothers from Liverpool who did not believe in paying tax. When in 1914 the new Finance Act proved painful, they went abroad. In 1919 they asked the Inland Revenue for tax exemption, saying (inaccurately) that if they paid British tax they would be left with only £17 2s 0d in every £100. The Revenue proved obdurate so they kept away.[13] Their businesses were located in Chicago, Moscow, Petrograd, Riga and Shanghai and all over the Americas, besides Australia, New Zealand, South Africa, Madagascar, France, Holland, Germany, Spain and Portugal. William Vestey owned the Blue Star Shipping Line and during the war, had supplied the army with bully beef from Fray Bentos, in Argentina. He exported cotton goods to the Chinese in exchange for Chinese eggs, beaten up, tinned and sold to Joe Lyons for sponge cakes. (Later on, when the Vesteys got a coat of arms, it showed three eggs on an iceblock).[14]

In both cases, the honours citations were false. Robinson was said to be a banker although his bank had been liquidated in 1905. Vestey was said to have given free cold storage to the Government in wartime although it had been paid for.

The King's letter came after weeks of unrelenting pressure in Parliament from Oliver Locker-Lampson, Sir Frederick Banbury, Lord Selborne and Lord Henry Cavendish-Bentinck, among others, and much adverse press criticism. Lloyd George and Austen Chamberlain doggedly refused an independent enquiry or even a debate.

The spate of questions asked in Parliament, predominantly from die-hard Unionists and the ensuing press coverage eventually led to a climb down and a full debate was scheduled in both Houses. A motion was moved by Locker-Lampson and seconded by Sir Samuel Hoare 'That it is expedient that a Selection Committee of seven members of this House be appointed to join a Committee of the Lords to consider the present methods of submitting names of persons for Honours for the consideration of His Majesty, and to report that changes, if any, are desirable in order to secure that such Honours shall only be given as a reward for public services'.

There were two postponements – one when Field-Marshal Sir Henry Wilson was assassinated, another when Austen Chamberlain fell ill. When the debate began, the Government tried to shift the blame, saying General Smuts had passed Robinson as a suitable candidate. He had – fifteen years before. Two former Governors of South Africa spoke in the Lords. 'Nobody, white or black, considered that either by his service or his record he deserved this honour,' roared one of them.

Robinson was visited at his room in the Savoy by Lloyd George's Private Secretary A.J. Sylvester and induced to refuse the barony. He was rather deaf, and is said to have thought at first that the deputation had arrived to ask for yet more money.

The debate got fiercer. As Lord Salisbury listened to it, he decided to ask who had recommended Robinson's peerage in the first place. As I listened to the Lord Chancellor [Lord Birkenhead] I gathered that nobody seems to have recommended it. . . We know Sir Joseph Robinson himself did not ask for the peerage. Who did ask for it for him? And why did he ask for it? It is a most mysterious thing. [15]

Robinson responded with fury to the Prime Minister's letter Sylvester had given him at the Savoy. 'This is not in accordance with what was arranged with Mr McCurdy. This is a breach of faith and I shall be covered with ridicule. . . I particularly did not desire that the King should be approached.' [16]

As the debates continued, four out of the five men Lloyd George had recommended for peerages in the 1922 Birthday Honours list were referred to, with the implication that they were unsuitable persons for ennoblement. In addition to Vestey and Robinson, attention also focussed on Samuel Waring. The former managing director of the Waring and Gillow department store had fallen on his feet so far as the war was concerned. When the business went bankrupt in 1910 Waring founded a new concern at White City in West London where he was later to make a vast sum of money from war time Government contracts. Roland McNeill MP told the Commons that during the reconstruction of the bankrupt company:

> . . . a very large figure was put down in the balance sheet as assets representing the value of the stock. The stock must have been very much overvalued, since the debenture holders holding £100,000,000 in debentures were obliged to take 75% of their holding in preference shares in the new concern, and these preference shares of £1 now stood at the value of 10 shillings a share. Subsequently, when the war came on Lord Waring made a very considerable fortune in constructing and turning out equipment for aeroplanes on government contracts, no part of that fortune went to paying the shareholders or making up the deficiency for the

debenture holders in the concern. . . for what reason was this particular businessman singled out at this time for this very high honour? [17]

Waring, who was listening to the debate in the Strangers' Gallery, caused a sensation when he stood up and shouted at the chamber below, "'That is a lie!' The following day, when he took his seat in the Lords he immediately attacked McNeill and threatened him with legal action'. [18]

McNeill then turned his attention to Archibald Williamson, whose oil firm, Williamson, Balfour and Co, had been accused during the war of trading with the enemy. Williamson too, on taking his seat in the Lords as Lord Forres, sought to fend off the accusations and was given a helping hand from the Lord Chancellor, Viscount Birkenhead. [19]

Robert Borwick, the fifth of the Birthday Honours peers must have thanked his lucky stars that the notoriety of the other four nominees had apparently deflected the press from asking why this wealthy seventy-seven year old Lancastrian custard and baking powder manufacturer had been awarded one of the highest honours in the land.

On 17 July the Duke of Northumberland gave a trenchant response to the question of where these seekers after honours were coming from. He quoted a letter from 36, Wilton Place, Knightsbridge, about a 'social matter of a very confidential nature which it is thought may be of interest to you,' signed H. Shaw, and addressed to Whitby Shipowner Walter Pyman. [20]

The letter was published in the Unionist die-hard *Morning Post* the next day. It is significant that the testimony flourished by Northumberland implicated the Coalition Unionist tout Harry Shaw and not Gregory, whose name was never publicly mentioned.

Shaw was a property developer with an office in Knightsbridge of which the telegraphic address, promisingly, was Doorway Knights. He shared the huntin', shootin', fishin' enthusiasms of the upper classes which made Maundy feel like a grocer. In 1921,

Shaw had suddenly bought Stowe House. Stowe was the exquisite seventeenth-century palace of the Grenville family, Dukes of Buckingham, who had loved and improved it over many generations. It was a vast mansion with staterooms and a chapel, gardens and a park, temples and fountains. Shaw bought it and sold the contents and the statuary. Within a year, he had, in today's parlance, flipped it: he sold the remaining shell to the Association of Preparatory Schools for a proposed new public school. [21]

THE KEY MOTIVATION OF NORTHUMBERLAND AND
THE *MORNING POST*, IN EXPOSING SHAW, WAS TO DRAW
THE UNIONIST LEADERSHIP INTO THE HONOURS MIRE.
IN SO DOING, THEY HOPED TO PROVOKE A SCHISM
BETWEEN THE LEADERSHIP AND THE BACKBENCHERS, AND
ULTIMATELY THE RUPTURING OF THE COALITION ITSELF.
IRONICALLY, AFTER HIS SHORT BURST OF PUBLICITY
IN THE MORNING POST, HARRY SHAW RETURNED
TO RELATIVE OBSCURITY. IT WAS TO BE MAUNDY
GREGORY AND LLOYD GEORGE THAT POSTERITY
WOULD REMEMBER IN CONNECTION WITH THE SALE OF
HONOURS, NOT LAW, CHAMBERLAIN AND SHAW.

CHAPTER NINE

New Opportunities

Nearly eight years had passed since Frances Stevenson confided to her diary, on St Valentine's Day 1915:

> . . .what I want him to do is go outside *party* politics. . . He could do it now, for his reputation is established, and both sides admit his capacity. He could leave his party and the Cabinet without it being said that he had been obliged to leave it, as they would surely have said after the Marconi affair, or at any other time when his schemes were meeting with opposition.[1]

Had Lloyd George read this at the end of 1922, he would regret having paid no heed. His position had been in doubt for well over a year before hearings of the Royal Commission on Honours drove another nail into his reputation. The Duke of Northumberland was to submit as his evidence:

> However corrupt and immoral it may be to make a subscription to party funds the sole condition for bestowing an honour, it could at least in former days be urged in extenuation of such a system that the person who subscribed sincerely believed in the tenets of the party which he thus assisted, but if anybody of any party can receive an honour by subscribing to a fund of which the Prime Minister of the day has the sole disposal, it must mean the institution of a system of the most shameless and cynical corruption.[2]

Today, the myth that Lloyd George was forced from office by a chain reaction ignited by the 1922 Birthday Honours List is virtually unquestioned. Furthermore, the fact that Lloyd George never again held government office is equally attributed to the honours issue. The reality was somewhat different.

A truce between Greece and Turkey had been concluded on 4 October. Rather than reassure Unionist backbenchers it seemed to have sparked further anxiety and disquiet. Would the truce lead to a permanent peace or would there be another breakdown between the two sides? Many feared that Lloyd George's policy towards Turkey was a sign of things to come and could drag Britain into an unwanted foreign war.

On the morning of 11 October Unionist Cabinet ministers had met and agreed to support Lloyd George in calling an immediate General Election. Party Leader Austen Chamberlain then insisted on a pledge of secrecy prior to official announcement of the election. Within hours, however, word of the decision had been leaked to former leader Bonar Law who immediately told Lord Beaverbrook. His reaction was to confront Birkenhead and try and persuade him to break with Lloyd George. Birkenhead replied confidently that although there would of course be a Unionist split, 'the majority would back Lloyd George and the Unionist cabinet ministers. Then a Centre Party would be formed commanding Lloyd George funds, followers and the Daily Chronicle'. With the addition of Unionist Party funds and the immense power of patronage, a triumphant victory, he believed, would be delivered. [3]

All now hinged on whether Lloyd George could win the support of a majority of Unionist MPs. A meeting was to be convened at the Carlton Club on 18 October, but was later postponed until 19 October as Lloyd George and Chamberlain were convinced that the result of the Newport by-election, due that morning, would aid the coalition cause. [4]

Those like Beaverbrook and Baldwin who were agitating for the Unionist Party to break with Lloyd George and fight the election as a separate party knew that their success depended upon Bonar Law's presence at the meeting. Law himself appears to have been in two minds as to whether he should attend and speak. Beaverbrook later observed that:

> Either he would go to the Carlton Club meeting as the alternative Leader or the malcontents must suffer defeat. Mr Baldwin at that time. . . was an obscure figure. He could not carry the banner of leadership. Men would not have rallied to his side. [5]

As it was, Law made a last minute decision to attend and gave the decisive speech. In a secret vote it was decided by 187 against 87 to withdraw from the Coalition. Again, contrary to myth there was no sense of defeat in the Lloyd George camp as a result of the vote. To them, victory had only been postponed by a few weeks. On the contrary, it was Law who was plunged into despondency. After all, he had not set out to become Prime Minister. Now he faced not only the trial of office but the uphill challenge of winning the forthcoming election. Lloyd George fielded 131 Coalition Liberal candidates, hoping to win around 100 seats. In addition, he could still reply on a group of Unionist ex-ministers[6] whose continued presence in his camp made the electoral hill Law had to climb somewhat steeper. Throughout the keenly contested election, the honours issue was noticeable by its absence as an issue.

Although convinced he faced defeat, come Election Day Bonar Law made a net gain of ten seats. Lloyd George's Coalition Liberals actually won more votes than in 1918 but saw their seats fall from 133 to 62, principally due to the emergence of the Labour Party as a major force in urban constituencies. Asquith's Liberals also rose from twenty-eight seats to fifty-four. In this temporary and unique four party situation, Bonar Law found himself with a majority of eighty-seven.

1922 had been a year of remarkable departures. Northcliffe had died in August. Horatio Bottomley was in jail; he had been convicted of fraudulent conversion and sentenced to seven years in prison for the 'Victory Bonds' scam which had swindled the poor out of their savings during the War. After his conviction in May, a privately printed book appeared. It was a scathing diatribe against Bottomley and incidentally, against Northcliffe, Rothermere, and all other press Lords of the right, most of whom had been given honours. The author, Herbert Ainley who wrote as the 'working man', loathed everything they stood for and thought less of the Prime Minister for making a Faustian pact with such people. F.E. was a loyal friend, and sorry to see him go.

F.E. was now embittered by the Carlton Club decision. He had misjudged the mood. He had underestimated the extent of resentment that Lloyd George was 'pulling a fast one'. His biographer wrote:

> F.E has usually been assumed to have been deeply implicated in Guest's and Gregory's activities. . . he was a known cynic who mixed freely and with pleasure in the raffish political underworld peopled by the likes of Gregory and Bottomley, from whom he was happy to take both hospitality and substantial gifts.[7]

F.E. was very good company. He had been Sir Frederick Smith in 1915, Sir Frederick Smith, Baronet, in 1917, Baron Birkenhead in 1919, Viscount Birkenhead in 1921, and the Earl of Birkenhead in 1922. Drink, drugs and dancing with Mona Dunn were his favourite pastimes, especially when depressed, as he now was. He had given up spirits for a year during 1921-22 and got a lot of work done, including the Irish Treaty.[8]

Bonar Law did not remain Prime Minister for long. In May of 1923, ill health forced his resignation and Baldwin, his Chancellor, became Prime Minister.

The Royal Commission on Honours, under Lord Dunedin, had heard from Chief Whips Viscount Fitzalan and Leslie Wilson (Unionist), Freddy Guest and C.A. McCurdy (Liberal), and Sir George Younger. The politicians claimed to know nothing. The Whips explained that they had seen lists prepared by worthy referees. The Liberal Whips were asked whether they had delegated the vetting of candidates. The very idea of doing so had never crossed their minds.

The Royal Commission made its recommendations. Its brief had been:

To advise on the procedure to be adopted in future to assist the Prime Minister in making recommendations to us of names of persons deserving special honour.

Its conclusion was:

To ensure that honours for political services were conferred for merit and not on account of any contribution to political funds, before submitting names to His Majesty, the Prime Minister should submit them, 'together with the reasons for the proposed honour and a statement that no payment to a political fund was associated with the recommendation', to a Committee of the Privy Council appointed by him, for a report on the fitness of the recipient. An Act should be passed imposing penalties on persons promising to secure honours in return for money payment and on persons offering to make such a payment.[9]

Labour's Arthur Henderson was the only dissenter. He would have preferred that honours be abolished altogether. He had to shrug and concede.

Lawyers and civil servants began their deliberations. A bill for presentation to Parliament would, in due course, appear.

Pending the anticipated change, the honours trade went deeper underground. It did not entirely stop. In fact, the 1925 Honours (Prevention of Abuses) Act in many ways made Gregory's life easier. When the Act finally reached the statute book in August 1925, some three years after the Royal Commission had recommended legislation, its clauses contained some decidedly unique aspects. The delay in implementing the legislation was very much an indication of the fact that outlawing the sale of honours was not something any Prime Minister wanted to do willingly. It had though been a key recommendation of the Royal Commission and there was now no way of avoiding legislation. However, the Commission had not been specific in terms of the precise form the recommended legislation should take and Stanley Baldwin, Bonar Law's successor as Conservative leader and Prime Minister, took his time in drafting a Bill to put before Parliament. He and the drafters of the Bill were particularly concerned to ensure that sufficient loopholes were incorporated so as to ensure that it would still be possible for future Prime Ministers to boost party funds in the traditional way. When it finally emerged in the summer of 1925 it was primarily noticeable for its brevity, covering less than a page of paper. Secondly, and most uniquely, it made the person who had paid money in the expectation of an honour equally liable to prosecution as the tout or official who sold the honour. Prior to August 1925 only fear of ridicule had ensured the silence of a donor who had paid money and not received an honour. From now on, a donor would risk a custodial sentence of up to two years if they reported or admitted such an action. Those who had received an honour as a result of a payment were equally deterred from ever disclosing this fact.

Gregory's life therefore became easier. Although his ability to market real honours had now been halted since the departure of Bonar Law in May 1923, he could now pocket money from individuals knowing full well that the failure of the honour to materialise would not result in his victim reporting him to the authorities. His office at 38 Parliament Street, administered by the 1920s equivalent of today's Parliamentary Estates Directorate, remained in his keeping as nobody dared to get rid of him for fear of what he might do or say.

There are several specific examples in 1923 of Gregory taking advance payment for an honour. Walter Kent, a hydraulic engineer whose firm made a good showing in the *Whitehall Gazette* was seeking a knighthood.[10] In another case, a would-be Baron was Sir George Watson, owner of the Maypole Dairy chain of grocery stores and baronet since 1912. Sir George, who had handed over securities to the value of £30,000 seven years earlier, died in July 1930, still without his barony. He would return to haunt Maundy Gregory.

Perhaps remembering the good fortune of his friend Jumbo (still the Vicar of Stiffkey, although now engaged in a mining-shares scam in the Strand), Maundy appears to have latched onto the possibilities of Church of England livings and deaneries. F.E, as a great friend of Maundy's, had been Lord Chancellor, and in his office was a chap called Colonel G.W.H.M. ('Buns') Cartwright who was his Ecclesiastical Patronage Secretary. 'Buns' Cartwright never saw any of F.E's family after F.E's death in 1930. He lived on until 1977, when his memorial service in the Guards Chapel was addressed by Brian Johnston speaking to 'a congregation of several hundred Old Etonian cricketers'. F.E's biographer remained puzzled by Cartwright.

> How he lived for fifty years is a mystery, but at the very end of his life there was about him a strong whiff of Maundy Gregory, of whom he could proudly display a number of mementoes.[11]

Maundy knew people at the Abbey, across Parliament Square, and could always do them a favour. On Christmas Eve, 1922 he was present for Sunday Service and the dedication of a superb processional cross in ivory, gold and sapphires, donated by Rodnan Wanamaker.[12] There was no particular reason why Rodnan Wanamaker, a flier, philanthropist and second-generation department store magnate from Philadelphia, should present such a magnificent gift had Maundy Gregory not suggested it. They had been great friends since the summer. Wanamaker had been eulogised in typical Maundy style in 'Officials I Have Met' as Special Deputy Commissioner of New York City in charge of Police Reserve – for 'although the names of conquerors whether Generals, Knights or Kings are preserved in themselves in effigy or record, yet the lasting fruits of a man's labour which endure down the ages belong to the work of the peacemakers. . . British-American Entente. . . advocate of international goodwill. . . tributes to the British nation. . .' – and so on, with Rodnan sandwiched between Mr Arthur Jordan, inventor of Rapid Rims, and Mr Albert Barratt of Barratt & Co (makers of Black Jack Chews, four for 1*d*).

Wanamaker had proved useful on several fronts. His enthusiasm for equestrian sport, for instance, assisted Maundy in retaining his cosy relationship with Scotland Yard, despite poor Thomson being now a mere journalist and private detective (and how delicious that BT must lower himself to the two trades so long pursued by Maundy). Rodnan had been delighted to present the Wanamaker Trophy at the Metropolitan Police Horse Show, Thames Ditton. Lieutenant Colonel Laurie, Assistant Commissioner already profiled in the *Gazette*, and General Horwood were most gratified.

In 1919, long before the horse show and the presentation at the Abbey, Rodnan Wanamaker had been made a Commander of the Royal Victorian Order, adding further sparkle to his *Légion d'Honneur*, Order of Leopold, Order of the Crown of Italy and other decorations. He had been picking up honours for years, partly because he gave generously of his time as well as his money to good causes. Had Maundy Gregory helped him get the R.V.O? It was awarded by the Prince of Wales on a visit to America in 1919, so possibly not. The King's biographer, writing of an entirely different episode a decade later, is dismissive:

> That anyone could hope to buy his way into the Royal Victorian Order, bestowed personally by the sovereign without ministerial advice, reveals both the gullibility of the ambitious and the extent to which touting continued even after the fall of Lloyd George. It was a familiar gambit of the honours broker to suggest that a donation to a hospital or other institution under royal patronage was a sure passport to a Buckingham Palace investiture.[13]

The same source informs us that Maundy Gregory's main contact at Buckingham Palace was 'Sir John Hanbury-Williams, Marshal of the Diplomatic Corps and thus a senior member of the royal household.' There were others, over the years. Tom Cullen mentions 'an equerry'. The only person from the Equerries' department whose name pops up from time to time is Ralph Harwood – later Sir Ralph, Deputy Treasurer to the King and Accountant to the Crown, who had begun life as a telegraph clerk in Battersea. But there is no reason to allege that these people were corrupt. On the other hand it is possible that the King, and those in his immediate circle, occasionally played into the hands of people like Maundy Gregory while remaining unaware of any manipulation going on behind the scenes.

How did he become a close associate of the Russian Royal family? Maundy Gregory flaunted jewels he had been given by Grand Duke Nikolai and he claimed to have provided the Grand Duke, and the Duchess in her widowhood, with a pension.[14] This is an odd thing, since King George V already provided generous assistance to those exiled Russian royals who appeared to need it. Unless, of course, a regular income was supplied in return for services, information or 'Pawnbroking by Appointment'. He had the cash in abundance and they had the jewels, but pretty soon he had the cash *and* the jewels.

F.E. is an interesting point of contact with the Russians as well. He was often invited to sail on the yacht of Robert Houston, one-time MP for West Toxteth, and client when F.E. was a Liverpool lawyer in 1906. Houston was:

> The first of a line of adventurous rogues whom the reckless side of F.E's nature could never resist; most notably, Horatio Bottomley and Maundy Gregory in later years. The founder of his own line of steamships. . . Houston enjoyed a reputation as an unscrupulous pirate. . . As a colleague in the House from 1906, F.E. was soon a regular guest on Houston's palatial 1,600 ton yacht *Liberty*, and the friendship flourished into the 1920s.[15]

London's 'White Russians' were often fellow-guests on Houston's yacht. Birkenhead's own friends aboard may well have included Maundy Gregory, who knew Houston from *Mayfair* days. They certainly included Winston Churchill. When war was declared in 1914, Houston – then a Unionist MP, while Churchill was in the ruling Liberal party – would have loved a War Office (supplies) job and the kind of contracts that later came to such as Lord Lever. So it must have been entirely coincidental that he promptly sent Clementine Churchill a superb emerald and diamond ring. She, equally promptly, returned it. Winston, when she told him, said she had done absolutely the right thing. 'Clemmie is very "particular", isn't she?' smirked Asquith to Venetia Stanley, in guarded reference later.[16]

Another frequent visitor was Lady Byron, who had made friends with Grand Duke Kyril Vladimirovich in Monte Carlo, and learned from him her horror of Bolshevism. In 1921 or 1922, Robert Houston – then over seventy – had been introduced to her, and was smitten.[17] Lady Lucy was a game old bird. She had begun life as the seventh child of a box-maker from St Paul's Churchyard, had become a soubrette, and had been installed in a Paris apartment in the 1870s by Fred Gretton, a millionaire brewer (Bass Ale) and the father of Colonel Gretton, Winston Churchill's friend. When Fred Gretton died, leaving her £7,000 a year for life, she set up a London home in Portland Place where she entertained Rhodes, Fisher, Roberts and others, before marrying Lord Byron for his title.

In 1921 she was a well-off, opinionated, lively widow in a blonde wig, looking for a husband. Sir Thomas Lipton introduced her to Houston and in 1924 they married. She was sixty-five if she was a day, and wore a two-string necklace of black pearls that had cost £100,000. The Houston millions were expected to go to F.E. They didn't; but that is a story for later. Lucy Houston was madly anti-Bolshevik and very fond of her Russians.

Grand Dukes were not Maundy's only Russian contacts. The Zhivotovsky's were going to prove important to him and his ambition to acquire the Deepdene Hotel in the early 1920s.[18] The Zhivotovsky family were pre-war Petrograd associates of Moishe Ginsberg, the important Yokohama-based Russian trader. Until the Bolshevik revolution they represented the Russo-Asian Bank of St Petersburg and were extremely wealthy. They were also engaged in dealings with Sir Basil Zaharoff and Vickers. Two of the brothers had been arrested in Russia as part of a crackdown on corrupt arms trading in 1917. The whole family wisely fled into voluntary exile with enough money to set up as dairy farmers, of all things, in the South of France.[19] In spring 1920, David Leonteivich Zhivotovsky and his daughter appear to have bought

Deepdene, near Dorking. His daughter, Princess Nizharadzy, ran it from the summer of that year as an hotel.

Deepdene, in the previous century, had been a stately home to rival Stowe. It was twenty-five miles from London, set in wooded, dramatically rolling countryside, close to a steep natural declivity in the hillside. A member of the Roman Catholic Howard family had lain low in a modest house on the hill during Cromwell's Parliament, and after the Restoration a great mansion was built there. Over the centuries the surrounding estate grew to 4,000 acres thanks to a succession of devoted owners, mostly connoisseurs and possessors of great wealth. By 1880 it had an ice-house and an orangery, a billiard room and a sculpture gallery, stables, grottoes, lodges, a lake, many reception rooms, bedrooms and boudoirs, sculleries and kitchens, a nursery wing, a warren of servants' rooms, a kitchen garden, a butler's pantry and cellars. For two hundred years no expense was spared. Deepdene was magnificent. Its glorious setting and aspect enraptured dozens of distinguished guests from John Evelyn to Benjamin Disraeli.

The Hope family, who owned the Hope diamond, made an Italian palazzo of it, and occupied it for over eighty years. In the 1890s, Lord Francis Pelham Clinton Hope, who had inherited Deepdene and was functionally bankrupt, let it to Lily, Duchess of Marlborough. She lived and entertained there until her death in 1909.

Deepdene was then leased to other occupants in turn, including Almeric Paget MP (later Lord Queenborough), and the military in 1914–15. When valuers from Christie's arrived to list its contents in the spring of 1917, the place was minded by a single caretaker. A grand sale of precious pieces – furniture, carpets, paintings, silver, smaller sculptures and objets d'art – was held in July. By September only the larger, less transportable and less desirable artefacts were left, and they were offered for Auction by Messrs Humbert & Flint, of Serle Street WC2. The British Library retains a case-bound copy of their final catalogue:

The Final Portion of the Hope Heirlooms

Important Six Days' Sale, On September 12th, 13th, 14th, 17th, 18th
     and 19th, 1917
The Contents of the Mansion
Embracing the
Costly Appointments of 40 Bed Rooms, Billiard Room,
Statue Gallery, Nine Reception Rooms, Halls and
numerous Offices.
Greek and Roman Statuary and other Marbles. Fine Bronzes.
Empire Furniture including bedroom suites, wardrobes, cheval
     glasses, bookcases, cabinets, escritoires, tables and many other
     items in mahogany, a Chippendale card table, mahogany chests
     of drawers, dressing tables, cupboards and chairs, well-made
     bedding, iron and other bedsteads, beautiful curtains and bed
     quilts, carpets and rugs
Full-sized billiard table, by Burroughs and Watts
Two grand pianos, by Erard
Decorative China and Porcelain. 2,000 volumes of books
Pictures and Prints. Electro-plate. Candlesticks, Cutlery, Coppers,
     a few Outside effects, Garden seats and Miscellanea.

Wandering through the building one found over 2,000 lots, room
by room: in the Still-room Maid's room No. 13. . . the Under-
Housemaid's room No. 12 . . . The Housemaid's Closet, Upper Gallery
floor . . . Yellow Bedroom No. 16 . . . Etruscan Room . . . Flaxman's
six feet high marble copy of the Apollo Belvedere on its plinth . . . a
9 feet high statue of Napoleon . . . an 8 feet high figure of Jason with
his golden fleece . . . Buhl cabinets . . . Persian rugs . . . a deal kitchen
table 9 feet long . . . miles of underfelt . . . scores of brass fenders and
coal-scuttles . . . ormolu candelabra fitted as chandeliers . . . a wardrobe
in ebony and amboyna wood. . .

   When the last Lot had been sold, the last piece of statuary removed,
the estate was carved up. Developers bought 200 acres here, a
hillside there, 500 acres of wood and arable land perfect for desirable
residences – So well placed for Town! – All services, front and back

gardens and even a *garage* for one's motor. Tarmac snaked over the hills where nightingales had sung; and where the land was not built upon, it was sculpted as a golf course.

Deepdene and its outbuildings, with 200 acres of surrounding parkland and gardens, awaited a buyer. In spring, 1920, *The Times* reported that Humbert & Flint had sold the house privately.

> The future of such houses is for hotels and institutions. . .
> Deepdene is a place of great beauty, close to Dorking and Box Hill, and the gardens are remarkable for their rhododendrons and azaleas. The service section of the house is adequate, at a small expense, for fully meeting the requirements of a very large hotel, and Deepdene may be one, for the upper floors could be divided into scores of bedrooms. It is understood that the hotel will be of the first class. . .

Ten days later another paragraph appeared:

> Following the sale of the Deepdene mansion, at Dorking, to Lansdowne Ltd to be adapted as a residential hotel . . . together with the pleasure grounds, the remaining portion of the Estate, comprising the gardens, lodges, parks and woodlands fronting on the Reigate Road and Punchbowl Lane, over 100 acres in extent, has been acquired by Major Maurice Chance OBE.

The profits that Lansdowne Ltd made from the sale to Major Chance − a successful local developer − could have been used to fund repairs and alterations. The building work raced ahead. Eager enquirers were directed to a company called Deepdene Ltd.

> OPENING IN JUNE
> "an epitome of Paradise" . . . grounds of nearly 50 acres
> . . . widespreading lawns, terraces, wooded walks, nooks for picnics, and magnificent views . . . Self-contained suites with baths . . . reception rooms among the noblest in the country . . . golf, dancing, tennis . . .

Tariff on application to the Secretary, Deepdene Ltd, Jessel Chambers, 88, 89 and 90 Chancery Lane, WC2, Holborn 562-563. Telegrams Telhammer, London.

Deepdene Ltd operated out of the 88-90 Chancery Lane office of Hammersley, Kennedy Ltd, a large firm of hotel valuers and auctioneers. Companies House reports that Deepdene Ltd existed only from 1919 to 1920. In March 1921, Messrs Hammersley, Kennedy & Co Ltd brought a case before the Court of Appeal against 'Nigeradse'.[20] David Zhivotovsky owned the place, along with his daughter, from 1923.[21] Zhivotovsky and his daughter had anglicised the spelling of their names to Givotovsky and Nigeradse, using a G where a J would have made a more Russian sound.

In 1915 Vladimir Davidovich Nizharadzy had been listed with Sidney Reilly as a fellow freemason of the English Lodge in St Petersburg.[22] So whether Hammersley, Kennedy sued Zhivotovsky's daughter, or her husband the freemason from St Petersburg, is unclear. From 1923 David Leonteivich Zhivotovsky and his daughter alone appear to have been the owners.[23] Their partnership was officially dissolved in April 1925.[24] Another company called Deepdene Ltd existed from 1925 to 1986.

It would appear that Gregory was, throughout the 1920s, a silent partner in the hotel with Zhivotovsky and his daughter. The initial link between Zhivotovsky and Gregory was Sidney Reilly. Reilly was a ruthless and clever fellow, a British agent of Russian origin, and the circles in which he moved in London overlapped with Maundy's; and had done, in fact, since he lived in London before the war. The Zhivotovsky brothers, now in late middle age, and Sidney Reilly went back a long way. Reilly had worked for both Abram Zhivotovsky in Petrograd (as an arms buyer in 1915) and their collaborator Moishe Ginsburg in Port Arthur (as a salesman during the 1905 Russo-Japanese war).[25] When, early in 1918, Reilly was establishing his credentials with the War Office, he submitted among other documents a Russian *laisser-passer* issued by Major General Erdeli dated 8 August 1914:

By order of the Chief of Staff of the Army, I request that the
bearers. . . the British subject Sidney George Reilly and the
Russian subject I.T. Zhivatovsky, be given assistance for the
purpose of expeditious and unhindered passage over the
frontier.

The above mentioned persons are commissioned by the
Chief of the Artillery Department to acquire material and
articles of armament for the needs of our Army.[26]

Reilly lived in London again from the late spring of 1919 until
October 1920,[27] except for a brief sojourn in Paris in March 1920
when he stayed at the Hotel Lotti, in the rue de Castiglione (an
hotel, coincidentally, linked to Maundy Gregory's story later); and
once more from January to July, 1923. But if we look for a connection
between Gregory and Reilly, we find it in Gregory's stories of
adventure in the Far East that he repeated, years later, to a young
Parisian lawyer, Jean-Jacques Grumbach. Gregory had never been to
the Orient but Sidney Reilly had. Reilly was a self-mythologiser but
his tales of adventure were inspired by the truth, and so vivid that
they inspired at least one novel – other, of course, than James Bond.
There is a letter, undated, in Russian on Deepdene Hotel headed
paper from Sidney Reilly.[28] He was executed in Russia in 1925.

In the 1920s the Deepdene Hotel did very well. It competed with
Brighton as a discreet weekend destination, and was much more
convenient for London, and its grounds more private, than anything
Brighton could offer. As newspaper reports indicate, it was used by
Ambassadors and consular staff. Guests were of a type sufficiently
well-heeled to enjoy a weekend in the country, but not so well-heeled
as to find life empty if they hadn't used the time to shoot something.
David Zhivotovsky died on 14 February, 1928, leaving over £45,000.
Princess Nizharadzy (the legitimacy of her title is untraced), ran the
place briefly after his death. After she sold the place in 1930, and after
Mazzina had taken it in 1931, with backing from Maundy Gregory,
she appears to have remained in residence.[29]

Maundy has been accused of having forged the Zinoviev Letter, a politically motivated doublecross that made headlines in October 1924. A man called Gregory was involved, but he was J.D. Gregory, a Foreign Office official entirely unrelated to Maundy.

The background to the Letter is as follows. After the election late in 1922, the new Conservative government under Bonar Law was weak and unsettled. Chamberlain, Birkenhead and Balfour, the ex-Coalition Tory leaders, remained in Parliament, a sulky presence that contributed little. Bonar Law resigned in May 1923 with throat cancer, and Baldwin took over. In October 1923 he called an election. The Conservatives won again but with a considerably reduced majority. The Tories could have compromised with the Liberals to retain their hold on power, but Baldwin refused this option on principle. And for the first time there were more Labour people in opposition than Liberals.

In January 1924, therefore, a Labour government dependent on continuing Liberal support came into office led by Ramsay Macdonald. It proved efficient and the Tories might have learned to live with it, had it not been for the Diehards' deep suspicion of Bolshevik Russia – which Macdonald did not fully share; on grounds of fraternal socialism, he was willing to negotiate trade agreements and generally keep channels of communication open. The Labour Party, unlike the Diehard Tories, had never banged a drum for White Russians, or believed in sponsoring an invasion. At the same time, the usual mass-circulation newspapers conducted a fierce campaign against the Red Peril.

The Labour government lasted nine months before disagreements with the Liberals led to its collapse. In October 1924 there would be another election and this time, the Conservatives wanted to regain power with a decisive majority.

The far right were determined to make victory certain. A few weeks before the election the Zinoviev Letter was shown to a few influential people and soon its text was splashed in the newspapers. It purported to come from the Executive Committee, Third Communist International (the Comintern), above a signature of the Comintern's president Zinoviev. It was addressed to the Central

Committee, British Communist Party and commanded specific actions directed at undermining the British state apparatus.

There was uproar between the Russian and British governments. The Russians dismissed it as an obvious forgery. Tories everywhere were horrified, believing it to be genuine, and promptly cast their votes against Labour – to no avail; when the results were counted, Labour had gained a million extra votes. However the Liberals had lost 100 seats to the Conservatives, so Baldwin was firmly in power. Scholarly opinion concurs that the Zinoviev Letter was forged in Berlin, by Russians, [30] and circulated in London by Admiral Hall, formerly of Naval Intelligence. This covert circulation preceded its exposure in the press. Given that Maundy Gregory had been similarly useful to Hall before, there is no reason to think he would not have shown a copy of the Letter about. But that is the extent of his involvement.

And in St John's Wood? Sadly, life at Abbey Road had not been the pleasant round of entertaining and marital harmony that it had promised to be. At the end of 1923 Frederick Rosse walked out on Edith.[31] We don't know why, although reading between the lines it seems that Edith felt she was the 'injured party'. His career prospered, and his private life is unknown, although some clue may lie in a score he wrote around 1923 called 'Nobody seems to want to love me now'.[32]

Maundy Gregory's close friend, Peter Mazzina, was gaining experience in restaurant management. The *Whitehall Gazette* reported in August 1924, that:

> . . . another West End Hotel and Restaurant de Luxe is being opened on May the 14th. This is . . . the Queen's Hotel, Leicester Square, the freehold of which having been newly acquired and large sums having been spent upon reconstruction and redecoration will emerge . . . as another rendezvous for those who frequent such hotels and restaurants as the Carlton or the Ritz, Claridge's or the Savoy. The new restaurant is pleasantly named, I hear – the 'Quai d'Orsay'- and the entire management is solely in the hands of Mr Peter

Mazzina, whose name is, I expect, known to many more than he realises, from his long association with the Carlton, the Berkeley, and the Savoy Hotels.

So that was Peter fixed up, for the moment.

Maundy and Edith stayed at 3 Abbey Road and were quite cosy. They sometimes stayed at Brighton, and later on took a small flat on the seafront. Maundy introduced Edith Marion Rosse to nearly everyone as his sister, although some assumed she was his wife; she, equally, introduced him as her brother.[33]

She was well provided for. She did not divorce Frederick Rosse and he agreed to give her half his income for the rest of her life. And Maundy, perhaps wanting some privacy or maybe out of sheer generosity, paid for Edith and a companion to take occasional holidays on the Mediterranean.

Maundy's taxi took him to the office in Parliament Street every day. He churned out articles for the *Whitehall Gazette*. (John F. Bodinnar, Bacon Curer, was one of his finer efforts in 1924. It started with the Crusades.) Colin Coote contributed measured and thoughtful pieces, from Rome, on the rising Fascist régime. He had lost his seat in 1922 but had been lucky enough to get work from *The Times* as its correspondent in Italy, and supplemented his salary with freelance work. The murder of Matteotti shook many English conservatives out of their complacency about Fascism.

Maundy kept in touch with Peter, now restaurant manager in an establishment that had taken the name of the French Foreign Ministry. Maundy enjoyed answering the phone, hand over the mouthpiece, whispering to whoever was in his office – 'Excuse me a moment. Quai d'Orsay on the line.' And the honours trade – which was still, technically, legal – went on providing a healthy income.

The Honours (Prevention of Abuses) Bill, which foundered at the end of 1923 when the Tories lost power, crept quietly back into Parliament and recommenced its journey towards the Royal Assent.

CHAPTER TEN

The Rot Sets in

Maundy Gregory knew too much. The impending legislation designed to make honours touting illegal promised to leave him untouched. Unless he retired, honours trafficking would remain a nuisance and Maundy Gregory would be its living symbol – protected by other people's secrets and his friends at Scotland Yard. General Horwood was still the Commissioner. Thomson had gone, and was no friend of Horwood, but his band of influential allies and supporters in Parliament remained loyal.

Thomson's further disgrace was achieved in 1925. Suspicion was first caused by an unorthodox pension plan he had made in 1922. In 1959, Peter Singleton-Gates wrote:

> In May of 1922 a person of some authority in London presented me with a heavy bundle of documents, with the comment that if ever I had time I might find in them the basis for a book of unusual interest. The donor had no ulterior motive for wishing such a book published; his gift was no more than a kind gesture to a journalist and writer.[1]

Perhaps this was a little disingenuous. May, 1922 was the month in which Basil Thomson had nearly lost his job over the IRA graffiti incident at Chequers. When he wrote his memoir *The Scene Changes* fifteen years later, he moved the IRA incident to October 1922 and claimed that Lloyd George's fury about it been the cause of his downfall.

But in May, 1922, Basil Thomson already thought he might lose his job, so it seems that he set about looking after himself. The full typescript of the Casement Diaries, to which he had access, would be worth a huge amount of money if published.

Singleton-Gates was an *Evening Standard* reporter. The transcript is exactly what he received from 'a person of some authority'.

> I was . . . given to understand that the three diaries from which the typescripts had been taken were the only ones found in the trunk in Casement's lodgings. They consisted of a Lett's diary for 1903; a Dollard's diary for 1910; and a cash ledger containing diary entries plus detailed accountings of payments large and small. There was also an Army memo book containing sundry trivial and obscure entries.

Singleton-Gates was given many other documents including police reports on enquiries into Casement's life, a list of possessions, the Thomson/Hall interrogation notes, and a letter from Casement to Inspector Sandercock, who had taken him into custody.

In the next two years Singleton-Gates read everything he could lay his hands on relating to Casement. This included the reports about the Congo atrocities and the Putamayo rubber plantations which had earned Casement his knighthood, for the diaries had been kept while he was undertaking those investigations.

> The documents I was then in possession of (I have them no longer) revealed the gross side of this otherwise generous and noble character.
>
> For me the whole constituted a passionate drama of a complicated man devoted to setting great wrongs right . . . of a true patriot who, seeking the freedom of his native land, gave his life with open hands; and I endeavoured to set it all forth in a book, *The Secret Diaries of Roger Casement*.

The Literary Editor of the *Evening Standard* gave him a preliminary notice – a review in advance of publication – on 10 January 1925. All hell broke loose. The Home Secretary, Sir William Joynson-Hicks ('Jix', also known in the House of Commons as Mussolini

Minor), summoned Singleton-Gates to an immediate interview. The following morning at midday, he faced Jix and Jix's 'grim' legal advisor Sir Ernley Blackwell in the Home Secretary's room in Whitehall.

> The first question put to me was bold enough. 'Where did the documents come from and who gave them to you?'
>
> 'Sir William,' I replied 'I am a newspaperman, and I must claim the privilege of that profession that we do not under any circumstances, or under any pressure, reveal the names of those who place confidence in us.'
>
> At that point Sir William thought it well to acquaint me with the Home Office view which rested firmly on sub-section 6 of the Official Secrets Act.
>
> 'Under this section, Mr Singleton-Gates, there is a penalty of two years imprisonment for one who refuses to give information to a police officer above the rank of Inspector, relating to an offence or suspected offence.'
>
> I replied that I saw no reason to change my expressed opinion, but suggested that he, being a solicitor himself, and having (here I inclined a cynical bow towards Ernley Blackwell, sprawled out at length on a settle) one of the most acute legal brains in the country to aid him, must certainly appreciate my wish to have a few days' consultation with my own advisors. Sir William agreed, with some reluctance.[2]

Big guns swung into action. In the course of the next week, F.E. and the Home Secretary told every London publisher that they were under threat of prosecution if they touched the book. Sir Ernley Blackwell wrote to demand an undertaking from Singleton-Gates that he undertook not to publish. And in the middle of it all Thomson's ex-War Office successor, Sir Borlase Wyndham Childs, got in touch. Singleton-Gates was well connected in Fleet Street and the Army, and had co-operated with Wyndham Childs in the past on criminal cases that demanded absolute secrecy. They trusted one another.

When I saw him at Scotland Yard, his one concern was as to whether an officer of his branch had been responsible for handing me vital papers. I was able truthfully to say, 'No'.[3]

Wyndham Childs then offered to arrange that he might see the original diaries.

Four days later, Singleton-Gates went back to Scotland Yard. He had brought with him some typescripts and prints of Casement's handwriting. He compared them closely with the originals and was sure that the diaries had not been forged. He remained certain, for various reasons, that Scotland Yard had received the diaries at least a year before Thomson said they had; but he knew he had seen the genuine article.

People of influence concluded that the person who had given the typescripts to Singleton-Gates was Sir Basil Thomson. On 14 May 1925 a shot was fired over his bows. An MP asked the Home Secretary whether Basil Thomson had used confidential material in his recent piece on Casement in *English Life*. Sir William Joynson Hicks said he had not, but that he had received a warning.

Blatant use of confidential police information, for purposes of gain, was not the done thing. Scotland Yard finally got their own back in December.

Ten days before Christmas, Sir Basil (sixty-three) was sitting in the cold and dark on a bench in Hyde Park with a young lady of seventeen. So engrossed in conversation were they that neither noticed the two helmeted figures approaching, tippy-toed, in big shiny boots from behind a tree.

'I'm surprised at you, Thelma,' smirked the Police Constable.[4]

The Sergeant and the Constable escorted them to the police station in Hyde Park. The dejected ex-Director of Intelligence trailed behind with the PC and apparently tried bribery. It did not work.

Sir Basil told the Magistrates that Thelma had been helping him with research for a book. That did not work either. He was fined, and any hope of restoration to high office was finally scuppered.

But Thomson's downfall came too little, too late, to weaken Maundy Gregory. Nor did Maundy have anything to fear from the

Honours (Prevention of Abuses) Act, which, as we have already noted, in many ways actually boosted his income. Previously, with Asquith, Lloyd George and (briefly) in 1922/23 with Bonar Law, he secured the money on their behalf and took a percentage or 'finder's fee'. Now he could pocket the entire amount for himself.

To an unscrupulous man like Gregory, this was also an invitation to blackmail. Anyone who handed over cash in anticipation of an honour would be as guilty as the person who offered to obtain it. So if Maundy took the money and failed to deliver the goods, the victim could do very little about it; particularly since – should he courageously go to the police – Commissioner Horwood was still Maundy's great friend.

For whatever reason (and since Maundy Gregory was by now acquainted with a number of *émigrés* from the Ukraine, Romania and Portugal he had probably expressed a willingness to sell information about them) Sir Maurice Hankey at the War Office decided to ask questions about Gregory. A note from MI5 is signed by Major Eric Holt-Wilson.[5]

Dear Hankey,

Here is a sketch of the man you mentioned to me this morning.

K [Vernon Kell, head of MI5] knows him well and likes him not at all.

Hope this will satisfy.

Yrs sincerely
E. Holt Wilson

Our records of him go back to 1910, and personal knowledge from 1915.

Pinned to this in the file is a short report, initialled by EHW on 23 March 1926 and marked SECRET: copies to Sir M Hankey GCB only.[6]

SUBJECT: J M GREGORY

We don't like him and don't trust him. We have often refused to employ him because of his character. Has run a private enquiry agency for many years, and tries to market volumes of general news of which a small percentage turns out to have an interesting foundation. He is difficult to shake off as he is an indefatigable 'Nosey Parker', perpetually on the prowl for something saleable. He succeeded in selling a good deal of rubbish during the war to BT, who responded by manipulating his exemption from military service in order to employ him further.

To sum up, his personal quality is <u>not</u> that of a high grade independent eclectic of nice discrimination, but rather that of the wholesale purveyor of likely fables some of which may prove to be true when tested. He has all the skill and failings of the professional inquiry agent, and nowadays tries to make himself useful to as many 'anti-something' societies as possible.

Independent verification is essential of any information offered by him. Before embarking on this private inquiry business he tried to float publishing companies and a bucket-shop investigation syndicate. It was the opportunity for 'German-hunting' in the war that switched him over to his more recent activities.

Sir Maurice was pleased with this. He returned the document 'which I have roughly memorised . . . It is exactly what I wanted.'

As for Maundy Gregory's influence elsewhere in Government, F.E. had become Secretary of State for India, but Colonel Cartwright clung like a limpet and went with him to the India Office as 'private secretary'. Cartwright fulfilled exactly the same function when F.E, in need of money, resigned to take directorships in the City in 1928. F.E's biographer remarked about Cartwright:

He may well have helped F.E. with the murkier aspects of his always chaotic finances; he is thought to have had some connection with stockbroking. It is not impossible that there was even an element of blackmail in his hold over F.E. He certainly spoke darkly in old age of all the things he could reveal if he were so minded; on the other hand, those of his recollections that could be checked proved largely false.[7]

1926 was of course the year of the General Strike. The *Whitehall Gazette* printed an article by Lex denouncing it as illegal, another by Gellius saying that the Bolshevists were behind it and yet another saying that socialism was 'pernicious'. What interested Maundy Gregory rather more was a new opportunity that had opened up in the West End. He could see a way to have Peter Mazzina front an exclusive club, where he could invite contacts to luncheon and impress them with fine food and champagne. The profits would be made in the evenings, for as everyone knew, night clubs were a licence to print money, as long as you induced the police to look the other way.

Night clubs had been a rather bohemian endeavour in the early years of the century. With the First War, and DORA (the Defence of the Realm Act) they had become notorious for prostitution and out-of-hours drinking. Between 1919 and 1925, with the relative liberation of women, they were at their height. Girls from 'good' families bought cocaine from Brilliant Chang, Avery Hopwood the playwright slashed his wrists in a night club lavatory, Nancy Cunard caused scandal by living with Hutch (Leslie Hutchinson) the black jazz pianist, and one night at the Savoy, Fahmy Bey's wife shot him dead when he returned from the '43'. There were protection rackets, hold-ups at gunpoint and fights over girls. 'Jix' fulminated. *Daily Mail* readers were pop-eyed. One or two policemen at Vine Street and other West End stations did quite well.

Night clubs became fashionable: daringly 'in' among the fast set. In June 1921, Frances Stevenson confided to her diary after a weekend house party at Cuckoo Bellville's (her hostess being an upper-class woman who had a rather smart Mayfair shop):

Cuckoo asked McKenna why he did not dine at the Embassy Club sometimes? 'A man in my position could not be seen there,' was McK's answer. 'Why, everyone goes there – Horne, Montagu, Churchill,' Cuckoo said. 'Oh, but as the head of a great bank I consider myself to be in a far more important position than a Cabinet Minister,' was McK's answer.[8]

When the Charleston was already all the rage, around 1926, the racier young things moved on to bottle parties, and night clubs became so mainstream that even bankers could be seen there. The Prince of Wales had graced the Embassy and Ciro's with his presence for some time. Now, at last, Maundy Gregory felt he could safely catch up.

26 Curzon Street had been at one time a fashionable dress shop called Redfern's. It was re-incarnated in 1926 as a night club but closed within a year, allegedly because of business lost due to the Strike (although the Strike proper lasted less than ten days and if anything, increased attendance at other night clubs, as public school boys poured into town, well scrubbed and ready to drive trams all day and party all night). It came on the market again and in 1927, Maundy Gregory took it over with a £20,000 mortgage from Barclays.[9] Only Mazzina and a bank nominee had their names on the documents, but a lot of money was spent on refurbishment, and it re-opened in April 1927 as the Ambassador Club with Peter Mazzina in charge at a salary of £3,000 a year.

This was a stupendously generous sum, in the range that could be expected by the Chairman of a public company. Maybe this was why Maundy Gregory impressed most strongly on his accountant, Pengelly, that Edith Marion Rosse (whose accounts he also did) must *never* know that he had a financial interest in the place; she must think of him as a member only.

The Ambassador Club was in a tall building at 26 Conduit Street, just off Regent Street; with a direct line to the House of Commons, but sufficiently far away to be out of reach of the division bell. There were uniformed flunkeys at the door, two gold coronets adorning the exterior brickwork, and men in velvet knee-breeches inside. 'Exclusive . . . culture . . . the best surroundings . . . forty-eight hand-done portraits upon vellum. . .' purred Maundy in his *Whitehall Gazette* article, not forgetting to remind his readers of ancient

London traditions, taverns, gamesters, and so forth. The restaurant had a balcony and a glass roof; the prevailing hue was Rose du Barry, with drapes, and marble columns. There was an American Bar and a 'richly appointed grill room,' an oak-panelled library with stained glass windows and bound copies of *Hansard* and *Punch*.

Maundy made a point of holding his nose and distancing himself from 'those institutions specifically termed nightclubs. . . marred by an undesirable promiscuity'. Promiscuity being shorthand for *indiscriminating in their admissions policy*. At the Ambassador Club, on the other hand, they were very choosy about whom they let in. Upstairs were private rooms, and some mystery.

Whatever these rumours were, they surely did not reach the ears of the new Dean at Westminster Abbey, at whose installation at Christmas 1926 Maundy Gregory had been a prominent guest; or the ears of Sir Chartres Biron, London's Chief Magistrate, who – just one month before that – had joined Maundy Gregory, among others, at a Guildhall banquet in honour of the Prime Minister.

When Maundy Gregory entertained his guests for luncheon at the Ambassador's, two magnums of champagne were put on ice by his table. This is not merely a mark of its status as his 'social alpine club'. He couldn't trust the wine. It was re-corked. He once confided to a friend that he kept a bottlers' corking machine and bought corks by the gross so that bottles could be re-filled routinely. This was entirely typical of Maundy, who exploited style over enduring substance whenever possible. (He once paid for some expert gilding at Westminster Abbey and basked in the gratitude he received. The gilding soon wore off.)

The Club was an odd hybrid – men only at lunchtime, a place for serious gossip and influence-peddling; an excellent band in the evening, and dancing. The guests at the High Table were like goats tethered to stakes.'[10] Major-General Sir John Hanbury-Williams, from the Royal Household, lunched with Gregory quite often, as did Lord Southborough, and F.E. Lord Southborough was nearly seventy, but had been for many years a senior civil servant at the Admiralty. Unusually for one who frequented the likes of Maundy Gregory, in 1921 he had become a Fellow of the Institution of Engineering and

Technology – in company, in the 1920s, with Marconi, Edison and Ferranti.

In 1925, in exchange for £10,000 from the Conservative Party, F.E. had been persuaded to stop supplementing his income by journalism. Baldwin had insisted he remain in Cabinet, but he insisted that he couldn't afford to; hence the payoff.[11] That was Davidson's story, anyway; but was it really all about journalism? It would have taken F.E. many years to earn that much by writing for the papers. Was it, in fact, to put an end to some other means of earning a living, such as ensnaring punters for Maundy? Whatever the reality, by 1927 he saw financial embarrassment on the horizon again, and was considering his next move, to the City.

There were persistent stories of blackmail surrounding F.E. These arose from his drinking and 'doping', as they called it then; his affair with Mona Dunn; and in the early years, the prodigious fees he earned for taking criminal cases that looked hopeless – coupled with his chronic need for yet more cash. Also, of course, there was his association with the slightly sinister Maundy Gregory.

F.E. simply lived above his means. There is no hint that he gambled. He did not sail a yacht or fly a plane, as so many rich men did. He drank, and had expensive tastes, and lived as his peers did with houses in town and country and a wife, servants and several children – but he had not, as many of his peers had, inherited wealth. His mother had been a widow, and he had a mentally ill brother whom he supported for many years in an asylum. There is no reason other than rumour to think that Gregory, or Cartwright, was blackmailing him outright in the sense of demanding money; but that he 'looked after' Gregory, in the sense of facilitating introductions, is possible.

Another of Maundy's favourite lunchtime companions was His Majesty the King of Greece. This was not King Constantine but King George II, one of Constantine's sons, who was at this time only thirty-six. Prince George had been excluded from the succession during the war because of allegedly pro-German sympathies. When Constantine abdicated in 1922 one of his sons had died, and another refused to be king, so Prince George was the last choice. The country was being run by a military dictatorship, and the new King's party were plotting a *coup d'etat.* When this was exposed late in 1923, he and his wife Elizabeth wisely decided to leave. In his absence Greece became a republic.[12] He was a King without a throne, who lived in Brown's Hotel and hoped, one day, to get his country back.

Maundy was flaunting his influence, which seemed unbounded. He seemed richer than ever in 1927. He opened the Ambassador Club and continued to churn out public relations for rich men in the *Whitehall Gazette.* Two years later he would move to a house almost next door to a Harmsworth; he had an interest in the Deepdene Hotel. A 1933 Vatican file on him, having named the source of his wealth since 1918 as the sale of honours through Freddy Guest, continues.

These activities brought him considerable sums of money which he appears to have invested in a number of ventures. He has a particular interest in Russian matters and has, since 1919, been associated with a number of Russian emigrés with whom he has participated in business ventures. These include a hotel in Surrey, England, property in Sussex, England, and agricultural holdings in the south of France.[13]

'Agricultural holdings in the south of France' were exactly what were described in a London court as belonging to the Zhivotovsky clan from about 1918.[14] The details remain murky, but there seems to be more than coincidence at work.

Domestically, also, he was getting things his own way. Edith's niece Ethel had worked in Winnipeg before returning from Canada in 1925. She had afterwards gone back there, against Edith's wishes, with Maundy placing £300 to her credit at the Bank of Montreal from his account at Drummonds. He had also booked her passage on SS *Montroyal.* But although she had been able to support herself, Edith asked her to come back because she was ill with cystitis. Ethel's own version of her return, which seems to lack a thread of cause and effect, is that she volunteered to come back because her aunt had just disposed of some flats.[15] Anyhow she was now living in a bedsitter in Lancaster Gate and doing some secretarial work for Maundy Gregory.

All this indicates an inward flow of cash. What he did not know, as he entertained his friends and zipped about London in his private taxi with its faithful driver, was that he was being watched, his contacts noted, and his affairs investigated.

Honours trading remained a murky area. In August 1927, the far-right *Morning Post* ran a series of articles which hinted heavily at something iffy on Lloyd George's watch, during the Coalition. Lloyd George was living in discontented retirement. All his pipedreams about retiring to Mesopotamia and making the desert bloom, which he and Frances Stevenson had discussed on Valentine's Day in 1915, were cast aside: the man was a politician and nothing else, and never had been; he required adulation and scheming in order to function, and still expected to return from the wilderness. Frances Stevenson, after their many years together, now saw him as he was. He had never been young, she wrote; unlike Disraeli, whom they both admired, he had never been fashionable or a man-about-town; he had been absorbed by politics all his life. On 18 August 1927, she added:

> Rothermere came over to Criccieth to see him last week. He is going to back D & his land policy, & says he will be PM again soon. He has been defending D over the *Morning Post* articles on honours. Max [Beaverbrook] on the other hand seems to be in league with the *Morning Post* & intended to write an article defending Bonar Law at D's expense. D told him, however, that if he did so, he would contradict it flatly and give the facts, which would not be flattering either to the Conservatives or to Bonar. I gather he and Max had words on the telephone. D is furious with him.[16]

Bonar Law, of course, was in his grave and unable to defend himself.

In May of that year, incoming Conservative Party Chairman J.C.C. Davidson had appointed Major Joseph Ball from the Secret Service to be the Party's Director of Publicity. J.C.C.D as a new broom was determined to squeeze out those whose activities were not only outside of his control but potentially siphoned off money from those individuals who might well have donated their money directly to party funds had the likes of Gregory not got to them first.

The articles were probably prompted by an opening salvo – Ball's carefully placed drip-feed of information detrimental to Lloyd George, and the old Coalition Tories. It took a while, but at the end of November Lloyd George rose to the bait in feisty defence of himself. This elicited a cold response from Austen Chamberlain, who was about to leave by train for Geneva from his home in Victoria:

> I find in this morning's papers your statement about your Party Fund. I have taken no part in any controversy that has arisen on this subject and I am sorry that you thought it necessary to introduce Bonar's name and my own into your statement. Of what passed between you and Bonar I have, of course, no knowledge, but your words would seem to imply that I had canvassed with you the personal merits of your nominees. If they were intended so to be read they would throw upon me a responsibility which I cannot accept. . . I have never considered myself and do not now consider myself in any way responsible for the selection which you made.[17]

Hurriedly he added a handwritten note that this was simply a 'friendly warning not to force me to take part in a controversy from which I should wish to continue to hold aloof.'

Lloyd George wrote a furious reply. He had been held personally responsible, he said, not only for the recommendations from the Liberal Whips but from the Unionist ones too, and had been entirely innocent at the time. If he had known then what he knew now, he would have vetoed them. He had been attacked about two cases in particular, and had defended himself with a clear conscience.

> Subsequently I was informed on credible authority – which if called upon I must quote – that substantial cheques had passed in respect of both these cases to the managers of your Party Fund. There are other cases of the same kind, particulars of which I am prepared to furnish – they range from Bonar's time to Baldwin's. . . I have been charged by some of your

colleagues with selling honours for money – without a word
of protest from either you, George Younger or the PM. I do
not mind the *Morning Post*. It is another matter when Ministers
take a hand in circulating this slander. That is why I have come
to the conclusion that if Joynson Hicks, Douglas Hogg, J.C.
Davidson and others persist in their charges I shall be driven
in self-defence to mention these and other cases publicly . . . I
have just had enough of it. I do not mind your taking part in
the controversy, inasmuch as that would release me from any
obligation of secrecy.[18]

The caution of the solicitor he had once been was far behind him.
He might have sent the letter, too, had Austen Chamberlain not been
in Geneva.

But he waited. Instead he scored it through and sent a shorter,
considered reply with a sting in the tail:

At least two of those cases mentioned during the discussions
in 1922 came from the Unionist Whip. I have no objection
to a parliamentary discussion or investigation. I have been
held purely responsible for a traditional method of collecting
money for Party Funds, which continues as I know up to the
present hour, and I have had enough of it.[19]

He and Chamberlain held weapons of mutually assured destruction.
It was their Bay of Pigs, and Chamberlain backed down.

J.C.C.D and Ball were still on the case, though. In October 1927,
at the height of the newspaper campaign against Lloyd George, a new
War Office file had been opened because of 'information received'
that Maundy Gregory was engaged in honours trafficking, which
since 1925 had been an indictable offence.

CSI was instructed by the Attorney-General [General Sir Thomas
Inskip] to institute enquiries with a view to ascertaining what were
the actual activities of this individual.

Subsequent investigation disclosed that while there were definite
indications that MAUNDY-GREGORY had been engaged in the

traffic in Honours and was still unsuccessfully attempting to continue this unsavory business no sufficient evidence could be obtained to prosecute...These facts were duly reported in detail to the Attorney-General and instructions were eventually received that there was no necessity to pursue the matter further.[20]

The note was initialled 1 December, 1928 – fifteen months after the matter had been raised. Even allowing for Inskip having sat on the file for a while, this indicates a pretty exhaustive investigation. Yet only two documents are appended. One was sent, four days later, to Kell at MI5 from J.C.C.D (J.C.C. Davidson, Conservative Party Chairman).

> As there is now no possibility of any of MG's recommendations appearing in the Honours List and in view of the fact that neither the Lord Chancellor, the Attorney General [nor] the PM believe that a prosecution is practical politics I don't see any reason for continuing any special measures of surveillance. I wish we could have jugged the devil but it is clearly impossible.[21]

On 3 January 1929, immediately following announcement of the New Year's Honours, a War Office memo was appended by a Captain Salter. *All papers connected with this investigation have been destroyed by me personally on the instructions of CSI.*

Too hot to handle, then. But the ground on which Maundy Gregory stood *had* shifted, nonetheless. Among his valued acquaintances was J.C.C. Davidson himself.

Davidson had been a very young Private Secretary to Bonar Law during the War, and later to Baldwin; now, still in his early thirties, he was Chairman of the party in power. He was astute, and had been friendly with Joseph Ball since the War. He was a high-flier whose actions indicate that he prioritised organisational change and set about getting it. He first got rid of dead wood, and then set about his most difficult task: to increase the Party's income without selling honours in the same way Bonar Law and Chamberlain had done. This meant that large donations from those outside the membership of the party could no longer be anticipated. Davidson's attitude to this was, first, that he could happily do without the donations of the unprincipled; second, that short-term losses were a small price to pay for achieving his objectives; and third, that his well-led party machine would undertake to increase funds by encouraging thousands of smaller subscriptions and donations.

He saw no point in attacking the job piecemeal, tearing down the stalls in the marketplace, so to speak. He must put Maundy Gregory, the wholesaler, out of business. As he discovered in the first couple of years:

> ... the problem was how to achieve this without precipitating a major public disclosure. Gregory's methods were so effective that many prominent persons were involved to some extent in his organisation, and a public revelation would have provided a *cause célèbre* of dramatic proportions.[22]

If Maundy Gregory were pushed into a corner, he could bring all the political parties down with him. When the 1927/28 investigation was stopped after fifteen months, MI5 and the Tory Party had some idea of the scale of the revelations he could make. A war of attrition might have to go on for several years, but it would, he hoped, ultimately work. In the same way, Davidson was to drive Harry Shaw out of the honours business.[23]

Maundy's business would collapse if unsupported by great wads of cash. Quite early on, Davidson decided to undermine its foundations; to work away, undercover, like dry rot until one day the Maundy Gregory edifice collapsed into dust. He would introduce a spy into the Gregory camp. This person would find out exactly who had paid for honours and Davidson would make sure that should their name be recommended from a Conservative Association or indeed any other source from within the party, they would not receive an honour.

Maundy would inevitably lose. Either he would be forced to hand money back, or he would decline to do so and undermine his own reputation. Or, typically, he would make excuses. A man who could blame the non-delivery of a baronetcy on the General Strike, as he did, would say anything.

Devious Mr Davidson put this plan into action: and he had the perfect spy in his sights. The Prime Minister was persuaded to write to Sir George Younger, the Party Treasurer, about someone whose duties would be 'the maintenance of a good subscription list'.

> I have been having a word or two with David [J.C.C.D] and he is genuinely worried, and of course you are I know, that the number of annual subscribers to the Party has been diminishing in recent years. . . It would not be fair to ask you to organise a drive amongst our supporters. There is, however, a man who is very rich, has plenty of time, and great energy, who has volunteered to do the work, namely A.J. Bennett, MP for Nottingham Central.[24]

So far as Davidson knew, Gregory was marketing knighthoods at £10,000, baronetcies at £30,000 and a peerage at £50,000 to £100,000 or more. When individuals explained to him that they had paid Maundy Gregory – and some did, he quite ingenuously told them, truthfully, that the payment in itself invalidated their candidacy unless they could obtain a refund from Gregory and could prove they had done so. If they did this and subsequently re-directed their donation, an honour would most likely, in the fullness of time, be forthcoming. [25]

The worm began to eat away at Maundy's business. The watchers watched and Mole Bennett reported. In 1929 Ramsay Macdonald and the Labour Party took office and in 1931, Macdonald headed a National Government – another coalition.

But still the House of Gregory remained impregnable because of 'practical politics'.

CHAPTER ELEVEN

The Dangerous Mr K

Summer, 1928, saw the departure of another of Maundy's protectors. According to Lieutenant Colonel John Baker White, Director of the Economic League (a belligerently anti-Communist organisation of the 1920s) Maundy Gregory was shielded by Brigadier-General Sir William Horwood.

Baker White related one episode in particular to Tom Cullen. Thanks to information from the Economic League, he said, Colonel Harker of MI5 investigated Gregory's activities as an honours tout. With Baker White peering over his shoulder, Harker compiled a dossier designed to result in a prosecution. This individual had refused to pay on non-delivery, and had received a blackmail threat; that one had tried to pull out of the deal and had been refused; and so on. Having investigated, Harker was confident that his evidence was more than adequate to mount a prosecution.

Harker and Baker White made an appointment to see Horwood, the Commissioner at Scotland Yard. They met in the foyer and called the lift. It seemed to be stuck on the third floor. When the cage swayed down and clanked to a stop, who should bounce out but Maundy Gregory himself, dapper as ever and beaming like the cat that got the cream. Baker White was dismayed. 'Colonel Harker, who had Gregory's dossier under his arm, looked at me, then his shoulders came up to meet his ears in a comic shrug and he said "That does it. There's no point in going up." With that he tore the dossier into small pieces which he deposited in a rubbish bin as we went out. That was the end of the matter.'[1]

Horwood's credibility was in tatters, and in 1928 he was made to resign when the *Daily Mail* insisted, on behalf of its 16 million readers, that a certain Miss Savidge was a virgin, and should have been treated like one by the Metropolitan Police.

Miss Savidge was twenty-two, and had been caught one evening in Hyde Park sitting too close to Sir Leo Money on a bench. (Sir Leo had once been Lloyd George's Private Secretary.) She was hauled away and given the third degree at Scotland Yard, even though her father, a salt-of-the-earth type, and all who knew her said she was a 'good girl'. The implication was that the police were out of control.

There was a lot of politicking behind this as well as some genuine beliefs. The old gang of Thomson supporters were determined to demonstrate that Horwood, who had been appointed in 1920 during the Coalition, was incompetent to run the Met. They demanded constantly that the force be cleaned up. Horwood had admitted long ago that the post-war intake were not the upright and sober Bobbies of popular fiction. A great many damaged and intemperate types had joined at around the time of the police strike in 1919, and the West End police were notoriously corrupt.

Sir William 'Jix' Joynson-Hicks, the Home Secretary, expressed a particular fear and loathing of night clubs. Kate Meyrick, London's night club queen, flourished despite several convictions and a sentence – two of her eight children were able to run the clubs in her absence. The West End would remain, in Jix's view, a sink of iniquity and filth after dark until the vice squad stopped taking bribes. He (and many another like him) was a Victorian, and horrified by what he saw as licentious behaviour, greed and random violence.

Across the Atlantic, *Time* magazine was much amused. From its cover glared Lord Byng of Vimy, the new Commissioner. Examining General Horwood's descent into ignominy, *Time* remarked:

> The retiring Commissioner, Sir William Thomas Francis Horwood, who offers 'age' as his excuse for resigning, is fifty-nine. Lord Byng is sixty-five.

Some Conservative MPs said the *Daily Mail* should lay off. The police had virtually downed tools, so frightened were they of infringing the privacy of young girls and being pilloried in the press. 'Conditions on the park benches and behind the shrubbery are becoming indescribable,' thundered one of them. Nobody asked how he knew.

Byng was brought in to clear things up. Within a year, Luigi Ribuffi of Uncle's club and Ma Meyrick – who had emerged from Holloway and fled to Paris in her cloche hat and furs before returning to face the music – appeared in court along with shamefaced Sergeant Goddard of Vine Street. The prosecution managed to make it clear that Goddard's goings-on had been common knowledge before Horwood left. The Sergeant (on £12 a week) had stashed about £12,000 in a Selfridge's safe deposit box and another in the Haymarket, had a financial interest in Alexander's and other clubs, and was frequently witnessed cruising around Streatham in the comfort of a large Chrysler.

The Ambassador Club evidently had nothing to fear from all this, whether or not Horwood was in charge. It was at the smarter end of night-club culture and now the Prince of Wales and his party had begun to arrive after midnight from time to time. The band was always good, and people came attracted by big names like Ray Starita, Eddie Norris, or Jack Hylton. Good musicians were a huge draw, and extremely well paid – though less so than they had been in the immediate post-war years when Kate Meyrick opened her first club:

> In the early days of post-war cabarets good bands could command enormous salaries. It is true that today [1932] you can get an excellent band at a very low rate, but in those times you had to pay, on an average, £150 a week, and Teddy Brown's orchestra used to cost me £350 per week … It was by no means an uncommon occurrence for two or three of our bandsmen to ring up an agency and hire an aeroplane to take them over to Ostend for the day. They would set off somewhere about nine o'clock in the morning, spend the day in Ostend, visiting the Kursaal and having a gamble there, and then return in the evening in time to be in their places at the 43, or whichever club it was, to provide the dance music for our guests.[2]

The Ambassador even took on an artistic flavour, for Maundy Gregory had made friends with young A.J.A. Symons. They had in common a passion for the work of Baron Corvo, the pseudonym of Frederick Rolfe. Rolfe had been a writer of cult novels and homosexual erotica. He was a selfish schemer who had been much in vogue when Maundy Gregory was at Oxford. There was something self-destructive, as well as bohemian, about Wolfe, an unattached student a generation before Maundy. He had lied and unapologetically demanded money from his friends and died destitute in Venice in 1913.

In Maundy's time at Oxford that other theology student, 'Jumbo' Davidson, shared rooms with C.J. Masterman, whom Compton Mackenzie described as a 'poor imitation of Baron Corvo'. Masterman claimed that he could not cross water without a compulsion to throw himself in. To get to France, therefore, he boarded the ferry in a coffin accompanied by Jumbo wearing a black armband.[3]

No doubt this was one of the stories with which Maundy Gregory entertained young Mr Symons. In the foreword to his successful book, *The Quest for Corvo*, published in 1940, A. J. A. Symons stated that his own hobbies were 'collecting musical boxes, the study and practice of forgery, and literary conversation.' He helped to found the Wine & Food Society and he knew Christopher Millard, one-time secretary to Robert Ross, later an antiquarian bookseller. It had been Christopher Millard who first recommended Symons to read Corvo's *Hadrian VII* and lent him Rolfe's letters. Symons had also been able to read correspondence from *The Times Literary Supplement* about Corvo's work, and a piece on their hero from Harry Pirie-Gordon, who had known him well; he had been a great friend of the much older Corvo/ Rolfe at Oxford in the early 1900s. They called each other Prospero and Caliban. Pirie-Gordon and his friends – Vyvyan Holland, Shane Leslie, Ronald Firbank and others less well known, most of whom were Catholic converts – discussed the foundation of a secular semi-monastic Order. They envisaged a sort of big boys' dressing-up box, with scrolls, mantles, coats of arms, insignia and so on.

In 1929 Maundy Gregory bought *Burke's Landed Gentry* and installed its office upstairs at 38 Parliament Street, with Harry Pirie-Gordon as Editor. Harry and Mabel Pirie-Gordon (Harry wasn't all that monastic in the end) became regular visitors to the Ambassador Club.

Maundy impressed Symons at once by paying a vastly inflated asking price for a single Corvo poem in manuscript. He also dazzled him – Symons' own rooms in Bedford Square were papered in silver – with flash, cash and bling. Not only did Maundy own his own taxi, have a mysterious air and 'very beautiful boots' but he exuded opulence beyond compare:

> It was not the gold cigarette case he produced (a gift of the King of Greece), nor his superb sleeve links (platinum balls covered with diamonds), nor the beautiful black pearl in his tie which produced this impression of vast wealth, so much as the implication behind everything he said. . . [4]

Symons positively drooled. They were soon firm friends. Maundy, ever 'The Cheerful Giver', bestowed generous presents, among them Mussolini's old passport and a rare Corvo manuscript. He also paid Symons £150 for Rolfe's 'Venice Letters'. These were like Casement's diaries in being mainly slavering descriptions of boys, but more literary and set in Venice.

He subsidised research for the book that would become *The Quest for Corvo,* and wined and dined Symons and his large circle of arty associates at the Ambassador Club; in the euphoria of the moment they invented the Corvine Society for like-minded people. Maundy Gregory would be Treasurer. They would hold an annual banquet. The food was described in somewhat eldritch terms (shades of Marinetti's futurist cookery) but seems to have been conventionally delicious.

The euphoria wore off, and there were only two banquets. The reason it didn't last was rather sad. Gregory in that company seemed a shallow old attention-seeker, unable to keep up, and he knew that they made catty remarks. Unlike many of the Corvines he had not seen active service and was not at ease with the intellectual background to Marinetti and Wyndham Lewis. Wyndham Lewis, who came to the second banquet, was then well known as a Vorticist painter and wartime soldier. (Many years later he wrote a book called, coincidentally, *Self-Condemned.*) One cannot imagine that Maundy was familiar with Vorticism and he would have been out of his depth with Tancred Borenius too, Professor of Fine Art at University College and contributor to the *Burlington Magazine* – at least, had they discussed art, he would. But Borenius, a scented owl of a man, was also a Finn who had in 1919 been his country's diplomatic representative in London. There exists at Glasgow University, in the collection of Dugald Sutherland MacColl (then Curator of the Wallace Collection) a tantalisingly undated, unsigned message:

> Professor Borenius has been summoned to lunch with the King of Greece. He still hopes to be able to be present, but may not be able to get away in time.[5]

A small, but very black cloud appeared on Maundy's horizon in the early part of 1930. Sir George Watson, of the Maypole Dairies – who had handed over securities to the value of £30,000 in 1923 – finally despaired of their delivery, and demanded restitution. On 27 March 1930 Maundy gave him receipts for the securities, but made excuses for some delay in giving them back. The delay continued and Sir George demanded he hand them over to his order at Lloyds Bank. Still nothing happened.

In July, Sir George died. Maundy breathed a sigh of relief. Having been disgorged from the jaws of disaster, he hoped he would hear no more about it, and turned to other things.

Maundy Gregory had for many years exploited foreign 'causes' which would give financial support to the *Whitehall Gazette* in return for promotion in the magazine. In 1930, Sir Arthur Willert at the Foreign Office was 'a little disturbed to find that at least one foreign power regarded this journal as, at any rate, 'semi-officially' inspired. This appears in a report of a friendly call paid by an MI5 agent to Sir Arthur in response to his query. He found that Sir Arthur was a thirty-four year old high-flyer who had never heard of Maundy Gregory, and told him:

> . . . the history of this individual's activities; omitting however to touch on his important connection with the sale of honours. I emphasised the fact that Maundy Gregory

ran the Ambassador Club, and was very friendly with such people as Sir William Horwood, Lord Birkenhead and Lord Southborough; and suggested to Sir Arthur Willert that he would probably find that there were persons at present employed in the Foreign Office who knew Maundy Gregory quite well and thought him a charming fellow.[6]

Best not to make waves, then.

But MI5 were not inattentive. In fact they were monitoring Maundy's phone calls and were well aware of what he was doing.[7] Early in 1932 the Anglo-Ukrainian Committee, with its headquarters at 38 Parliament Street and its 'Committee and Reading Room' at the Ambassador Club, 26 Conduit Street, came into sharp focus through a Ukrainian, a former diplomat called Vladimir Korostovetz, who had visited the Home Office Aliens Department, and was evidently anxious to discuss goings-on at the Committee.

Maundy's association with the nationalist Hetman [Ruler] of the Ukraine seems to have begun quite early on. An article in the *Whitehall Gazette* in 1921 condemns the Hetman as a former puppet of the Kaiser. But this attitude would change.

The Hetman, Paul Skoropadsky, was a Cossack, a former General who had run the Ukraine for the last six months of the war with German support. From whom did Maundy Gregory obtain this article, or the information in it? Maybe, as early as 1921, he had met Vladimir Korostovetz, a White Russian; who, to the best knowledge of an MI5 correspondent in 1926,[8] had been private secretary to Sazonov, who was Foreign Minister to the last Tsar. There had been a file on him at MI5 since his arrest in 1921, by the Poles. When the Hetman, Korostovetz and other Ukrainian refugees began to make their presence felt in England ten years later, their association with the German far-right made them rather an unknown quantity. This, in time, contributed to a later rumour (unfounded) that Maundy Gregory supported the Nazis during the war.

According to an account Vladimir Korostovetz published in 1931 in Germany,[9] he had visited the Hetman in Kiev in 1918 and the Hetman said he took German protection because it was the only protection available. Korostovetz found reason to believe him; in his experience in Kiev, the intelligentsia and the aristocrats preferred to think that the Bolshevik threat to Ukraine would blow over and everything would go back to the way it had been in Romanov times, while the White Russian leader von Denikin and the Allies wouldn't help the Hetman's nationalist party either. Skoropadsky assured Korostovetz that he'd rather have had American help than German, if only it had been on offer. But beggars can't be choosers, and in Kiev in 1918:

> ...it made a strange impression to see German patrols guarding the offices of the Okhrana...which was working for an uprising and the occupation of Kiev while the intelligentsia made the most of the momentary calm and enjoyed itself, and while the Hetman was vainly seeking support among those he had saved.

Korostovetz, at least, knew that good times would not return any time soon. His own family had been very grand before the Revolution. His father in the 1890s was senior Colonel of the élite Preobrazhensky Regiment; young Vladimir was brought up in St Petersburg, attended its University and belonged to the smart English Club. The family wealth came from a vast Ukrainian estate. He remembered travelling around it on childhood holidays.

> We set off in three carriages each drawn by eight farm horses (for on these occasions my grandmother would not allow our own horses to be used), and preceded by outriders. Before we entered the carriages, she would have them thoroughly warmed by the primitive method of making farm-hands sit in them for several hours.

He understood why the Bolsheviks had gained support, but he also understood the violence of which a rabble was capable. He and his family had been horrified by pogroms in 1905, when the local Governor deliberately diverted outlaw bands to hideous violence against landowners and Jews. His grandmother, on their estate, did everything she could to protect 'their Jews.' Khorostovetz in this account is at pains to deplore case after case of hideous treatment meted out to these people, for whom (in 1931) he expresses both compassion and admiration.

His visit to the Hetman in 1918 took the form of an enquiry into what the man stood for, and Korostovetz made a point of asking him how Jews would be treated in the Hetman's ideal Ukrainian state, which would co-exist (in the Hetman's dreams) with Bolshevik Russia. The Hetman had a Jewish Minister for Commerce and said he intended to treat minorities as fairly as everyone else.

This was not true. The Hetman quickly repealed inclusive laws passed by the short-lived liberal government. Yet it seems oddly anachronistic to find this awareness of the dangers of anti-semitism in a book written by a Ukrainian, published in Germany in 1931 – particularly since some MI5 reports imply that both Skoropadsky and Korostovetz subscribed to Nazi ideology. According to this book, he was well in advance of upper-class British understanding at the time because he had seen the ghastly events of 1905 and earlier, which had made an indelible impression in his youth.

When the Ukraine was taken by the Bolshevik government at the end of the War, the Hetman Skoropadsky escaped to Western Europe. In Poland, Korostovetz was arrested, then released, and ended up in Berlin, where Mr and Mrs Korostovetz socialised with British diplomats and journalists and he wrote reports on what they both discovered. His political stance then became still further confused. 'Without any shadow of a doubt', an MI5 man said in 1926, during his time in Berlin he was paid $200 a month for this work by the Soviet Legation:

> It is of interest to note that the present foreign policy of the Russian Government is viewed with utmost sympathy by the majority of the Monarchists, to which party Korostovetz has always given himself out as belonging.[10]

Another note (to Captain Harker) arrived at MI5 in September, 1930, two and a half years before the Nazi régime began:

We received further information to the effect that Korostovetz was one of the most active members, in 1927, of Skoropadsky's group in Germany and that he was subsidised by the Germans and acted as the chief of a sort of Ukrainian Information Bureau... He was a friend of Mr Gregory...

We are now received [*sic*] information ... to the effect that Korostovetz has recently been in Holland and England as an agent of Von Schleicher of the Reichswehrministerium. We should very much like to know whether his presence in England can be checked, with a view to testing the reliability of the report.

Von Schleicher, German Army chief, was murdered as a political opponent of the Nazis in 1934. (This does not mean he was a liberal.) An undated MI5 officer noted in reply:

[Korostovetz] applied for a visa to proceed to Great Britain in November last, giving as reference his brother... [living in Wandsworth], the Editor of the *Whitehall Gazette*... and Count Bobrinsky, 9/10 Marble Arch, Hyde Park, London. On being asked for more particulars, he did not press the application further.[11]

The address would seem suspiciously like Number 10 Hyde Park Terrace and the Count's name fictional; Maundy Gregory lived there from June 1929.

At some time around 1930-31, unaware that Harker of MI5 had any interest in what they were doing, Skoropadsky was introduced to Maundy Gregory, and Korostovetz became a regular contributor to the *Whitehall Gazette*.

The Council of the Anglo-Ukrainian Committee formed in November, 1931 consisted of Lords French, Strathspey, Southborough, Brigadier-General Horwood, and Vladimir Korostovetz. The President was His Highness the Hetman Paul Skoropadsky and the Chairman was A.J. Maundy-Gregory, Esq., O St J (Order of St John of Jerusalem).

Within three months of the Committee's inception Vladimir Korostovetz had grown very suspicious indeed of Mr Maundy Gregory. At this point he and MI5 had a useful meeting.

It was February, 1932; but Captains Miller and Harker must have thought it was Christmas. For the first time they were listening to an outraged insider with absolutely nothing to lose. They interviewed Korostovetz several times over the following weeks and confirmed what he told them with 'an irrefutable source' (possibly A.J. Bennett). The twenty page memorandum that resulted is a small ironic masterpiece, a Dickensian pastiche.[12] Describing 38 Parliament Street through Korostovetz's eyes when Korostovetz was a mere visiting journalist in 1928, Miller observes that:

> At each successive visit it was borne in upon one that one was moving on the verge, or perhaps even not far from the centre of the most influential circle of all. There was a general sense that the word of the Chief, as he was invariably called in the office, was listened to in high quarters, and that on that word money was available or obtainable for those causes which tended to support or revert to the ancient order of things. It emerged, almost casually, that the Chief was the Director of 'Secret Patronage' and though it was some years before Korostovetz got a definite statement that Maundy Gregory was the Chief of the Secret Service, the implication that this was so emerged in many forms and from a variety of directions.

Maundy made free with the names of his closest friends – the King of Greece, of course; Prince Danilo of Montenegro and his brother; Arch-Duke Otto of Austria; the Finnish authorities; the Portuguese . . . even the British royal family.

At Christmas time Mr Maundy Gregory's sanctum blinked like Aladdin's cave with jewels, cigarette boxes and pocket books in, or decorated with, the more precious metals, to be sent as reminders of good will to royal, noble and influential personages.

Maundy's dearest friends were rarely less than 'personages'. One floor above *Burke's Landed Gentry* (prop. M Gregory) upstairs, were offices associated with the Order of St John, and a flat which had only recently become the English mission of the Papal Order of St Sepulchre.

Korostovetz wished to raise funds in support of the Hetman and Ukrainian Nationalism. Maundy was delighted, and could think of loads of people who would be happy to help. Subscriptions? Nonsense! What they wanted was 'good substantial sums from good substantial people.'

One awaits the familiar phrase about Sinews of War. Lloyd George used it. Maundy Gregory used it. It meant: *Large Round Sums, without which we can do nothing.*

And now, had Mr Korostovetz any suggestions? Korostovetz named a few people, including Sir Henry Deterding, but he could not help feeling that the whole matter had been raised to a higher plane.

It was the Messina Benefit all over again. Gregory, who did not necessarily know that the Hetman got his money from Germany, had scented the Anglo-Ukrainian Committee passing by and swallowed it whole as a means of fund-raising. Mr Korostovetz began to perceive something . . . not quite right.

Accustomed to find the task of financing his movement both painful and laborious, [he] never quite succeeded in tuning his mind to the larger harmonies Mr Maundy-Gregory appeared to have the gift of composing. When Mr Korostovetz spoke of 'subscription' lists Mr Maundy-Gregory continued with a gesture to substitute the word 'donations'.

Mr K was careworn: a personal cashflow problem. Maundy Gregory pressed upon him a £100 loan; afterwards, more; until finally he had accepted £630. At some stage he signed IOUs.

Mr K provided introductions. Maundy Gregory talked to the right people: Sir Henry Deterding for one. He reported (confidentially of course) that Sir Henry – a Dutchman – would be happy to spend £40,000 on the Anglo-Ukrainian Committee! And there were almost no strings. It would come out of the £75,000 he would be paying Maundy Gregory for a peerage.

Through rifts . . . a colder light was beginning to fall on things hitherto very accountable. Mr K got in touch with Sir Henry's secretary to confirm, and was disappointed. Sir Henry (of Royal

Dutch Shell) would not be appointing a representative to the Anglo-Ukrainian Committee since this might be construed as an abuse of British Government hospitality. After all, Britain did have diplomatic relations with the Soviet Union.

Mr K was now cultivating humbler friends than the Chief at 38 Parliament Street. Information must have poured forth from Mr Blackmore Beer the Assistant and Mr Pengelly the Accountant as from a broken dam. Dismayed, Korostovetz found out about Sir George Watson.

Back in 1923 Sir George had handed over £30,000 to Maundy Gregory in expectation of a barony and had died, never having received it, in 1930. His legatees wanted the money back. Maundy had spent it, so to save face, he borrowed it from Drummonds Bank. The Bank agreed to take security, but expected to retrieve the loan in three quarterly instalments of £10,000. The first instalment had been paid. But the promised security had not been provided and the second instalment was overdue. Officials at Drummonds parent bank, the Royal Bank of Scotland, were tight-lipped, pitiless and drumming their fingernails on the desk. He needed money.

Then there was the Royal Duke, to whom Maundy Gregory claimed to be lending £100,000, and from whose family he was, allegedly, assured of gratitude. There were the phone calls from Number 10. There were the enormous outgoings. It was all beginning to look as flimsy as stage scenery.

Mr K was by now making enquiries in earnest, and discovered that since the 1925 Act Maundy had collected £380,000 in return for which he had provided not a single picayune knighthood. Outgoings were huge. The *Gazette* didn't make a cent. Nor did the Club. Maundy had almost conned another of his backstairs toilers, a young man called Tufnell who had acted as Secretary to the Anglo-Ukrainian Committee, out of £1,000.

The little community at 38 Parliament Street consisted of individuals in varying stages of belief and disbelief, with a cross-section of exploiters and exploited... Most curious, and apparently most influential of all were the Ambassador Club and Mr Peter Mazzina... The Ambassador Club belonged to Mr Maundy Gregory. The question that arose was whether

Mr Maundy Gregory did not, almost, belong to Mr Peter Mazzina.

Korostovetz told Harker and Miller that Mazzina was getting £500 a week for Ambassador Club expenses and that this was probably five times the required sum; that Mazzina had an interest in Kettner's; that it was Mazzina who had refused to allow a merger between the Ambassador and the Anglo-German Club. And that no 'personage' who went to the Ambassador ever paid. Ordinary punters did, but their bills were so inflated and the staff so surly that they never returned. The place was sumptuous and romantic, with excellent food, very good bands and a regiment of waiters. It was usually empty.

Korostovetz also told them that the waiters at the Club were part-time sleuths for Mazzina and Gregory. The implication was that some kind of blackmail racket was going on. Meanwhile Mazzina, they reported, 'contrived to be informed of his patron's affairs.' Peter Mazzina knew everything about Maundy Gregory because he too, had a Mole at number 38. It was apparent that Peter Mazzina had a pull over Mr Gregory. No one quite knew why. Perhaps Major Pendennis, whose surname Mr Maundy Gregory used in signing his telegrams, might have supplied an answer.

The reference is to Major Pendennis in Thackeray's novel *Pendennis*; a social climber and blackmailer who was himself blackmailed. As *noms de plume* go, it seems rather like a sign with a pointing index finger.

Harker and Miller suspected some connection between blackmail and the upstairs rooms at the Ambassador Club. Maundy was in the habit of confiding that in one of them, gold had been made by a German whose release from a German jail he personally had effected.

Mercury and sand conjured by electricity and uranium oxide (but one must be sure it was not sea-sand) displayed gold in fair proportion. The patents, as Mr Maundy Gregory would say with quiet authority, were vested in the Monarch.

The writer of the report wondered if Peter Mazzina's rejection of the Anglo-German club as a partner might be significant. 'In any case, Peter Mazzina is very near the heart of the mystery.'

Mr Zachs, the Correspondent in Rome, both of the *Whitehall Gazette* and, more curiously, of *Burke's Landed Gentry*, had made the acquaintance of a nephew of the Pope. Through his influence it was proposed that Mr

Maundy Gregory should become Grand Almoner for Great Britain of the Papal Order of St Sepulchre.

Maundy had paid the £750 requested by Mr Zachs, but to preserve the formalities must convert to Catholicism in double-quick time. Monsignor Luigi Barlassina, Patriarch of Jerusalem, arrived on a flying visit to Europe from Palestine. He was put up in Russell Square. He was driven to the Ambassador Club to find a crowd murmuring with excitement: a welcoming party of leading members of the Italian community. The Patriarch blessed them all. They were the Club's waiters, in hired morning coats. The Order of St Sepulchre opened for business at number 38, while in Paris, Peter Mazzina knelt in reverence as the Patriarch of Jerusalem received Maundy into the Church of Rome.

Back in London Korostovetz confronted Maundy Gregory. What had happened, he asked, to the money that was to be raised for the Ukrainian cause? It had been promised; it had not been forthcoming; and what with a Deterding here and a Tufnell there, he doubted it ever would be; so he intended to advise the Hetman to disband the Committee. Ah, said Maundy. That would not be a good idea. He had at his fingertips IOUs signed by Mr Korostovetz to the value of £900. And he had only to pick up the telephone to the Home Office, and who knew what might not happen?

Korostovetz talked to the Hetman. The Chairman of the Anglo-Ukrainian Committee, he told him, was a con man. The Hetman withdrew support.

The august Anglo-Committee members were persuaded – only Maundy knew how – that there was nothing to worry about. There was to be a small change of plan. (Most regrettable, but unavoidable – some unpleasantness associated with a young Secretary called Tufnell.) They would henceforth be sitting on the Anglo-Finnish Committee.

Mr Maundy Gregory visited the Finnish Minister ... [He] had already interested himself in the affairs of Finland and a Dr Borenius had off and on acted as his agent in London and occasionally in Finland for that purpose.

The Finnish Minister would get back to him.

Korostovetz went to the Home Office, who arranged his interview with Captains Harker and Miller.

> Korostovetz was extraordinarily frank throughout the
> interview and gave the impression of a man who was anxious
> to place all his cards on the table and was at the same time
> definitely labouring under considerable apprehension as to
> what might happen to him in the future.[13]

The above ended a brief update to the British agencies in Berlin,
written on 9 March 1932. According to the latest information
Korostovetz brought them, Maundy had a single knighthood in the
pipeline, insufficient to keep the show on the road, so he had got
his friend Major Malabisse-Beckwith working on Lucy Houston.
The impressive Major was to plead, in the weekend of 6–7 March
1932, that as an emissary from the head of the Secret Service, he
could tell her that a mere £100,000 would save the country from
the Bolshevik threat about which the new National Government
seemed unconcerned. (Whether or not he got it we do not know.
Lucy Houston was no pushover. Accused by Houston's family –
resentful about their legacies – of being insane, she invited a house
party of internationally distinguished psychiatrists, all expenses paid,
to a weekend at her Jersey mansion. In each guest's room was a blank
cheque and a statement for signature to the effect that their hostess
was perfectly rational. She retained the Houston millions.)
    Written on 8 March 1932, the full MI5 report on Korostovetz's
information said:

> The success of Mr Gregory's last venture is still . . . in the air.
> It is presumably linked in some way with the League for the
> Protection of Western Civilisation centred in Berlin, in whose
> affairs Mr Gregory plays a part.[14]

Was Maundy Gregory turning into a Nazi?

CHAPTER TWELVE

Keeping up Appearances

The German commander who had supported the Cossack Hetman in Kiev in 1918 was Baron Werner von Alvensleben. He was rich – a successful businessman as well as a soldier, who had lived in Canada – and opposed to social-democratic governments of the kind then in power in Germany and Finland. He was politically active in the twenties as part of the old, conservative German right wing. He was jailed several times after the Nazi accession in 1933. He became an honorary member of the Ambassador Club in 1930.

Tom Cullen, in his book on Gregory, says Skoropadsky was able to pay for articles on the Ukraine in the *Whitehall Gazette* and that his money came from Germany; specifically, Cullen names the racist ideologue of the Nazi party, Alfred Rosenberg, as its source. He implies a direct connection between Werner von Alvensleben and the National Socialists.

This is contradicted by the facts, and also by the MI5 file. The misunderstanding is easily explained by Cullen's having confused Werner with the SS Gruppenführer *Ludolf* von Alvensleben, who was Hitler's Major-General of Police and superintended the massacre of up to 20,000 Poles during the War.

Gregory certainly held right-wing views, insofar as he cared about such things, and published racist rants (probably in return for payment) but so far as we can tell, he was not an active member of any Fascist party. Any direct link between Gregory and the National Socialists or the British Fascists is unknown. It seems that in November 1930 Gregory and the Hetman went to Berlin to a rally of von Alvensleben's 'League for the Protection of Western European Culture' which Horwood was to address.[1] Maundy seems to have been thrilled, for the Sportpalast was an impressive space with a thundering crowd in it and he liked men in uniform. The League was unhealthily far to the right but to the best of this author's understanding it was not a Nazi party organisation.

His Finnish connections were rather different. Whether Gregory ever visited Finland is unlikely, although he wrote about the wonders of General Mannerheim and the Schutzkorps in the *Whitehall Gazette*. Mannerheim, a former Russian general of Swedish extraction and far-right sympathies who became President of Finland 1944-47, had led the 'White Guard' – largely Finnish volunteer troops of the German Schutzkorps – in vicious fighting against Finnish and Russian 'Reds' after the first War. In the early thirties the far right was in the ascendant in Finland as it was in Germany, and Maundy was awarded the Order of the White Rose.

Korostovetz, from November of 1932, contributed to a pro-Hetman newspaper called *The Investigator* which bore the message of Nazi anti-semitism to the apathetic English. This was an ideological reversal of his views in 1931. He wrote as 'V de K' or 'Vladimir de Korostovetz' at that time.[2] If this is so he had taken Hitler's shilling.

Had Gregory understood what he was getting into? According to Tom Cullen, Gregory seems not to have taken Ukrainian politics seriously. As far as he was concerned they were a bunch of squabbling windbags playing a game of Bulava, Bulava, Who's got the Bulava? (The Bulava was a mace in the possession of the Hetman.) Maybe he felt the same way about the Germans. His fate, and his attitudes, during World War II would not indicate any claim to friendship with the Nazis on his part.

He adopts, in the mind's eye, the arguments of the person he happens to be buttering up at the time.

Also, his stance must be understood in its historical context. Many English politicians and MI5 officers at this time expressed qualified enthusiasm for Italian and English Fascism and either had no idea how dangerous the Nazis were, or did not associate the two. In 1930 Esmond Harmsworth and Winston Churchill put up Oswald Mosley, then a Labour MP and Chancellor of the Duchy of Lancaster, for membership of the Other Club. Winston Churchill at the time was obsessed with the dangers of German rearmament and a fierce non-appeaser but it was several years before he and others like him dropped Mosley. Wyndham Lewis went to Nazi rallies in Berlin and thought it all rather fine, and as for the Jews – the Nazis didn't really mean it. Rothermere newspapers supported the British Fascist cause until 1934, and MI5 did not fully wake up to the danger of 'armed revolution and pogroms'[3] until the thirties. John Baker White, of the Economic League, claimed first to have heard of Hitler in 1929 from a friend in Intelligence.[4]

Cullen alleges that Maundy went back and forth to Berlin more than once. If so, one connection could have been Gerald Hamilton, who lived there in the late twenties and was part of the Isherwood set. They had met in London – 'Symons took me to see him, thinking we could be useful to one another.'[5] Hamilton's relationship to Gregory is odd, for he claims that he and Maundy had right-wing views in common. Hamilton wrote all this in *The Way it was with Me,* published in 1969, by which time he was a true-blue Tory. He had become a Mosleyite before the war and was interned in 1940 under rule 18b (imprisonment without charge or trial) as a Fascist. And he was consistent in remaining an Irish Nationalist all his life. But he had been round the political block in his youth, and during his time in Berlin as a *Times* correspondent he sympathised with the German communists. His 1937 account of those years, *As young as Sophocles,* indicates as much.

In *The Way it Was with Me,* he wrote of his association with Maundy:

> I had no interest in these English titles and decorations. My job was to help to secure for his clients foreign ones. One particular foreign decoration was the Order of Christ of Portugal, because this order could be worn with a bright red ribbon which most people mistook for the French Legion of Honour. Any expenses incurred while travelling were generously reimbursed. . .

Maundy increased Hamilton's guesstimate of expenses by 50 per cent. There are two Orders of Christ, both originally 'of Portugal'. The one Hamilton means – with the red ribbon – is awarded by the Papal

States. By his own detailed account elsewhere, Hamilton had been friendly with people in the Vatican since his youth. Monsignor (later Cardinal) Ceretti is mentioned in the early 1920s. Maundy Gregory pops up in *The Times* on 3 May, 1932, as a guest at Spinks's opening, by Cardinal Bourne, of an exhibition 'Treasures of the Cathedral of Mainz'. He had often been seen with Church of England dignitaries in the past. He boasted that he had raised money for Westminster Abbey. He even belonged to the exclusive Protestant Order of St John of Jerusalem. And now here he was, hob-nobbing with high-ups in the rival outfit.

Late in 1932, in response to a query from Monsignor Barlassina, someone associated with the Vatican made discreet enquiries about Maundy Gregory's probity and financial situation.[6] Their file, #118265, began with brief facts about his place of birth and education ('failed to graduate') at Oxford. It continued:

> After some involvement in theatrical entertainment he became associated with John Keen-Hargreaves and Henry Keen-Hargreaves, art dealers in London. In partnership with these gentlemen, Maundy Gregory established a society publication *Mayfair and Town Topics*. In 1918 he became involved with a Government official, Frederick Guest, in procuring those willing to pay for official titles and honours. These activities brought him considerable sums of money which he appears to have invested in a number of ventures. He has a particular interest in Russian matters and has, since 1919, been associated with a number of Russian *émigrés* with whom he has participated in business ventures. These include a hotel in Surrey, England, property in Sussex, England, and agricultural holidings in the South of France. He has donated sums of money to anti-Bolshevik organisations and publicised the anti-Bolshevik cause in his newspaper The *Whitehall Gazette and St James' Review*. In 1926 he acquired the Ambassador Club in London. Maundy Gregory has also donated money to many charitable causes in England and Europe.

Presumably this information came largely from Maundy Gregory's conversation, via perhaps Cardinal Bourne or Father Chichester, who was involved at the time in instructing Maundy in the precepts of Catholicism before he was received into the Church. Only the reference to the Keen-Hargreaves brothers as 'these gentlemen' has the unmistakeable whiff of Scotland Yard about it.

Maundy was becoming a sort of international commercial traveller, on the lookout for honours to trade. He was certainly more concerned with money than he was with ideology.

Sinister political movements were on the march in the late twenties. It could be argued that Maundy had become more discriminating about what he printed in the *Whitehall Gazette*, since he now hedged opinion pieces about with a disclaimer. Such articles included those of Sir Warden Chilcott, a Conservative MP who found Baldwin much too flaccid a leader. 'Can we afford ever to suppress brains? It should not be overlooked that that great Italian patriot, Mussolini, arose out of the Socialistic and journalistic ranks. What chance have we to discover *our* Mussolini under the Party system?'[7] Germany wanted to dominate Europe commercially; Jews of all nations were at fault. Keynesian economics could work and full employment must be obtained even if it meant forcing men out to dig ditches.[8] The Conservatives were supine in government, and the Socialists arrogant and dishonest. The nation demonstrated only 'sulky apathy,' and wanted consensus rather than brutality to solve the problem. 'Eleven years of political life, plus £22,000 of good, hard-earned cash in subscriptions, has sickened me for the hypocrisy of that hollow game of 'Party Politics.'[9]

Chilcott's *Whitehall Gazette* and other articles were reprinted in book form in 1928 with thanks to Maundy Gregory and a picture of Austen Chamberlain as the frontispiece, inscribed *To Warden Chilcott, on whose yacht Dolphin I have twice carried forward the policy of Peace in Our Time, this token of our friendship. Austen Chamberlain May 9, 1928*. Taken as a whole, the articles advocated a return to National Government under Austen Chamberlain. What took over, of course, was a National Government from 1931–1935 under Ramsay MacDonald.

Maundy may have received some money from Sir Warden Chilcott and others for printing articles in the *Whitehall Gazette*; he may have made a profit out of *Burke's Landed Gentry*. Apart from that, it seems that Maundy Gregory got away with taking £380,000 in the six years since 1925 without giving anything in return.[10]

His outgoings were enormous. He bought Burke's Landed Gentry and employed its staff. He maintained his office at 38 Parliament Street, and its staff, on Parliamentary property. He continued to arrive every day in his taxi with its full-time driver. He continued to produce the *Whitehall Gazette* at a loss.

He and Edith Marion Rosse moved, in June 1929, to 10 Hyde Park Terrace; he immediately had some building work done there. It was a more prestigious address than 3 Abbey Road. His housekeeper and gardener were paid and so were his household bills and his private secretary, Mr Pratley.

For many years he and Edith had spent their free time at the Royal Albion Hotel, one of two owned by Harry Preston, a legendary dandy, sportsman and hotelier in Brighton. Now Maundy had taken a flat for himself and Edith in Brighton, over the Imperial Restaurant. And of course there was Vanity Fair at Thames Ditton, which they still adored – their little summer dacha with its electric canoe.

And the Ambassador Club. The sheer expense of going there was behind the times; the upper-class and young no longer spent money like water. The Ambassador Club had never been at the cutting edge and it had lost its freshness now. In 1930 the popular and expensive Jack Hylton band had its contract suddenly terminated, and Hylton was taking the Club to court.[11] Peter Mazzina had a growing family. He decided that he would prefer to live outside London.

Down in Dorking, the Deepdene was failing under the erratic management of Princess Nizharadzy. In 1929 her high-handed behaviour towards a faithful retainer of her father's brought her before the High Court, charged with wrongful dismissal and false imprisonment. Her case was put by the eminent King's Counsel Rayner Goddard, but despite his eloquence the jury found against her and she was ordered to pay the plaintiff considerable damages and arrears of salary.[12]

In August 1931, Peter Mazzina and Arthur Giordano – that is, Mazzina of the huge salary and surly team of waiters, and Giordano who had just presided over the bankruptcy of Kettner's – took the lease of the ninety bedroom former stately home, Deepdene. Rumour had it that Mazzina was merely a front for Gregory. While this was actually true, few if any, at the time could prove it. [13]

Deepdene had been highly profitable when David Zhivotovsky and his staff ran it, but Princess Nizharadzy's stewardship had been disastrous. Within months of Mazzina having taken it over, the hotel suffered a terrible indignity: a huge electric sign, DEEPDENE HOTEL, was erected on the roof to make it visible to distant motorists. It also served as location for a film, *Lloyd of the CID*. It developed a salacious reputation, and began to lose money. Peter Mazzina, as manager, was running it into the ground.

Maundy also had to contend with the poker-faced men from the Royal Bank of Scotland. They had no security for the outstanding £20,000.

Was he, by 1932 if not earlier, living on capital? Had J.C.C. Davidson's strategy worked? The truth is that Maundy was a little overstretched.

CHAPTER THIRTEEN

Uncle Jim

In retrospect, the pinnacle of Maundy Gregory's career can be identified to the day and hour. Maundy's glorious moment was the Derby Night dinner held at the Ambassador Club on Thursday 2 June 1931, the evening before the great annual race meeting at Epsom. In his life, this was the Last Supper, *Babette's Feast* and *Big Night* rolled into one: a life-affirming banquet to celebrate the sheer joy of being in this place, at this time, setting aside pressing concerns and the underlying certainty that a great upheaval is afoot.

This was not the moment when Maundy was at his richest, or most powerful. It was not even the first Derby Night Dinner. Until 1927, and the death of their inspirer, the dinners had taken place every year at the Carlton Hotel. Maundy had been hosting them at the Ambassador Club since 1928 and always made sure that the Dinner and its guest list of about 150 government ministers, press men, industrialists, lawyers, aristocrats and artists were reported in *The Times*. But it was the last time he would sit, unthreatened, at Britain's top table.

The occasion was presided over by Major-General Jack Seely. He was from a distinguished family in the Isle of Wight, a great friend of Winston Churchill who had known Maundy Gregory for years. He was the only member of the War Cabinet to have seen active service in the War; he was mentioned in despatches five times, and gassed in 1918. In 1917, as a widower in his forties, he had married a widow, the Hon. Evelyn Izme Murray, JP, who happened to be Alick Murray's younger sister.

On either side of Jack, glowing merrily above the damask and silver and crystal, beamed the faces of Maundy Gregory's friends, enemies, and others who barely knew him. Here was Sir Austen

Chamberlain . . . a little further on, the Duke of Marlborough . . . The Duke of Sutherland, who had sold his London home, Lancaster House, to Lord Lever in 1921 . . . Rufus Isaacs the Marquis of Reading who had weathered the Marconi scandal to become Viceroy of India . . . And Viscount Elibank, Alick's younger brother who had succeeded his father to the viscountcy in 1927. Lord Southborough of course . . . J.H. Thomas the trade unionist and Dominion Secretary in the current National Government that had Ramsay MacDonald at its head . . . Winston Churchill . . . Viscount Esher, 'Reggie' Brett, old now, who had known everyone in Edwardian and late Victorian England and had understood so much about the Cleveland Street intrigue of 1887 and its use by Arthur Newton.

Viscount Craigavon was there, the Prime Minister of Northern Ireland. He had been a Parliamentary Secretary during the First War, and part of the group with F.E. and Carson which later negotiated the Anglo-Irish Treaty. Many of those present would have toasted the memory of F.E. with sadness. He had died (allegedly of boredom and brandy) in the autumn of 1930, just two years after leaving politics to pursue a more financially rewarding career in the City.

Freddy Guest . . . Lord Jessel the railway king and philanthropist . . . Sir John Simon . . . Sir Warden Chilcott . . . Lord Queenborough, who had taken Deepdene at the outbreak of War . . . The Marquis del Moral, who as an Australian intelligence officer working with Australian troops around Pretoria in the Boer War had been instrumental in the capture and trial of Breaker Morant . . . This was a brace of Admirals.

Dudley Ward, son-in-law of Viscount Esher but mired in a divorce, having finally lost patience with his wife's affair with the Prince of Wales (which had been going on since she and the Prince met at a party in the blackout in 1918). The Marquis of Linlithgow . . . Major G.R. Hennessy, so prominent in munitions during the War . . . Lord Cushenden, who had in 1928 signed the Kellogg-Briand pact by which Great Britain and scores of other nations renounced war for ever . . . J.C.C. Davidson . . . Gwynne, Editor of the *Morning Post;* Lord Camrose, owner of the *Daily Telegraph* among other papers; and Colin Coote, who would one day become one of its most successful editors . . . Sir Ralph Harwood was there, and General Horwood.

'Woolfie' Barnato the glamorous inheritor of millions from his father Barney; Brendan Bracken; the Honourable Everard Baring, of the banking family . . . More politicians, more Lords, more millionaires, philanthropists and opinion-formers than you could shake a stick at.

From the arts came Charles Graves the writer, Detmar Blow the fashionable architect and Sir Edwin Lutyens, who had designed New Delhi. Also included were Vyvyan Holland, writer and son of Oscar Wilde; Tancred Borenius and A.J.A. Symons, as well as Charles Gulliver who owned the London Palladium. There were a good many policemen, including Colonel Sir James Sleeman, photographer, who wrote the classic *From Rifle to Camera: the reformation of a big-game hunter.* People from intelligence, property development, and Harry Preston the Brighton hotelier (it is unclear whether this Harry Preston, and Basil Thomson's eponymous brother-in-law, were one and the same); Knapp-Fisher, Chapter Clerk at Westminster Abbey; Sir Julian Cahn, the wealthy cricketer and hunt Master whose father had made a fortune from furniture; the grocer David Greig, Harley Street surgeon Mr David Levi, explorer Sir Sven Hansen . . .

At this point the eye rests, and returns, and interprets. The next chair is occupied by Mr T.W. Byford. The only Byford we know of in Maundy's life was a *fence.* Surely not.

Mostly, the guests assembled at the Ambassador Club were from the wartime generation. A later one, the generation that had been too young to fight in the War – that of Oliver Messel and Noel Coward, Evelyn Waugh, Cecil Beaton and David Tennant – was already in the ascendant, and they were very different. For one thing younger men, regardless of their sexual orientation, enjoyed female company.

Women barely figured in Maundy's life. Peter Mazzina's wife Josephine did not interfere in his relationship with Maundy. Maundy's mother, an erect and dignified figure in her white coif and black dress, was safe in Bishop Morley's College, a select residential home in Winchester.[1]

Edith Marion Rosse, on the other hand . . . he worried, sometimes, about Edith. In the cold spring light of 1932, his worries about Edith, and his worries about money, were beginning to coalesce.

He had always made a great fuss of her. He called her 'Milady', while Edith liked to call him 'Uncle Jim'. He had been Uncle Jim to Ethel, Edith's niece, when she was a schoolgirl. It suited him; he was a few years younger than Edith, but avuncular. From the nickname alone there probably emerged the myth that Edith was his sister, which is how he usually introduced her.

Now that Ethel was no longer a schoolgirl, but in her late twenties, she was downright tiresome. It did not help that Edith had no comprehension of this post-war generation and treated her niece as though she were sixteen. Although she was counting on Ethel to stay at home and be a 'companion' – as if a young girl, in London in the 1920s, would happily settle for the company of a woman in her fifties – either she or Maundy Gregory always ended up sending her away. Edith had very little to do all day. She sat on a Ladies' Committee here and there, and had some property to administer, but she was not fully occupied. Fruitlessly, she devoted much emotional energy to managing her niece's life.

Ethel had education enough to pass as middle-class, but her father was an unemployed carpenter, and young people generally required parental approval before getting 'engaged' in those days. The parents of a young bank manager from Surbiton or wine merchant from Finchley would find that Ethel came from a questionable background: a father in slummy Islington, an Aunt who had been on the stage and shared a house with a flashy man, not her husband, whose money came from who-knew-where ... Ethel had been brought up with bourgeois expectations, yet she had no settled family life and her secretarial jobs never proved permanent.

Some of Aunt Rosse's sisters had done well in life but she was the moneybags of the family. She owned, to Ethel's knowledge, four houses on Thames Ditton Island including Vanity Fair, five flats at 34a Hinde Street, off Manchester Square, a flat at 8 Thayer Street off Wigmore Street and a seven-roomed flat – 6a Hyde Park Mansions – close to the Edgware Road.[2] This was extremely valuable property, all of it in the West End except for the island summer-houses. In August 1928, when Ethel was staying at Abbey Lodge, Edith had made a will in favour of her niece, with a legacy to her housekeeper Mrs Howard.

It was drawn up in her married name of Liechtenstein by a solicitor, Stanley Brooke.[3]

Ethel had an intermittent income from secretarial work, no sense that she belonged anywhere and no expectation of a permanent relationship and a family of her own. She was a troubled young woman with an uncontrollable temper[4] who enjoyed a good time. The predictable result was a love-hate relationship in which Ethel came to her aunt for handouts and Edith tried to control Ethel's life by using money as a weapon. They had been having rows since 'the girl' was about sixteen. Within months of signing the will,[5] Edith tore up her copy in front of Ethel and said 'You have now burnt your boats with regard to your future.' She fell ill that winter and was cared for by Dr Blair of St John's Wood.[6]

However, she did make another will in Ethel's favour. This time she did not mention it to her intended legatee. 'She appeared to have an obsession that she must save all the money that she could for her niece Ethel,' said Mr Pengelly, the accountant, later.[7] He added that Edith had put £6,500 in the name of E.M. Davies – Inscribed 'Stock 5 per cent'– 'which she told me she had bought for Ethel; but for reasons of her own she had the stock transferred on 5 November 1929 to her name, E.M. Rosse, and then sold it, to re-invest in: £1,550 War Loan, and £5,050 5 per cent Conversion, which she held up to the time I last did her accounts in April 1932'.[8]

In the winter of 1929 Ethel spent a few weeks working for a journalist in the South of France.

She spent the winter of 1930-31 living in a convent near Hyde Park and her earnings as a secretary were supplemented by the 30s (£1.50), which came from Maundy Gregory from March until August 1931.[9] This came to an end on the instructions of Mrs Rosse, who ordered her solicitor to stop the allowance. One might infer that Stanley Brooke, of McColm and Brooke, of Lewisham in south-east London, saw Mrs Rosse's affairs, and Maundy Gregory's, as closely entwined. He had 'acted for Mrs Rosse and Mr Gregory for many years.'[10]

One wonders whether or not Mr Brooke knew that Maundy had been – since February 1931 – pursued through the courts by the executors of Sir George Watson, who were demanding the return of his £30,000 in securities. Edith certainly didn't.

Maundy insisted that the securities had been a gift. A year passed. In January 1932, certain letters from Sir George, concerning honours trafficking, seemed about to be made public; and all of a sudden Maundy agreed to pay the whole sum. He now had to raise the money, besides fulfilling a number of other urgent commitments.

In January 1932[11] Mrs Howard left, and in February Ethel came to look after her aunt until another living-in housekeeper could be found. When Edith went to Thames Ditton for a few days, Uncle Jim and Ethel, left in the house together, quarrelled violently. Mrs Rosse, who had had an angry phone call from Maundy, cast about for someone on whom to offload her woes. Pengelly took up the story:

> I knew of the existence of a previous Will made by Mrs Rosse in which her niece was mentioned as beneficiary. . . . With regard to the Will now mentioned, Mrs Rosse telephoned me at my house – then at Putney – and asked me to see her as soon as she got back . . . as there had been such a row between Uncle Jim and Ethel and that 'Uncle Jim' wished her to destroy the Will. A few days later I saw Mrs Rosse at Hyde Park Terrace and she was very worried and asked me if I know if anything was wrong with Mr Gregory because he had been so bad tempered and gave the impression that he was financially worried and she led me to believe that Mr Gregory had been asking her for money. She seemed surprised not to be able to think he was a wealthy man, and asked me if I had told Mr Gregory of her deposits at the bank and the Abbey Road Building Society.
>
> Another thing that appeared to worry her . . . was that Mr Gregory had approached her with a view to the destroying of the will which was in favour of her niece Ethel.
>
> I did not know that this will had been destroyed until I went to Somerset House after her death and saw the will proved by Mr Gregory.[12]

She also asked Pengelly, when he visited her on that occasion, whether in his view the Abbey Road Building Society was giving her value for money, because Mr Gregory insisted that she should not have all her eggs in one basket, and should take some of her money out of her deposit account at Lloyd's and buy into War Loans because it was easier to raise money on them . . .

She had always taken Maundy's advice. But now the worm of doubt sneaked into her mind.

On Saturday 27 February 1932 the new housekeeper, Mrs Lottie Eyres, moved in, as well as her husband, Charles. Whether or not Mr Eyres was employed in the household is unknown.

On the Monday or Tuesday, aunt and niece had a row. When Edith asked about a ring she had given to Ethel for her twenty-first birthday ('Why don't you wear that lovely ring I gave you?'), Ethel had to admit she had pawned it. She produced the pawn ticket and Edith demanded it. 'Mr Gregory', she said, could have that, and once he had redeemed it, he could keep the ring. (She did not address the notion that Mr Gregory would have been almost equally pushed to find the redemption money.) Ethel threatened to get in touch with the police if he did. Matters were as bad as they had ever been between the two women and this is a clear instance in which Gregory was set up as a rival for Edith's affections.

Maundy Gregory had been generous to Ethel in the past but now he took Edith's side. On 1 March, a Wednesday (1932 was a leap year) Ethel was turfed out of 10 Hyde Park Terrace. Maundy let it be known that should Ethel darken their door again, he would be insufferably angry. Edith began to send her niece a weekly allowance of 30 shillings. He continued to tell her she should cut the girl out of the will once and for all.

But the aunt and niece were what we would call co-dependent. Ethel, to give her her due, at twenty-eight was socially, financially and emotionally insecure, and her combative attitude did not help her. As for Edith, she needed someone to whom she mattered. Since her estrangement from Frederick Rosse, she had no-one else to love, or to think about. She was lonely, with a tendency to drink too much and none of the open-handedness that people liked in Maundy. In the past, she had advertised in the *Morning Post* (the Diehard Tories' favourite paper) and found 'companions' – women friends 'to go out and about with'.[13] And she was not very well; she had high blood pressure, and believed herself to have heart trouble. Bouts of illness, in 1925, 1928 and 1932, followed major quarrels with Ethel.[14] She was at the same time demanding a lifetime spent in gratitude and pleading to be paid attention.

In the spring of 1932 they met in secret, for Maundy must not know that Edith and Ethel were still communicating. Sometimes they walked in Hyde Park; sometimes Ethel was even invited back for the afternoon. If she was still there when Maundy came back to dress for an evening out, she was hidden in Edith's bedroom until he had gone out again.

In June 1932, two things happened to Edith which are important but unconnected. Stanley Brooke committed suicide, so she could no longer rely on a long-standing relationship with her solicitor. And her attitude to Ethel changed.

In a letter written on 29 June she demanded to know whether Ethel had another source of income, because if she had, she intended to stop her allowance.

> . . . You write me lengthy letters all about a lot of gossip 'I' 'I' 'I' marriage and a lot of nonsense. . . . Mr G has talked it over last night and wants to know what you are doing for your future as he is disgusted with your idleness and living on others all these years and now openly tells me that he is not going on paying this 30s weekly. If you had behaved as a decent and proper companion to me and filled the emptiness I have suffered in my life he would have done anything for you, but now he sees how impossible you are and have been for years he (like most men) is fed up and doesn't see why he should go on. He has put up with you <u>for my sake</u> . . . If I hear of any lies disloyalty or gossip I shall enlighten <u>everybody</u> – Mr Simmons included.

Ethel most probably had a suitor. Her financial life-support was a bottomless pit, but accusations of parasitism were a bit rich coming from somebody who had taken half Frederick Rosse's income for a decade and – according to Mr Pengelly – had only intermittently paid rent on her smart accommodation; Edith's occasional cheques to Maundy Gregory amounted to about £1 a week.[15]

Three weeks later Edith found new lodgings in Endsleigh Street, Bloomsbury, for Ethel. She wrote to her brother Fred

> I saw her room, beautiful with pink casement curtains – a lovely lounge with Grand Piano, wireless, &c. All young ladies – students and secretaries but all refined.

It was hopeless; Ethel wanted her freedom, and rebelled at the ghastly thought of sharing accommodation, however refined, with a lot of other 'young ladies'.

> Whilst I kept her I had the right to forbid a bed-sitting room especially after the dreadful thing I was told and which she admitted to me. I've given her all today to change her mind and go to Ashley House tomorrow but she has written insulting letters and says I am legally bound to pay for her and a lot of rot like that...

Aunt Rosse was obsessed. 'It has been the biggest blow I have ever had and has left its mark on me . . . Thank God I haven't many more years . . .' And so on. Maundy Gregory after a hard day fighting off the (still metaphorical) bailiffs, had to come home to this fractious, self-pitying woman. One almost feels sorry for him. Unfortunately he had contributed to the mess in the past, by effectively paying Ethel to go away.

Finally, Ethel decided to resolve the quarrel and come back to Hyde Park Terrace. Edith relented, and told her the decision was not hers (Edith's) to make, but she should write to Maundy Gregory, explaining that she would like to stay at Hyde Park Terrace with her aunt. Her letter was returned unopened, twice. The day after it came back for the second time, Ethel received a note from Edith saying that she would visit that afternoon and that Ethel's future depended on it.

Edith arrived at the bedsitter in York Street where Ethel was staying. Her attitude seemed – according to Ethel – 'strange' and she 'glanced at my dressing table, swept everything off, picked up her husband's photograph and deliberately broke it in two.' She then informed Ethel that if she did not leave her lodgings now and go to the YWCA she would be left penniless and destitute. She followed this up with a special-delivery letter of confirmation and a spiteful phone call to Ethel's landlady.

What was Edith thinking and why? She was very close to Maundy Gregory that year. During Ethel's stay in February the two older ones had spent every free evening together. Did he tell her something to Ethel's detriment about a relationship between the younger woman and Frederick Rosse? It would have been untrue, and there is only that one, strange visit to Ethel's bed-sitting-room to indicate anything of that kind. But subsequent letters she sent to her niece were harsh and unfriendly. Edith's brother (Ethel's father) Fred, saw Edith from time to time and also testified to the police that Edith had expressed annoyance with Ethel in July and early August of 1932.[16]

Edith was unreasonably insecure about money, so much is plain. This had become belatedly apparent to Maundy Gregory when, hard pressed by the executors of Sir George Watson and with nowhere else to turn that summer, he asked her outright for a loan.

She refused him. At some time that summer she did, in fact, take £4,500 out of her deposit account at Lloyds and put it into War Loans; but there was no other activity. Pengelly did not know about it at the time, because he normally reconciled her accounts in April and October.

Maundy had been generous to her over the years. He had paid for her holidays in Monte Carlo and Florence, had accepted only nominal rent. As Edith wrote to a stranger,

'We have three pianos and wireless &c and a lovely house (Home!) . . . My brother is in politics &c. He provides the luxuries and I the necessities!!!'[17]

The necessities included the dinners they ate together during the week. He paid her for those,[18] while she was his guest on weekend evenings. With a thousand little treats, Gregory had always presented himself as the 'Cheerful Giver' at home.

Gregory knew that Edith had accumulated a property portfolio, and in doing so had taken his own advice. He knew through Pengelly that she was well off. What he had failed to understand was that she would never gamble her assets on the judgement of anyone else, even him. 'Never a borrower nor a lender be' – she would almost literally rather die than lend money. She wanted to maintain total control in her lifetime and die rich.

His creditors were pressing, and he may have felt resentful.

Edith had alienated the two people who mattered to her. Both had asked her for money.

Ethel was worried, and mystified; her aunt had never been like this before. She seemed to have taken a dislike to her for some reason.

Ethel turned to Frederick Rosse for sympathy. They met at Russell Square tube and she received exactly that, and no money. Another unfriendly letter arrived from Edith on 15 August.

Maundy Gregory came and went. His money troubles showed no marked improvement, although his standing with the Almighty had risen heavenward like a rocket. On 17 January 1932, the priest who had been giving him instruction (Father Francis Colchester, formerly a teacher at Mount St Mary's College, Colchester) dropped dead of a heart attack at the age of seventy-two. By 22 January Maundy had sufficiently recovered from the shock to be received into the Church anyway, in Paris, in the presence of His Beatitude Monsignor Barlassina and Peter Mazzina. On 1 March he became a Knight Commander of the Equestrian Order of the Holy Sepulchre (of which Mons. Barlassina was the Grand Master). On 3 April he became Knight Commander of the Most Noble Order of Pius IX. This ranks third among the pontifical orders of knighthood. 38 Parliament Street was now a fully operational Chancellery for the Order of the Holy Sepulchre. That should attract some folding money.

Friday 19 August was a very hot day. At lunchtime, three people were indoors at 10 Hyde Park Terrace. Edith was on the ground floor, with Mrs Eyres her housekeeper there or in the basement. Maundy's housekeeper Mrs Wells was upstairs. Edith was looking forward to seeing young Hugh Donaldson, now in the colonial Police and briefly in London from Malaya, at 6pm. Also she had arranged to go away for the weekend.

Mrs Wells opened half a bottle of champagne for her, and she got some cheese and tomatoes for lunch.

A lady visitor arrived at 2.30. Mrs Eyres showed her into the lofty front reception room and left her contemplating an oversized poster from *The Desert Song* and the view across Bayswater Road. Then the housekeeper tapped on Edith's bedroom door and told her that her visitor had arrived.

'All right. I'll be there in a minute,' she said.

Mrs Eyres went down to the basement. A moment later the bell rang. She ran upstairs and found Mrs Rosse looking terrible. Mrs Eyres must tell the woman she couldn't see her today after all.

'I feel something's burst in my head.'

She collapsed onto her bed. Mrs Eyres let the lady visitor out and returned to the bedroom. Mrs Rosse had violent vomiting and diarrhoea and told her to get a doctor. Dr Blair was out. Mrs Rosse told her to call Mr Gregory.

'I don't know if he'll come in time – I feel so ill.'

Mrs Eyres called Mrs Wells down from upstairs. According to her own testimony, Mrs Wells

> . . . found she was vomiting and I assisted to get her into bed. . . I asked her what she had been eating and she said 'tomatoes and cheese' and complained of her head. She said 'Fetch a doctor. I have never felt so ill.' I phoned Dr Blair, he was not in, and Mrs Eyres went to find a doctor.

I phoned for Mr Gregory at his office and he arrived simultaneously with Dr Plummer.

Mrs Eyres also phoned Mr Gregory's office. (She believed him to be Mrs Rosse's brother.) Mr Pratley, the private secretary, would pass on the message at once. Between 3 and 3.30 Maundy Gregory arrived. Mrs Eyres later said:

Mr Gregory and the doctor appeared to be perfect strangers and I think they only met on the doorstep. Dr Plummer was called as a result of enquiries made by my husband who went out to find a doctor after failing to find Dr Blair at home.

Dr Plummer's practice was nowhere near 10 Hyde Park Terrace, or Dr Blair's surgery in St John's Wood. It was in Melcombe Street, close to Baker Street tube station. He was summoned by telephone. He had never met or treated Mrs Rosse before but he did later say that he and Dr Blair knew each other, so maybe this is how the connection was made.[19]

As it happened, there was a rather grand physician, Zebulon Mennell, living thirty yards away at number 8 Hyde Park Terrace on the opposite corner of Albion Street.[20] He had lived there for years. His entry in Kelly's Directory mentions nothing about his being retired.

Gregory told Dr Plummer as they entered that his sister had been taken ill.[21]

Mrs Wells had known Mrs Rosse for many years, and had worked for her before she worked for Maundy Gregory at Abbey Road. She went home every day at 2.30pm, so having done what she could for Mrs Rosse she left Dr Plummer, Maundy Gregory and Mrs Eyres in charge of the invalid.

Edith felt really dreadful and had a blinding headache. Dr Plummer prescribed icepacks and aspirin and said that she had heatstroke. She thought she was going to die. The windows were open but the day was stifling. She had known this would happen. Ethel had killed her. Ethel would be sorry.

But she needed to make a will. 'Jim,' she said faintly. 'I want to make my will. Get me a piece of paper and a pencil and put this down.'[22]

Dr Plummer suppressed a sigh. She was not *in extremis,* but if it would make her feel better … [23]

Maundy looked around. Where was the 'fountain-pen with a twenty-two carat nib half an inch broad' when he needed it? not about his person, apparently. But maybe, it being a hot day, he had left his jacket in the hall. He produced a stub of pencil and a Carlton

Hotel luncheon menu card, on the back of which he wrote hurriedly at her dictation[24]

> Everything I have, if anything happens to me, to be left to Mr J. Maundy-Gregory to be disposed of as he thinks best in accordance with what he thinks I should desire.

Weakly, she scrawled her signature, which meandered across the last two words in Maundy's handwriting and was too wide for the page.

'I want you both to witness this,' she murmured to the doctor and Mrs Eyres.[25] Maundy Gregory held out the menu card to the doctor.

'I think you had better sign it again, Mrs Rosse,' Dr Plummer said. 'That's not very clear.'

The sick woman took back the pencil and signed her name, straighter and clearer this time. Dr Plummer put the date and his signature and qualifications below *in ink*, and Mrs Eyres signed her name at the bottom of the page. Maundy also signed, with his own broad-nibbed pen, vertically along the left margin of the document, but there is no date next to his signature.[26]

Maundy Gregory asked her to look at the will. Was it all right? She read it – in Mrs Eyres' view she was perfectly capable of doing so at that stage – and said 'Yes'.

One does wonder why, if Dr Plummer was in the room when Edith asked for a pen, he did not produce his – at least when he asked her to sign a second time. No doubt there is a rational explanation, such as his doctor's bag not containing pen and paper. He did not take this will business seriously anyway, and later said that he was merely 'humouring the patient.'[27]

Dr Plummer gave his patient (who had just bequeathed her considerable estate to a man with an overdraft of £7 5s 4d) some aspirin and left. He was recalled three times that evening, and gave her morphia. On the Saturday, Mrs Howard – her former housekeeper who had since become a friend and occasional visitor – rang her but Maundy Gregory said she was suffering the effects of too much sun, and was asleep. She was still asleep when Mrs Howard rang back at

7pm. Mrs Howard was concerned, and Maundy admitted that his sister was really ill.

However, she recovered. After a few days, according to Mrs Wells later, Dr Plummer stopped coming and Dr Blair resumed his role as her doctor.

What happened 'after a few days' is interesting, because her brother Fred told Frederick Rosse, in a letter, and the police, that on Monday 22 August 1932 – just three days later – Edith met him at 7.30pm at Baker Street tube station, gave him a pound for his birthday the day before, and had a drink with him at the Globe, on the south side of the road opposite the station. He was with a friend who later testified that he saw her and she appeared to be 'in her usual health'.[28]

The implication of this is that she had recovered. Mrs Wells, who went home at 2.30pm every day, knew nothing of any evening appointments she may have kept. Mrs Eyres, who lived in, said Mrs Rosse did not go out at all between the Friday when she was taken ill and the following Thursday.[29] The medical records of Dr Plummer indicate that he visited her four times on the Saturday after her attack and two or three times on the Sunday and Monday. In his view, on the Monday she would have been unable to get up, dress and leave without assistance. On the Tuesday (the day after the alleged meeting at Baker Street), Edith saw the doctor again, and afterwards said she was well enough for him to stop coming and Maundy Gregory rang him up to say so. Every day when Mrs Howard rang up, though, Mrs Eyres told Mrs Howard that Mrs Rosse was too ill to be seen.

The next day, Wednesday 24 August 1932, Edith asked for Dr Blair, who came every day for a week. On Friday 26 August Fred Davies received a parcel of clothes from her in the post. On 29 August 1932 she had a long talk with Mrs Howard on the phone. Edith told her that she had had some kind of stroke, and *could not remember anything.*[30]

> 'I went to shut the window, because it was very hot,' she said, 'and something seemed to strike me down.'
> She appeared uncertain as to who was talking to her because she called me Daisy. I told her it was Howard speaking and she said 'You must not take any notice of what I call you.'

'Daisy' was Daisy Stafford, who looked after the properties at Thames Ditton. Mrs Howard promised to come and see her, but would ring again tomorrow. She did not, in fact, phone back until Saturday.

Just two days later, on 31 August, Dr Blair pronounced Edith 'practically well'.[31] His visits ceased. That week Pengelly rang, having heard she was ill and wishing to find out how she was; Maundy told him she was recovering and 'would soon be well again if she did not get a relapse.'

On Thursday 1 September Edith went for a drive with Gregory. She had told Mrs Eyres that she wanted to find treatment for her eyes that day, as she had been complaining of disturbed vision. As soon as she returned she went to bed, and on the Friday and Saturday, stayed there. She had been following a liquid diet (prescribed by one of the doctors) until the Friday, when she had stewed steak. Late on Saturday afternoon, 3 September, she got up to dine with Maundy Gregory.

Mrs Howard called again at around six that night, when Mrs Rosse had gone to Maundy Gregory's rooms for her aperitif. Mr Gregory answered the phone in the hall and said that Mrs Rosse was upstairs. He left the phone to talk to her, came back and suggested that Howard come to see her tomorrow, Sunday, between 12pm and 1pm.

There was nothing new in their dining together in the evenings. On weekdays, when he was at home, he normally ate supper with her in her dining room, or took something left ready in the half-landing kitchen by Mrs Wells. Mrs Wells cooked for both Maundy and Edith at the weekends. On this particular Saturday she was not present, but Edith had arranged for Mrs Eyres (who cooked for her during the week) to make liver and bacon for them, followed by stewed plums and cream. The household lived on the slow-cooked, meat-rich, fairly typical British diet of the 1930s.

They ate their meal and drank what was brought, as usual, by Maundy. They sat up until after eleven, when Edith went to bed. Her bedroom had once been a billiard-room, and stood in an extension out to the garden. Perhaps she felt vulnerable, either because of poor health or from a fear of burglars, for she had had a bell installed so that she could summon Maundy's help if she needed it.

6 Albion St, Gregory's home during the First World War and early 1920s

The Carlton Hotel, Haymarket, London; a favourite rendezvous for Gregory and his clients

Harry Shaw (right), Gregory's rival honours tout.

Gregory's home, 10 Hyde Park Terrace.

Premises of the Ambassador Club at 26 Conduit Street, Mayfair, London as they appear today.

Deepdene hotel luggage label.

Edward Billyard-Leake, who reported Gregory to the police for honours touting in 1933.

Gregory leaving Bow Street Court, 16 February 1933.

Gregory in Paris, July 1933.

Gregory's father.

Gregory's mother.

Gregory's Grandfather, Lt Col George Wynell – Mayrow. Rode in charge of Light Brigade and demonstrates that in respect of this, Gregory was telling the truth about his forebears.

Gregory's brother Stephen.

The Keen-Hargreaves brothers pictured with the Duke and Duchess of Teck, 6 July 1911.

> "The keen-eyed Captain strains into the storm,
> With an experienced gaze, that finds a course
> To safety 'mid the jarring elements;
> Knowing his ship is staunch, and well-tried skill
> Shall, under Providence, the haven win"
>
> Dowe's Fragments. (1786)

"THE CAPTAIN."

Four very pertinent pro-coalition Lloyd George political cartoons published in the *Whitehall Gazette* 1920–1922.

"By archers taught that never-slackened bows
Will wane in strength and at some juncture fail,
Wise men give to affairs a playing space,
And so in sport the energy renew
That makes them masters of the arduous hour."
WILLIAM BROWNE, 'Miscellanies' 1763.

"RECREATION."

"Alas, poor Yorick! I knew him, Horatio: a fellow of infinite jest, of most excellent fancy: he hath borne me on his back a thousand times; and now, how abhorred in my imagination it is! my gorge rises at it." *HAMLET Act V. Scene I.*

Tabard

"EXHUMATION."

"There are in every age Statesmen who tower amid the Political throng as Swift's Man-Mountain did amongst the Pygmies. The arrow-flights of malice and envy from their puny enemies may sting and irritate, but cannot bring them down or check their course. Such see their goal and will not be deflected."

REV. DR GRAYCOTT, "Sermons on the Times," 1836.

"TENACITY."

Maundy Gregory and his dog.

Frederick Rosse and his solicitor, C.A. Madden, visit Paddington Mortuary on 23 April 1933 to see the exhumed body of his wife Edith.

<u>BURN</u> as soon as <u>READ</u>   17. Park Lane-

                                                    May 17. 1920

Dear Prime Minister-

        I have to write you a few lines to supplement
the information that Dudley Ward will convey to you when
shewing you my recommendations for the coming
Birthday Honours.

        Firstly let me say that I have been very carefully indeed
through the claims of the candidates and am satisfied
as to their general merit. In other words they are
well up to the average and their promotions will
give at least <u>local</u> satisfaction.

        Incidentally they are all very strong reactive supporters
of your Government and of yourself in particular.

        The Municipal Honours (knighthoods) have been very
carefully selected + always add to the popularity
of the list. So much for the Baronetcies
                                        + Knighthoods-

Peers
        I very much hope you will approve of Reginald Cox
head of Cox's Bank.
        The Bank did marvellous work during the war.

Above: First page of F.E. Guests's 'Burn as soon as read' letter to the Prime Minister, 17 May 1920.

Opposite: 10 Downing Street notepaper, regarding a posted-dated cheque that had been presented for a knighthood in the 1919 New Year's Honours List (the seal and notepaper, not printed).

You will have noticed
that Mr Marple
post dated his
cheque — Jan 7 1919
in order to set his
honour on Jan 1,
and to enable him
& his sponsors
say that when he
received his Knighthood
he had paid nothing
for it
The first thing is surely
to return his cheque & the

An Act for the prevention of abuses in connection with the Grant of Honours. [7th August 1925.]

BE it enacted by the King's most Excellent Majesty by and with the advice and consent of the Lords Spiritual and Temporal, and Commons, in this present Parliament assembled, and by the authority of the same, as follows:—

Punishment of abuses in connection with the grant of honours.

1.—(1) If any person accepts or obtains or agrees to accept or attempts to obtain from any person, for himself or for any other person, or for any purpose, any gift, money or valuable consideration as an inducement or reward for procuring or assisting or endeavouring to procure the grant of a dignity or title of honour to any person, or otherwise in connection with such a grant, he shall be guilty of a misdemeanour.

(2) If any person gives, or agrees or proposes to give, or offers to any person any gift, money or valuable consideration as an inducement or reward for procuring or assisting or endeavouring to procure the grant of a dignity or title of honour to any person, or otherwise in connection with such a grant, he shall be guilty of a misdemeanour.

(3) Any person guilty of a misdemeanour under this Act shall be liable on conviction on indictment to imprisonment for a term not exceeding two years or to a fine not exceeding five hundred pounds, or to both such imprisonment and such fine, or on summary conviction to imprisonment for a term not exceeding three months or to a fine not exceeding fifty pounds, or to both such imprisonment and such fine, and where the person convicted (whether on indictment or summarily) received any such gift, money, or consideration as aforesaid which is capable of forfeiture, he shall in addition to any other punishment be liable to forfeit the same to His Majesty.

First page of the 1925 Honours (Prevention of Abuses) Act.

Now she did – and she rang. He went downstairs – not carrying a poker against intruders, so far as we know – and found that she was very ill and had 'almost collapsed' trying to phone a friend.

Maundy knocked on Mrs Eyres' door to wake her up and called Dr Plummer. He arrived soon after midnight. She had been sick and was sleepless; he gave her morphia. In his opinion, she was not as ill as when he'd seen her in August and had merely been eating and drinking too much liver and bacon and champagne. She also said she had taken a cocktail and a liqueur. Mrs Eyres could not confirm this.

> I do not know whether Mrs Rosse had anything to drink when dining with Mr Gregory on the Saturday but I surmised she had had some lager beer because I found the empty bottle in the room and two glasses on the table.

Mrs Eyres cleared the table on Sunday morning. Mrs Howard arrived that Sunday at 12.30. Mrs Wells was already there. Edith was confused and frail. Mrs Howard stayed to nurse her and relieve Mrs Wells, who had to go home for the afternoon. From then on, Mrs Howard slept in the same room as Mrs Rosse.

Maundy Gregory was extremely solicitous, constantly dropping in to soothe his 'sister'. No-one saw any medicine being administered in his presence and Mrs Howard, who was there constantly, never saw him give her anything at all; she was adamant about this. He came in often to see the invalid, and always enquired of her how she was feeling; that was about it. In Mrs Howard's view, he did not suspect that she might be on her deathbed. Edith lived on jellies and milk puddings, and the mild remedies prescribed by Dr Plummer.

Dr Plummer visited three times on the Sunday and twice every day that week, for such was the care a rich woman could expect in the great pre-NHS days of private practice.

According to her brother Fred, he rang up and spoke to her on 9 September. It has to be remembered that so far as we know, there was only one telephone on the ground floor, which would, as was the custom, have been in the hall. Fred Davies said that his sister explained she had had a heart attack, brought on by Ethel's behaviour.

9 September was a significant day for Maundy. He was promoted from Knight Commander to Knight Grand Cross of the Order of the Holy Sepulchre. This rank was usually exclusive to 'ecclesiastical or secular princes, Ministers, and Ambassadors' who had visited the Holy Land. In terms of precedence, he was now the equal of Cardinal Bourne, Archbishop of Westminster, and the Earl of Denbigh, head of the Order in England and Wales.

On the Friday, 10 September, the doctor was feeling uneasy. Edith did not seem to be getting better; in fact she was becoming comatose, more and more difficult to awaken. He sent a note to Dr Parsons Smith of 23 Harley Street asking him to call at Hyde Park Terrace that afternoon. Dr Parsons Smith, a heart specialist, diagnosed uraemia, as a consequence of alarmingly high blood pressure and kidney disease. He also noticed that she had an enlarged heart. 'I regarded the outlook of this patient as extremely grave and saw little chance of recovery.'[32] He prescribed complete rest and more morphia.

On Monday 12 September two nurses were engaged to help Mrs Howard around the clock. The patient was intermittently confused, and complained of headaches.

On Tuesday 13 September Dr Plummer arrived at 7.30pm for the second time that day. He was taken up to Maundy Gregory's first floor reception rooms to wait, as a Mr David Levi, a Harley Street surgeon, had made an appointment to to meet him at the house.

Mr Levi had been called in by Peter Mazzina, who knew him because he had operated on one of his children. Mazzina had kept him waiting for three quarters of an hour at the Savage Club before accompanying him to Bayswater in Levi's car. Like Dr Plummer, David Levi was told that Mrs Rosse was Maundy Gregory's sister.

The general practitioner and the surgeon saw her together. She was unconscious and breathing stertorously. Mr Levi testified later:

> I examined her and I considered – one, that she was a medical case and out of my province; two, that she was dying.[33]

Now that it was pointed out to him, Dr Plummer could see that she had had a stroke. She was paralysed on the right side. It had happened 'since my previous visit that day.'[34]

Mr Levi told Maundy Gregory that a physician should be called, preferably a neurologist. 'I'll give you the name of a Harley Street chap I know.' He suggested a Dr Wilson. Maundy Gregory anxiously rang, and Dr Wilson arrived despite the lateness of the hour when Mr Levi was still there.

According to Dr Plummer he diagnosed the stroke as 'the outcome of the complaint previously diagnosed by Dr Parsons Smith and myself.' The doctors left.

When Dr Plummer was called back at ten to one in the morning Edith Marion Rosse was dead. [35]

CHAPTER FOURTEEN

Acting Fast

On Wednesday 14 September 1932, Maundy Gregory woke up with a funeral to arrange. Edith lay dead downstairs. He had let Dr Plummer leave, but then called him back to the house to open one of her veins. He explained to the doctor that she had thought it important to be quite sure.

He would have just a select few close friends of Edith's at the funeral. Her relations would find out soon enough. With luck Frederick Rosse would be touring, as usual, but he must be informed right away otherwise he could make trouble. But he wouldn't be expecting anything. Begging, Ethel might, but she could whistle for it. And the brother too, wherever he was.

On this day, Maundy had £1 1s 9d (one pound, one shilling and ninepence) in his Drummonds account.[1] There had been three wills. The first, in favour of Ethel, had been torn up in 1928. The second, also in favour of Ethel, had still been in existence this summer. Whether or not a copy had been lodged with Stanley Brooke before his death, and what Maundy knew of its whereabouts or its fate, we do not know.

And the third, the pencilled note that gave him carte blanche, was safe from prying eyes. Nobody had asked about it; not Dr Plummer, nor Mrs Eyres of course ...

Nor Edith.

He felt fully entitled to inherit the lot. He had put property in Edith's name, beginning with Vanity Fair more than twenty years ago – and when he thought of the dinners, the outings, the trips abroad ... All the same, questions would be asked about this will, if only because it was written in pencil. Frederick Rosse probably counted as next of kin, or even the brother he had never met, and Ethel would be sniffing around. Mrs Eyres would tell everyone who asked that Edith was dead and then where would he be? There were sisters in Canada as well. *Possession is nine points of the law.* He needed to get hold of Edith's assets in double-quick time before the telephone started to ring. Get onto the Royal Bank of Scotland and reassure them that he should soon be in a position to pay the second, overdue instalment of £10,000.

He was out of bed already. Thoughts tumbled over each other. He would have to act fast. The Cause of Death form had been signed. Dr Plummer had put down something about a cerebral haemorrhage and kidney disease. He would need copy death registrations to show to the Probate Office. He must register the death this morning, and find a funeral director, and find a burial site, and make a start on the paperwork. Edith wrote everything in a big locked book, a sort of diary-*cum*-cashbook. It would be in her bureau. He would ring Harrods funeral service first, then go down and make sure Mrs Eyres was kept busy while he emptied the bureau and brought all the paperwork upstairs.

Pengelly had known since the summer that Maundy's financial state was worsening. On 8 August the Drummonds account was overdrawn by £559, but £1000 was paid in the following day. Maundy's liabilities at the time were £3,264. These figures shone in Pengelly's mind like the lights of Piccadilly Circus, especially the liabilities. They indicated that a wheel was close to spinning off the Maundy Gregory wagon and the whole rickety affair could end up in a ditch.

Maundy had always told Pengelly that he was engaged on Secret Service business, and for a long time Pengelly believed him, since satisfyingly enormous sums could be relied on to turn up twice a year in crisp pound notes. The accountant had also grown used to cheques with several noughts on the end leaving Maundy's account at Drummonds, at the northern end of Whitehall, to the credit of the Ambassador Club's own Drummonds account (Royal Bank of Scotland branch) – as well as to Maundy's private account at Lloyds Bank. But recently, Maundy had complained that he could not possibly go on supporting the Ambassador Club.

Pengelly agreed. But he didn't like it. Retrenchment such as this on Maundy Gregory's part indicated that his employer anticipated a permanent reduction in income. Another job in accountancy would not be easy to find. He could not walk without crutches and must rely on his car. There were young children to educate and feed. He rather hoped that Maundy was going to come into some money, because otherwise, he feared for his own immediate future.

Maundy ordered a lead-lined coffin and accepted an estimate of 100 guineas for the funeral. Nothing was too good for Edith. The funeral would be this Friday, he told Mr Mann from Harrods, at Whitchurch, near Pangbourne on the Thames. On Thursday afternoon he had Bramley drive him along the Thames Valley to Whitchurch, where there was an old church near an island in the river. Edith had always said she wanted to be buried next to the Thames.

The taxi passed through the busy London suburbs. The Vicar of Stiffkey was all over the newspaper hoardings again. Maundy's career since the War, and Jumbo's, had diverged dramatically. Maundy's fortunes had risen throughout the 1920s until the summer of 1931, while from what the papers said, Jumbo's had fallen, and now seemed about to hit bedrock.

In 1919 Jumbo had returned from extended service overseas as a Navy Chaplain to greet his four children – all under twelve – at the rambling rectory at Stiffkey, and his wife Kitty. Kitty had put on a bit of weight. In fact she turned out to be three months pregnant. Which unless this were a virgin birth. . .

Jumbo was appalled, and needed no encouragement to seek feminine company elsewhere. He met Rose Ellis in Leicester Square. She had been a Land Girl in the War, he told her; so he took her back with him to Stiffkey, where she took over gardening duty at the rectory, under Kitty's nose.

Rose Ellis had to go back to London to get medical help for syphilis. While she was being treated he found her a suitable place to live. Oddly enough it was in Endsleigh Street, Bloomsbury. Then he ran into Arthur John Gordon, a Canadian, and started to spend time with him at the Emerson Club off the Strand. Together they began a bucket-shop, selling mining shares. His pastoral duties were not forgotten; indeed, he was expelled from the Overseas League because of the fallen women who used to hang around outside.

They were expensive, these girls. He made a habit of taking Rose to Paris – and some of his actress friends too – to find work for them, he said. His behaviour in Soho was benevolent. He gave money away, much as Maundy, whose own enterprise was thriving a mile down the road, disbursed meals and entertainment. The similarities between them are striking. Both were generous, though in both an ulterior motive might be detected by the suspicious.

In 1925 Jumbo overspent seriously, and borrowed at high interest in order to pay the rates on the rectory. As a result he was forced to file for bankruptcy, and lost half his living to creditors.

This did nothing to cramp his style. He caused more and more talk up in Norfolk. He seemed to revel in attention, on one memorable occasion cycling down the aisle to his pulpit (probably because he was late off the train). A lot of his parishioners thought the world of him. He was kind, a good preacher and deeply caring – when he was there. But Rose Ellis was one of many girls he had brought to Stiffkey from London in the guise of domestic help, and after twenty-four years of his ministry some of the more strait-laced parishioners thought they knew a trollop when they saw one.

When Jumbo failed to turn up for service on Armistice Day, 1930, Major Hamond was outraged. He complained to the Bishop of Norwich. Sunday service was never on time; the Rector was hardly ever there to tend his flock; the man was slack, unpunctual and the loose girls he invited down were depraving village youth and leading them into immorality. One of those girls was Barbara Harris, whom he had met at Marble Arch only this year. In his capacity as the Prostitutes' Padre – which was what the newspapers would call him later – he got her a job with Lady Paget-Cooke. She left, for unknown reasons, and he found her another, with Lady Waechter. He certainly was persuasive for a country vicar.

The Bishop decided to take action under the Clergy Discipline Act. In January, 1931, he told Jumbo to resign his living. Jumbo refused.

That summer, he knew he was being spied on. Strangers were unusual in Stiffkey especially if they hung around on Sundays and came to church, and asked questions about the Rector in the pub during the week. But in the summer of 1931, he guessed they were snooping for reasons associated with his finances.

The Charles Arrow Detective Agency – which was based, coincidentally, at 89 Chancery Lane, like the offices of Deepdene Ltd in 1919 – had been commissioned by the Bishop. In November 1931, Rose Ellis was approached by Christopher John Searle (ex military intelligence) and Mrs Ettie Schwab, whose business cards showed that they came from Arrows. They would like to ask her about her relationship with the Reverend Davidson.

In March 1932, when Maundy was beginning to feel financial pain, Ethel had been shown the door, and Captains Miller and Harker were poring over their fascinating discoveries about the Ukrainian independence movement and Werner Von Alvensleben, Jumbo was called before a Consistory Court. There was a possibility that he might be criminally prosecuted for keeping a disorderly house. A stream of girls testified to his character and only one or two, whose profession was indeterminate, went into titillating detail about rather more than that. Unfortunately for Jumbo, there was photographic evidence for some of this.

Numerous waitresses and actresses complained of being pestered. One of his more annoying habits, said the waitresses, was to serenade them with *Queen of My Heart*. He informed the court that this was from a musical called *Dorothy*. Photographers besieged the prettier girls. Stiffkey, the name of which had hitherto been associated only with oysters, became quite a tourist attraction. The *Daily Herald* was sued, in a related case, for contempt of court by the Bishop of Norwich. And now, in the autumn of 1932, Jumbo was about to be defrocked.

Maundy sympathised. But he had no intention of letting the authorities catch up with *him*.

Whitchurch was hopeless. He had Bramley drive him back to London along the winding Thames, visiting every village church on the way. It was the same wherever they went. Either the graveyard was full or it was restricted to parishioners. Finally they arrived at the little hamlet of Bisham, where after a wearisome time spent hunting down the Vicar, Maundy promised an enormous 100 guineas to the Church Fund and arranged the burial for Saturday. It was perfect, he thought; a quiet place at the very edge of the river. The funeral directors would work quickly, so with any luck, by the time Ethel and the unknown brother worked out what had happened, poor dear Edith would be safely under the daisies and her money spoken for.

Ethel had been ringing up to speak to her aunt since August. The housekeeper always told her that Mrs Rosse was ill or that she had gone out. Finally, one day in the third week of September, she stepped beneath the portico of 10 Hyde Park Terrace and knocked on the door. Hilda Howard answered. Ethel was surprised to see her; she had known her for years, since Mrs Howard had worked for Aunt Rosse since 1925 – but she had left in 1931.

She was even more confounded to hear that her Aunt Rosse was dead, and had been buried at a church near Marlow.

It was a great shock. Mrs Howard took her into the house. Mrs Rosse had received every care, she said. She had nursed her herself for three weeks, and there had been two other nurses and three doctors. Ethel asked whether there had been a Will. She was told yes. And it was witnessed by Mrs Eyres and Dr Plummer. Dr Blair had not been there.

Ethel rang Maundy Gregory and asked him exactly where her aunt had been buried and what had caused the death.

He said she was buried 3 miles from Marlow and the cause of her death was professional secrecy (*sic*). He did not wish to discuss the matter over the telephone as he was recovering from effects of 'influenza.'[2]

Ethel tracked down Dr Plummer in Melcombe Street and went to see him. She asked what had caused her aunt's death. He refused to give details, citing professional secrecy. He had no reason other than Maundy's instructions not to tell Ethel what her aunt had died of.

She went to see her father at 2 Providence Terrace, Upper Street, Islington.[3] She told him the sad news. It came as a shock; as, apparently, did the news that Edith had been separated from her husband for almost a decade when she died. He went out to telephone Hyde Park Terrace and left a message that Maundy Gregory should get in touch.

As soon as he was told that Ethel had called, Maundy wrote to Fred Davies.

Dear Mr Davies,

I would have written to you before to tell you of the sad, sad news; but I had not your address.

Poor Edith passed away peacefully early last Wednesday morning.

She had a heart stroke three weeks before and a relapse a fortnight later.

We did everything we could for her, 3 specialists and 2 nurses.

She did not suffer at all towards the end.

Yours very truly,
J Maundy Gregory[4]

Fred left his single unfurnished room in Islington and made his way to Lancaster Gate. At the millionaire's mansion where his sister had led, all those years, a life of which he knew nothing, he was admitted to the hall and left to wait, clutching his cloth cap. He was overwhelmed by the style in which she had been living; he had had no idea.

A man appeared who said he was Mr Pratley. Mr Pratley apologised for Mr Gregory's inability to see him and explained that Mr Gregory was very ill. Fred left a message for Mr Gregory to contact him by letter and arrange a meeting.

He brooded for a while; Edith had been a very rich woman.

Frederick Rosse, having received notice of the death from some form of 'heart-stroke' (*sic*) from Maundy, shortly afterwards got a letter from Ethel on the same topic but with a very different tone. She said Edith's will made in 1928 had been destroyed, and gave him details of the property Edith owned. On 23 September he wrote back, thanking her, and saying that Maundy Gregory had already told him of the death and that his solicitor (Mr Betts, at Long & Co in Lincoln's Inn) was looking after his interests. Mr Betts would be checking to see what had been registered at Somerset House.

Ethel had told her father that Dr Plummer wouldn't tell her the cause of death. Fred went into a phone box and hoicked up one of the big directories that were anchored there. He looked for Dr E. C. Plummer, the same E. C. Plummer who had witnessed the will. He rang up, and asked for an appointment to discuss his sister's death. The next day another letter arrived at Providence Terrace. This one came from 20 Melcombe Street.

Dear Sir,

Respecting your telephone enquiry about the late Mrs Rosse, I think no useful purpose will be gained by seeing you; you will of course understand that any information of a Medical nature is a matter of Professional secrecy, and I am not in any way concerned with her private affairs.

I have no wish to be discourteous, but there is no use in wasting your time and mine in a discussion which will lead nowhere.

Faithfully yours,
(E C Plummer)[5]

A scribble signed it off.

Fred swallowed the insult, the arrogance. . . That night he wrote to the Coroner's Court at Paddington Green. He asked for an interview and heard back by return that he might come in the following morning. At last, someone who could take action. At the Court, he told an official how something was not right about his sister's death. He felt information was being kept from him. Nobody would tell him anything about how she died or what had happened to her property and he was next of kin. The man told him he should get a solicitor onto it. Fred was crestfallen. He might as well have been told to go and out and hire himself a Rolls Royce.

He wrote to Maundy Gregory. There was a grave at Edmonton, a family grave. Edith had kept the details. And what was happening about the will? Ethel had made her intentions plain: she had said that she intended to remember him. She had also mentioned her husband. The following day, a letter came back, on the thick notepaper he had seen before.

Dear Sir,

Mr Gregory has asked me to say that he must thank you for your kind letter . . . he is having a search for the particulars you ask for regarding a grave at Edmonton . . . He has been intending to write to you for some days to tell you that he would like a little later to consider personally making you some little gift from himself as a memento.

Believe me,

Yours faithfully
G Pratley
Private Secretary[6]

In other words he might, if he was lucky, get a pearl-handled pen-wiper. What had happened to Edith's money?

Ethel's letter from Edith's husband had said something about wills being registered at Somerset House. It was just a bus ride away from where Fred Davies lived but it was like going into a palace. Huge grey stone walls, vast windows onto a courtyard, and row upon row of dark wood shelves full of records up to the ceiling. Your voice echoed. He asked to see the will. They kept a photographic copy, or for a fee of 3s he could see the original.

He saw the copy. His sister had left everything to Maundy Gregory. The handwriting in the will didn't look like hers. The signature was faint and he didn't recognise that, either.

He asked a friendly-looking man what to do next. How could he find out what she died of? The man told him that the cause of death would be on the death certificate and he could get a copy from the Paddington Registrar.

Ethel did not know what she could do, except get up every morning and go to her temporary job at Selfridge's. She wrote to Maundy ('regarding my financial position') to say how broke she was; and wrote again; she offered to work for him as before; she got no reply at all. She was borrowing money from a cousin in Hendon who had been helping her out since July.

The Paddington Registrar didn't seem too difficult. Fred Davies got the certificate, and saw the cause of death and the certifying doctor's name. He went back to Somerset House and paid 3s to see the original will. His suspicions were stronger than ever.

When Ethel next visited, he showed her the death certificate. Cerebral haemorrhage and Bright's disease. Then he dropped his bombshell: he thought the will was a forgery. She was horrified.

He said the will was lodged at Somerset House on 19 August 1932 and was witnessed by L.G. Eyres and E.C. Plummer.[7]

Dr Plummer's name was also on the death certificate. On 26 October Fred Davies wrote to Maundy Gregory.

> Everywhere I make enquiries people seem to be under the impression that you were Mrs Rosse's brother. As the Will states that her property be left as she desired, I must inform you that she desired me to participate. I must ask you to give me full details . . . we may be able to settle this dispute amicably – otherwise I must take steps to stop any disbursement of property until a Court of Justice decides.
>
> As her brother and next of kin I am entitled to the information I seek. Failing a reply, I shall instruct my Solicitors to act for me in this matter.
>
> Yours faithfully,

Fred Davies received no reply. In frustration he wrote to Frederick Rosse, saying he thought the will was a forgery and Maundy Gregory up to no good. He and Frederick Rosse began to correspond. Fred Davies agreed that copies of what he had to say should be passed to Rosse's solicitors; for his part, Frederick Rosse listed the sums he had paid Edith over the years. 'My income has been so crippled since 1924. . .' he wrote sadly; also gently pointed out that in fact he, as her husband and never divorced from her, was legally next of kin. Fred Davies would be second in line, after Rosse's death.

> I cannot help thinking that you have overestimated the amount of your sister's estate. I am quite unable to imagine how she could have accumulated such a sum; she was always very exacting in seeing that she got her absolute fifty per cent of my income down to the last half-penny.[8]

He wrote this in the second week of November in full confidence that his solicitor was looking after his interests. His solicitor, Mr Betts, demonstrated professional complacency on a par with that of Dr Plummer. He sent a couple of underlings down to Somerset House to have a look at the Will. They came back and said it looked right enough to them. He was 'keeping an eye', he told his client serenely. Frederick Rosse had no idea, as his solicitor had no idea, that Probate had already been granted.

Edith's sister Clara, in Canada, wrote to Fred Davies to ask whether she had been mentioned in the will.

Ethel and Fred Davies had no money and no hope of representation. By the New Year, they were both out of work. Ethel lived on charity in a convent.

Maundy had been positively buzzing around. Probate in the sum of over £18,865.18.11 was granted on 3 October, eight days before he wrote to Fred with his gracious offer of a 'memento' and only nineteen days after Ethel's death.

This speed of execution may have been easier to achieve because he had no problem proving that this was the most recent will, retrieving it from anywhere, or dealing with former executors (such as a solicitor in Lewisham who had killed himself last summer). For if the statement made by Ethel Marion Davies on 15 February 1933, when she reported what Fred told her he had seen, is correct, Edith's pencilled will had been placed in the care of the authorities on the day she signed it.

'He said the will was *lodged* at Somerset House on *19 August 1932*.'

Was this merely careless transcription by DS Percy Ruffett and DC Hodge, over the three days in February, 1933, when they took Ethel's statement? Or is it a phrase that stuck in Fred Davies's mind because he had seen it on papers accompanying the will?

If Fred Davies was right about the date and place of deposit (and Wills nowadays can be lodged for safe keeping at the Probate Registry), then this means that on that broiling August afternoon, Maundy took an hour out to leave the sick woman's bedside, shoot down to Aldwych in his taxi, and place her Will in safe custody for a small fee. 19 August was a Friday. Edith's deathbed scene (full dress rehearsal) had not begun until 2.30ish, and he would have had to get Somerset House by 5pm; in a taxi, with little traffic in 1932, on the sleepiest day of the emptiest month of the London year, a two-mile journey of no more than fifteen minutes.

This is significant. No-one other than the testator – Edith herself – would be allowed to see the deposited Will in her lifetime. If she asked about it, in order to rescind it, upon recovery from her crisis, Maundy could have told her that it since she made it when ill, he had destroyed it. And since she had previously made a Will in Ethel's favour – a 'second will', seen by Pengelly, which was to the best of Pengelly's knowledge still around, probably still in her desk, while a copy could have been with Stanley Brooke before he died – she may well have felt that there was no immediate need to make another.

If, on the other hand, she did remember having signed a scribbled will, in pencil, in her darkest hour, she would surely want to remake it in ink once she was up and about.

Fred Davies, who had heard from Edith that summer that a Will in Ethel's favour had been torn up at some point, and burnt, because the young woman was 'a lazy little cat' claimed that when he

> ...asked her whether she was going to make a new one she said she would, and I said 'Don't forget your little brother' (meaning myself), [and] she said 'Failing you my boy, my husband, failing my husband, you.' She then went on to describe a visit to Ethel's bedroom on which occasion she destroyed her husband's photograph.

Edith was disingenuous. The torn-up will, by common consent, was the first one. Pengelly had seen a second, in which everything was left to Ethel, and Edith never gave him any reason to think that she had destroyed that one. Whom do we believe – Fred or Pengelly? Pengelly had nothing to gain, and Askew, whose opinion as an experienced policeman should have been informed by more than mere snobbery, did not trust Fred Davies at all.

On 26 October, when Fred Davies wrote threatening that he would put the matter in the hands of his solicitors, Maundy Gregory was busy seeing off the King of Greece, as His Majesty boarded a train to the Continent from Victoria Station. And 'any disbursement of property' was also steaming forward at high speed. Probate had been granted on 11 October and Maundy was disbursing at full throttle to his creditors.

Maundy was a clever manipulator. He told half-truths all the time. A witness who testified to an agent employed by Maddin's Solicitors, said

> On Friday 9 September I called by appointment at 10.30am. I saw G [Gregory]. . . he said 'I am very worried. My sister is extremely ill. . . I think she got a touch of the sun when we were out recently. Since then she has been in a coma. I have had brain specialists and other doctors here. She has suffered for a long time from kidney trouble.'[9]

The 'brain specialist' could only have been the neurologist Dr Wilson, who did not arrive until the night Edith Rosse died, four days later. However, it is possible that the interviewee mixed up the date when Maundy said this to him (On 9 September Maundy was rather busy on Chancellery business.) After the funeral, in the course of a phone conversation the same interviewee was told:

> ' . . . My sister always said she wanted to be buried by the river. My dear friend Lord Southborough has been so helpful to me. You see nobody had been buried at Bisham for a long time. Being so near the river I had a specially deep grave prepared owing to the danger of floods.'

In practical matters, Maundy was totally hopeless. Most people are aware that there is such a thing as the water table. Had 10 Hyde Park Terrace, been engulfed by floods, presumably Maundy would have sought safety in the cellar.

The interviewee, who preferred to remain anonymous but would respond if necessary to a subpoena, had been discussing 'a continental job' that Gregory was about to hire him for. Basil Thomson? Maybe. Maundy brought out the Inner Slave in most people. Most people felt flattered to have the confidence of a good raconteur with an air of secret importance; reflecting his authority, they did his bidding. Dr Plummer carried out Maundy's orders on very short acquaintance. Edith Rosse behaved, until 1932, as his pawn in the matter of her niece, of whom she was genuinely fond. His housekeepers did exactly as they were told. If Mrs Eyres and Dr Plummer, together, suspected that Mrs Rosse was in no state to make a will, who were they to argue when Maundy consented?

On 6 January, a languid enquiry crossed a desk at MI5:

> <u>B</u>: Please see attached telegrams between Sir Basil Thomson and MG. Do you think DSS would want to consult 'C' as to whether any action was desirable? [10]

Thomson had sent his telegram from Jurançon, in the Pyrenees on 29 December.

> Agent Berlin propose meeting me Paris cost twenty pounds shall I go what can we pay for really satisfactory goods.

On New Year's Eve Maundy sent one back to Thomson in Jurançon:

> Just returned most decidedly meet friend in Paris sending twenty stop Promise anything in reason for satisfactory goods and agree payment in two parts stop Getting on past this end.

Another telegram arrived at Parliament Street on New Year's Day; this time it was from someone called Geronazzo in Egypt.

Best wishes good bye Milan.

The file is signed off 'No Action.' What on earth was he up to?

CHAPTER FIFTEEN

Downfall

In October and November of 1932 Maundy Gregory paid his overdue £10,000 out of Edith's estate, propped up his commitments in other directions and quickly ran out of money with which to make the £10,000 final payment.

Meanwhile at 11 Downing Street, an entirely unrelated (albeit relevant) correspondence was in full flood between Captain Clifford Sherburn, in Bournemouth, on behalf of himself and his widowed mother Lady Sherburn, and the office of the Lord President of the Council in Ramsay Macdonald's National (Coalition) Government. This was Stanley Baldwin, who had formerly been the Conservative Prime Minister.

Clifford Sherburn was the son of Sir John Sherburn who had died in 1926. Sir John had been an eminent surgeon in Hull. Born in 1851, he trained under Lister and for fifty years worked for the Hull Royal Infirmary and the Victoria Hospital for Sick Children, Hull, which he helped to found. He was a partner in a shipping firm later taken over by the Ellerman Shipping Line, and a partner in the Humber Steam Trawling Company, whose fleet had been taken over by the Admiralty during the War. He was an active member of Hull City Council for over forty years; Sheriff of the County in the year of Queen Victoria's Jubilee; and twice Mayor of Hull. He was Lieutenant Colonel of the Northumbria Volunteer Brigade and served for twenty-two years. He had served on various Army and Ministry of Labour Boards. He had three times – in 1900, 1906 and 1910 – given up safe Unionist seats to keep the Unionist Party's end up in larger, hotly contested Liberal constituencies.

The Sherburn family had owned property in Yorkshire since 'about 1150'. They held records of twenty-seven generations going back that far. Nine of them had been in Parliament between 1296 and 1558. Between 1272 and 1902, seventeen of them had been Knights. Sir Nicholas Sherburn was even a baronet, in 1685; but in 1717 his particular line (the Stonyhurst branch of the family) became extinct. His only daughter became the Duchess of Norfolk by marriage to the 8th Duke.

Clifford Sherburn's point (proved by letters he enclosed) was that Sir John had been promised a baronetcy in 1904 but the Unionists went out of office in 1905 and the baronetcy was never granted. The same thing happened again after the War.

In 1926, when Sir John was ill, Clifford Sherburn had written to remind Stanley Baldwin, as Prime Minister, of Bonar Law's post-war commitment. Mr Baldwin then said he was sorry, but the next list was already complete. Sir John Sherburn's name would come up next time. Sir John died on 7 July of that year.

Captain Sherburn took the view, which he reiterated by letter in October and November 1932, that his father's record of public service made him deserving of a baronetcy had he lived, and he had several times been promised one. His mother was particularly anxious that her son should inherit the title, as her husband had wished. There was now a National Government and surely the time had come for the baronetcy to be awarded, posthumously.

Baldwin replied in the negative. The reason he gave was that no record of any such promise could be found. The reason given inter-departmentally was that it was difficult enough to obtain sufficient honours for the living, without entertaining applications from the dead. This was, of course, the fallback of the bureaucrat since time began: that if they conceded to one deserving case, they'd be over-run by others.[1]

At the time of Gregory's arrest in February 1933, and in the decades following, the question was often posed as to how a confidence trickster of Gregory's undoubted calibre could have become entrapped by the Honours (Prevention of Abuses) Act, when for so long he had successfully navigated its un-chartered waters to his own advantage. Gregory himself, and indeed his family, believed that he had been set up for a fall by those who, for some time, had been laying siege to his activities. The instrument of his downfall was a man whose personality and motivation is still, six decades later, shrouded in mystery.

In December, 1932, Lieutenant Commander Edward Billyard-Leake, a handsome man in early middle age, acquaintance of a Royal prince or two and holder of the Distinguished Service Order, *Croix de Guerre* and *Légion d'Honneur*, received a letter from a person unknown to him called J.D. Moffatt. He knew his name from the racetrack. This Moffatt lived at Dial House, Datchet, wrote on Sports Club paper, and must be the person whose name he knew. Mr Moffatt asked for a private interview.

Commander Leake asked his secretary to write back requesting further details.

Mr Moffatt rang up. He told the secretary that the matter was highly confidential and could only be discussed with Commander Leake. Billyard-Leake thought little of this, and did not answer. Again Mr Moffatt rang up. He told Mrs Billyard-Leake that he wanted to speak to her husband and 'she probably knew what it was all about.'[2] She did not, lost patience and rang off.

On Friday 20 January 1933, when Mr Moffatt rang again, Commander Leake answered. Mr Moffatt requested a meeting. Billyard-Leake made an excuse but promised to ring back. His curiosity was aroused, and on the Sunday he did. He said Moffatt should come to his house at 15 Lowndes Square, Knightsbridge, at noon tomorrow.

They arrived more or less simultaneously at the door. Commander Leake was in his chauffeur-driven car with a lady. When he and Moffatt were alone Moffatt said how very confidential his business was. And

> 'Would you like to have a knighthood? I have been asked to get in touch with you about it.'
> 'Why?'
> He then said people thought I ought to have it. No such idea had ever entered my head.[3]

Billyard-Leake was mystified and began to think aloud. Was this something to do with his late father, perhaps? Charles Billyard-Leake, an Australian, and his Australian wife had donated Harefield Park, their Queen Anne mansion set in 900-odd acres near Uxbridge, to the nation in 1914, for use as a military hospital for Anzac servicemen.[4] His wife (Edward's mother) and his sister had been active members of the Hospital board. In 1921 the place had been sold – but not before his father, Charles Billyard-Leake, was offered a knighthood. He had turned it down, saying he wanted a baronetcy or nothing.

Mr Moffatt thought that illuminated the mystery. That must be why People in Authority were so anxious for him, as Charles's son, to receive a knighthood – or baronetcy – now.

> . . . and there was someone who wanted very much to meet me and discuss the matter. He said that it would cost about £12,000. He produced a copy of the *Whitehall Gazette,* which contained a list of people who had attended a Derby dinner. The list included the name of Maundy Gregory. He said 'I want you to meet Maundy Gregory. You see from this list the sort of people with whom he associates. He can get the knighthood for you.'[5]

Billyard-Leake was offered an appointment with Maundy Gregory this very afternoon after lunch. He accepted, to see what would happen.

He picked up Mr Moffatt at 2.30 from the Sports Club, and his chauffeur drove them both to 10 Hyde Park Terrace, where Mr Moffatt left him alone with Mr Maundy Gregory soon after 3pm.

'The highest authority in the country has been considering for a long time whether you ought not to have the baronetcy promised to your father,' Maundy confided. (Which was a clear untruth in the context of Stanley Baldwin's refusal even to consider the excellent claim of Captain Sherburn three months earlier; but he is unlikely to have known this.) He then began to talk about the Sinews of War. Prices were not so exorbitant as they had been in Lloyd George's time, of course. And the present Birthday List was already full. But the

New Year's Honours List of 1934 might have a vacancy and of course, a gentleman such as himself was deserving of a baronetcy. At the very latest, next year's Birthday Honours List would be the one.

Maundy Gregory then went on to talk about a number of highly placed friends of his, including the King of Greece and Mussolini. He also said he was the possessor of some order, the name of which I forget, which entitled him at all times to direct access to the Pope.

Billyard-Leake accepted his invitation to lunch at the Carlton Hotel two days later (25 January) and left. He made his way at once to his solicitor Sir Godfrey Thomas, to whom he told all that had happened. 'I thought that the authorities should know the sort of thing which was going on.'

Sir Godfrey Thomas told him to string Maundy Gregory along and come to see him after Wednesday's lunch. He also got in touch with Sir Patrick Duff at 11 Downing Street. Sir Patrick played for time. Baldwin must make the decision. He would have to consult the Party Chairman, J.C.C. Davidson, and the Attorney General Sir Thomas Inskip so that they were all prepared for whatever beans might be spilled about past events, and past honours, if the evidence proved incontrovertible and a prosecution unavoidable.

On Wednesday, Maundy Gregory appeared at the Carlton while Billyard-Leake was having a cocktail with a friend (a witness conveniently placed, probably on Sir Godfrey's advice). When lunch began, Billyard-Leake said he had spoken to his wife, who asked who his contact was. He really hadn't been able to tell her very much. Did Maundy have anything on paper . . . ?

Maundy had been asked before, and happened to have just the thing about his person. He withdrew from his pocket a folded document of three thick quarto pages.

'This,' he said solemnly 'is filed in the archives of the Vatican and most of the European courts.'

STRICTLY PRIVATE AND CONFIDENTIAL
Arthur John Peter Michael Maundy Gregory, according to the record of the Heralds' College, London, has a direct royal descent and pedigree from Edward III, which is officially

vouched for under the signature of the late Sir Henry Farnham Burke, KCVO, CB, FSA, Garter King at Arms.

His Honours

Commander of the Most Venerable Order of the Hospital of St John of Jerusalem in the British Realm

Deputy Director of the Venerable Order's Centenary Appeal, 1931–33

Grand Cross of the Equestrian Order of the Holy Sepulchre (special representative of the Order in England)

Knight Commander of the Most Noble Order of Pius IX

Receipient of the Apostolic Blessings of His Holiness Pope Pius XI, 29 September, 1932

Commander of the Most Noble Order of the White Rose of Finland

Grand Cordon of the Royal Montenegrin Order of Danilo

Grand Cordon of the Tunisian Order of Nichan Ifitkhar[6]

Background

During the War was occupied in the work of counter-espionage, in which he employed some 1,000 agents.

Assisted HIH Grand Duke Nicolas of Russia, towards later years, with regular quarterly emoluments paid entirely confidentially.

Materially assisted the Grand Duchess after the death of her husband, the Grand Duke Nicolas.

Actively concerned in the affairs of the Montenegrin Royal Family, whom he has assisted.

Works continually in propaganda for the monarchical cause in Greece and in paving the way for the return of His Majesty the King of the Hellenes

A principal co-organiser of the great secret anti-Bolshevist movement

Financed the entire gilding of the choir stalls in Westminster Abbey, an improvement long desired by the Very Reverend Dean and Chapter

Organised and obtained for Westminster Abbey the gift of a gold and jewelled Processional Cross, costing more than £5,000, from the late Hon. Rodnan Wanamaker, CVO

Obtained and confidentially handed over an anonymous gift of £20,000 towards saving the roof of St George's Chapel, Windsor, in the early and crucial stage of this most necessary and vital Appeal

Proprietor, Editor and Leader Writer of the *Whitehall Gazette and St James' Review*, in which he has since 1919 conducted a consistent and assiduous campaign on behalf of Monarchy and against the growth of Bolshevism and Communism and their ramifications in Europe

Has good relations with certain influential Authorities in his own country and abroad

Mr Maundy Gregory is Advisor to, and holds Power of Attorney of,

His Royal Highness the Prince Danilo of Montenegro

Her Royal Highness the Princess Militza of Montenegro

As waiters bearing silver trays flashed between the tables and the lunchtime conversational buzz grew louder, Commander Leake looked up and drew breath.

'Would you mind if I borrowed this? I'd like my wife to see it.'

Maundy consented, provided that Billyard-Leake would return it in person. He went on to reinforce his claim to be able to deliver the goods by pointing out . . .

. . . two or three people in the Carlton for whom he had been able to secure honours, among them a Lady Rathbone, who I gathered was the wife (or widow) of a wealthy Lancashire manufacturer. He also said that he had served in the Secret Service and that Admiral Hall and Sir Vernon Kell were intimate friends of his. Among other people he mentioned were Sir Lionel Halsey, General Seely and Sir Sidney Fremantle. I asked if I might refer to any of these for information about himself, and he said yes, with the exception of Sir Lionel Halsey, who had been mixed up with financial transactions of which he (Maundy Gregory) disapproved.[7]

This was followed by an invitation to lunch on Friday with himself and Lord Southborough. Lord Southborough was a member of the Ambassador Club. Was Billyard-Leake, by any chance, also a member? Oddly enough, he said, he had been invited to join some time before, and had been led to understand that Lord Southborough had put his name forward; which was extraordinary since he and Lord Southborough had never met. How very strange . . . and had he actually discussed the matter of the knighthood with his wife yet? Because Maundy had talked about it with People in Authority and in his case, they were willing to arrange everything for only £10,000. If he wanted to make quite certain of it, he should deposit £2,000 right away. Of course Billyard-Leake was probably wondering what would happen to the money, and he wanted to make it clear that not a penny went to party funds. 'No party question entered into it.' The implication was that because the money did not go to a party, everything was legal and above board.

Billyard-Leake and Maundy went their separate ways, the potential client saying that he now felt much better informed, and Maundy urging him to lunch on Friday.

Billyard-Leake returned to Sir Godfrey Thomas. Later that day, Baldwin's Private Secretary, Sir Patrick Duff, rang Commander Leake at his home and asked him to make an appointment to see Sir Maurice Gwyer, the Treasury Solicitor.

Billyard-Leake had promised to ring Maundy to confirm whether or not he could have lunch with him and Lord Southborough on Friday, but he neither rang, nor turned up on the day. Instead he attended a meeting with Sir Maurice Gwyer at the Treasury at 6.30 on Friday night and made a statement. With Sir Maurice, and his assistant, Mr King, in the room, he telephoned Maundy, apologising and explaining that he had been detained in the City and had been too busy to ring. Maundy Gregory suggested they re-schedule, and would he like to meet the King of Greece?

'I would very much like to meet the King of Greece,' said Billyard Leake, eyebrows shooting upwards at Gwyer and King. 'Unfortunately I'm going to Scotland early tomorrow and won't be back until the middle of next week, about Wednesday. Maybe we can talk then. And I'll be able to discuss it properly with my wife while I'm away.'

Billyard-Leake had to leave Mr King to transcribe the statement he would sign on his return to London. But he did not go on his way without adding that he thought Maundy Gregory and the Ambassador Club were the centre of some kind of racket run by a gang of extortioners.

A girl I once met there told me that she had been asked to make up to me, and that it was believed that I would be willing to pay a substantial sum of money for a baronetcy, in which case she (the girl) would get her share for what she had done. This happened some time ago.[8]

The one thing that might stop Maundy decisively in his tracks, and therefore make him dangerous by prompting him to blackmail, was publicity. There was a slight possibility, in the winter of 1932, that this could arise from a matter entirely unrelated to the British political parties. It came about, bizarrely, through another Australian sailor; only this one had re-invented himself and was now a twenty-eight year old Hollywood screenwriter, on the payroll of Cecil B. de Mille.

His name was John Farrow, he had come to London in April, 1932, and he was in love with an actress. When Maundy met John Farrow, the actress was back in Hollywood shooting a film called *Tarzan*. She was playing Jane to Johnny Weissmuller's eponymous hero and her name was Maureen O'Sullivan. She was a Catholic, and he wanted to marry her. She wouldn't marry him until he was a Catholic too.

He was invited to attend the Chancellery of the Order of St Sepulchre at Parliament Street. It was 'sumptuous', he said later, with a Chapel there as well. Maundy did not actually wear full regalia on this occasion, but opened a closet and reverently displayed it: the white robe with black facings, the insignia, the sash ... Maundy would have fixed – for a consideration, of course – a high-speed induction course and reception into the Church of Rome, but things were more complicated than that. John Farrow was divorced. What he needed was an annulment, *before* the religious conversion.

This was going to cost him.

He was sure something could be arranged. And would he like to meet Major-General Seely? They had lunch at the Ambassador Club with some Members of Parliament. Since Mr Farrow so admired the place, he simply must come to the Derby Dinner at the end of May ... He went to the Derby Dinner. Getting back to the point at issue Maundy thought that, say, £320, for distribution among Catholic charities, would be favourably received by the Church authorities and it was usual in these matters. Mr Farrow wrote out a cheque. Two weeks later, he told him the annulment was going through. Mr Farrow wanted to know exactly when it would be done. Maundy said if he really wanted it within a couple of weeks, a further charitable donation of £1,000 would work wonders. Farrow said he didn't have it. Maundy suggested a compromise: he would advance the £500 to the charities himself if Farrow gave him a £500 bill of exchange, payable on 30 September 1932. If the annulment hadn't appeared by then, of course he would cancel it.

Farrow was put off, and put off again, and on 20 August 1932 he cancelled the bill. He began proceedings to recoup his £320 through the civil courts.

A few months later, the police would state that they had received complaints over a four-year period about Maundy's having taken money in exchange for honours and titles which were not delivered. All had ended with the injured party getting cold feet when it became obvious that he would become a laughing-stock.[9]

Farrow's case in the civil courts showed no sign of ending the same way. But Mr Farrow's problem had nothing to do with the Conservative Party, and if he knew about it J.C.C. Davidson remained unperturbed.

As long as Maundy remained just about solvent, he had every reason not to betray anyone. At Christmas 1932, he was happy, as he had been happy in the old days during the war, with snoopery and intrigue, except that now he was paying Basil Thomson to investigate. Maundy relished this turning of the tables. The money would come in, one way or another. He travelled. He sent telegrams. He paid for information.

Those who have taken the view that Gregory was not a victim of a set-up but the victim of his own greed,[10] have argued that Billyard-Leake simply wasn't the right type. To them, J. Douglas Moffatt,

Gregory's contact man, had not properly researched his mark; Billyard-Leake looked a likely candidate simply because he had money; must have, since he was rich enough to pay for an evening's entertainment at the Ambassador Club. Moffatt had been lazy, perhaps consulting only the phone book in order to discover Billyard-Leake's address and write him a letter. It seems he approached him with no idea about Harefield Park or the philanthropy of Billyard-Leake's parents or the *Légion d'Honneur;* nor, necessarily, did he know that Billyard-Leake had heard his own name at the racecourse.

Billyard-Leake and his decorations were in *Who's Who* and if Moffatt had seen them he should have been wary. For Billyard-Leake did not fit the usual demographic. He was not self-made, not likely to be impressed by the appearance of wealth, but an active businessman and distinguished naval officer who had already achieved a place in Society. Was the approach to Billyard-Leake simply an ill-judged error on Moffat's part or was there something else that led him to Billyard-Leake's door? [11]

Dial House, Datchet, suddenly came under the spotlight. James Douglas Moffatt, his years of loyalty to Maundy loosened by lack of reward, and soon to be dislodged altogether by the threat of prosecution, was about to become a nark.

When he returned from Scotland, Billyard-Leake found a letter from Maundy Gregory.

I much hope to see you at lunch tomorrow with Lord Southborough – Carlton 1.30 –

Apart from this I should be glad if you would call upon me tomorrow morning in the neighbourhood of 11 o'clock, as I want just to complete certain data which I have practically complete.

Your great sporting effort, of which you told me, I am very interested in, and I think I have just the man to help you very materially in completing that matter.

Will you phone me about 10am in the morning, Padd. 7484. [12]

He also found a letter from Sir Maurice Gwyer suggesting that the Director of Public Prosecutions, Sir Edward Tindal Atkinson, hoped to meet him shortly. So he was kept busy until about 6.30 on the evening of Thursday 2 February when – returning home with a friend, Michael Isaacs, who was dropping in to Lowndes Square for a drink – he received a message; Mr Gregory had rung, and would he please call him back?

Commander Leake asked Michael Isaacs to sit near him and listen during the conversation. He began it by apologising; he had been busy and had only just come home. As to the knighthood, after discussing the matter with his wife, and thinking it over, he had decided against it. He definitely did not wish to go on.

Mr Gregory said: 'It is very regrettable as the matter is now practically agreed upon. If you adhere to your decision the matter is dropped and I cannot revive it. Couldn't you give say two or three thousand on account, to keep the pot boiling?' I said 'I told you before that my decision would be final,' and Mr Gregory said: 'Will you not consider the matter and talk it over again with your wife tonight?'[13] Commander Leake said he would, and if they changed their minds they would ring him.

Wheels were already turning. The following day, Chief Inspector Askew was summoned to the Assistant Commissioner's Office and told to visit the office of the Director of Public Prosecutions. There he received instructions in the case of Mr J. Maundy Gregory. He proceeded to Bow Street Magistrates' Court where he obtained a summons, at the DPP's instance, for a contravention of the Honours (Prevention of Abuses) Act, 1925.

Askew and Detective Sergeant Gillen waited, on the evening of Friday 3 February, for the return of J. Maundy Gregory to 10 Hyde Park Terrace. And when they were pretty sure he was there, they called at the front door. 'I was informed on each occasion that he was not at home and was unable to obtain any information that would assist me in getting an introduction.'

He and DS Gillen were on the doorstep again by 8am on Saturday morning. Maundy Gregory had kept Mrs Eyres on since Edith's death, although Mrs Wells still worked for him upstairs. They

... saw a servant who said Mr Maundy Gregory was not up and would not see anybody until after breakfast. I then told the servant I was a government official and must see her master very importantly and confidentially. She left me and some time afterwards another servant saw me and said that Mr Maundy Gregory was not in, that he had breakfasted early and gone out and the time of his return was unknown.

It was obvious that Mr Maundy Gregory was avoiding an interview and I told the servant that I was satisfied that he was in and disclosed my identity adding that I did not propose to leave the house until I had seen him.[14]

Maundy played for time by asking for a card to be sent up. Forty minutes after receiving Askew's card, he 'bounced into the room,' as Askew put it later, apologising for his earlier non-appearance but there were 'impostors' about.

I handed him the summons which he read carefully.

In the Metropolitan Police District

To Mr J Maundy Gregory of 10 Hyde Park Terrace W2
Information has been laid this day by the Director of Public Prosecutions for that [*sic*] you on the 23rd day of January 1933 at 10 Hyde Park Terrace W2 within the district aforesaid, did unlawfully attempt to obtain for yourself from Lieutenant Commander Edward Billyard Leake the sum of £10,000 (ten thousand pounds) as an inducement for endeavouring to procure the grant of a dignity or title of honour to the said Edward Billyard Leake.

Contrary to the provisions of Section 1(1) of the Honours (Prevention of Abuses) Act, 1925.

You are therefore hereby summoned to appear before the Court of Summary Jurisdiction sitting at the Bow Street (WC2) Police Court on Thursday the 16th day of February, instant at the hour of eleven in the forenoon to answer to the said information.

'What do I have to do?' he asked.

'You have to appear on the 16th to answer the charge which is set out,' said the Chief Inspector.

Askew and Gillen left. Back at Scotland Yard the Chief Inspector sent a message to Superintendent Canning of Special Branch. If Maundy Gregory (holder of a ten-year passport valid until 1934, the number of which Askew gave) tried to leave by any port, he was to be delayed and the DPP informed.

CHAPTER SIXTEEN

Nemesis

On Saturday 4 February 1933, Sir Vernon Kell visited Sir Edward Tindal Atkinson, Director of Public Prosecutions, on another matter and heard the news first. Maundy Gregory was on notice to appear in court, charged under the Honours Act.

As soon as his meeting was concluded he rang his office and suggested that telephone checks be re-instituted on the line in and out of 10 Hyde Park Terrace. Steps were taken to this end. Before the weekend was over, Kell had rescinded the order. MI5 was not involved, had not been involved since June 1932 and altogether would be better off out of it.

At the start of the week commencing 6 February, Captain Miller's note on Korostovetz and the Hetman was delivered to the DPP although 'it is not, I think, exactly what he requires.'
I understand that, before any proceedings were set on foot, Downing Street was consulted, and it was only after considerable hesitation that the decision to proceed was taken.[1]

Although the incumbent at 10 Downing Street, in the National Government was Ramsay Macdonald, the real power behind the throne was Conservative Leader Stanley Baldwin. It was he and not Macdonald who was to call the shots throughout the Gregory case. From the outset he and Sir Thomas Inskip, the Attorney General, knew that kid gloves would be required to prevent any inopportune revelations in court. The MI5 man reassured his reader:

> I understand further that the Attorney General is fully aware
> of all the implications of this case.

> What would be of most use to DPP is a list, if we can
> provide one, giving any indications of those who have been
> approached by Maundy Gregory in the past with a view to
> obtaining Honours through his good offices.
>
> I have told the DPP that I will consult our records ...

This had gone too far. A note in the file from Thursday 9 February
1933, reads :

> DSS [Kell] saw DPP this morning on this case, and it has been
> settled that the authorities will not require any information in
> the possession of this office.

Maundy Gregory had twelve days in which to secure his future. He
would, of course, plead 'Not Guilty'. Nothing must come out. His
taxi had never been so much in demand. In it he bustled up and down
the streets of Mayfair and Belgravia, St James's and Kensington, and
wherever he went he was admitted to see a Personage, alone, on an
Urgent and Private Matter. Several Lords, and any number of baronets,
found themselves required to speak to him most confidentially. It
would be so unfortunate if anything remotely damaging to their
reputations were to 'come out'. In the awkward corner into which
he had been so regrettably pushed, 'a couple' would hugely assist in
defraying legal expenses and assuring that nothing did ...

Two thousand in cash obtained from each individual visited
reputedly raised £30,000 in the hectic days pending his court
appearance. Maundy undoubtedly tried hard to extract emoluments.
He even visited Major-General Seely, who had nothing to hide and
'showed him the door'. These disgraceful and humiliating visits were
without doubt an acknowledgement by Gregory that whatever
the outcome of the impending prosecution, his career was ruined.
The Ambassador Club would have to go out of business. Personal
bankruptcy would follow upon his failure to meet all the other
demands that would now go un-met: bills, rent... Silver plates, vintage
wine and other glittering possessions were moved from Conduit
Street to Deepdene. Valuables were quietly smuggled out of 10 Hyde

Park Terrace to the flat above the Imperial Restaurant at Brighton. And George Pratley, who knew too much, must see nobody. He was despatched to lie low in rooms above the Ambassador Club.

Maundy briefed his solicitors, Kenneth Brown, Baker and Baker. He paid a fortune to ensure the services of Norman Birkett, KC.[2] He insisted that he would plead 'Not Guilty'. He felt he had no choice. Unless one of his erstwhile friends stepped in with more money, he and Peter would be ruined, and never again able to live in the style to which they had become accustomed.

He could see only one possible course of action. He must stick to his guns, protesting innocence and thereby threatening to bring the whole thing out in the open at the Old Bailey, until somebody panicked and came forward with an offer adequate to buy his silence and a quiet retirement.

Norman Birkett was not available until just before the hearing.

On Tuesday 7 February, the evening papers picked up the story and ran it as headline news. A man called Maundy Gregory was going to appear at Bow Street at the end of next week, charged with trying to sell a knighthood for a huge £10,000.

Ethel Marion Davies was still unemployed, and living on charity at the Convent of the Holy Sacrament, 60 Gloucester Gardens. Job-hunting as usual, she bought the paper and scanned it with shock and excitement.

Here, she exulted, was her chance to get someone to listen to her. *She knew something.* Maundy Gregory wasn't just a con man – he was probably a forger, a thief and even a murderer. Revenge at last! The following morning she went straight down to Scotland Yard, marched in and demanded to see the officer in charge of the case of Maundy Gregory.

She was taken into Askew's office. Understandably, she was in a rather over-excited state.

'She is a most garrulous person and I found her very difficult in keeping to the point,' complained the Chief Inspector. Exhausted after extracting the basics – she was twenty-nine, Edith Marion Rosse was her aunt, she had known Maundy Gregory since she was

twelve and had once been employed by him – and so on – he turned
her over to Detective Sergeants Ruffett and Hodge, who took a sixty
page statement over three days on Monday, Tuesday and Wednesday
of the following week. In the course of the interviews she outlined
her father's situation with regard to herself, her own in regard to her
aunt, her aunt's marriage – everything, in fact, that was pertinent. She
explained all she knew of the Will, which was that her father had
seen it at Somerset House and thought it was a forgery in Maundy
Gregory's favour. An earlier will that had definitely existed, which she
had seen, had been destroyed, and in that one Aunt Rosse had left
almost everything to her. Her aunt later re-made it but in February of
last year Maundy Gregory had urged her to destroy this second version.
She did not know whether or not that had ever happened. But her
father thought that the will allegedly witnessed by Lottie Eyres and Dr
Plummer looked like a forgery. Edith's husband Frederick Rosse had
solicitors onto the case because he was next of kin, even though they
were separated, but so far as she knew, nothing had come of it.

And then there was the illness. She still didn't know exactly how her
aunt had died because Dr Plummer and Maundy Gregory kept telling
her and her father it was a professional secret. But they were her brother
and her niece; they had every right to know. Why should Maundy
Gregory and this doctor make such a mystery of it unless there was
something to hide? Her aunt was a wealthy woman. She had letters to
show how volatile Aunt Rosse had been, but she had been kind to her
in spite of Maundy Gregory. Maundy Gregory had had a hold over her.

Fred Davies was interviewed on Tuesday 14 February. 'He is
apparently a man of rather low mentality and not a person upon whom
a great reliance can be placed.'[3] All the same the evidence he gave was
coherent (whether truthful or not, was for Askew to judge) and he
had been exchanging letters with Frederick Rosse, the husband and
next of kin who received nothing in the will. Everyone else he met,
he complained, seemed to think Maundy Gregory was Edith Rosse's
brother, not him.

Chief Inspector Askew was inclined to think that this might indeed
be a suspicious death. But interviews had to stop. The Bow Street case
was due to be heard.

The Magistrate was Mr Rollo Graham-Campbell. Maundy Gregory, a dapper but lonely figure opposite him in the wide dock under the high ceiling, pleaded 'Not Guilty'. There was a rustle of interest on the press bench, but Norman Birkett, KC, for Maundy Gregory, was already getting to his feet. He explained that since he had only recently been instructed he was asking for an adjournment, but were it not granted he would prefer to reserve his cross-examination until later. Mr Graham-Campbell was understanding. That day, he heard only the case outlined by Sir Thomas Inskip, the Attorney-General, which was the offer of a knighthood to Billyard-Leake and how Maundy Gregory and the Commander had met.

Mr Moffatt featured in the prosecution's story but was not a defendant. He sat in the public gallery. His presence there, allied with a single glancing reference to something he had said, in police paperwork, indicate that he had obtained immunity in exchange for spilling the beans.

Billyard-Leake entered the witness box, and was asked by Sir Thomas to describe these events in detail. He explained how he had asked Michael Isaacs to sit beside him while he talked to Maundy Gregory on the phone; he described the interview with Mr Moffatt. He was an excellent witness, describing in direct speech what had been said.

Norman Birkett reserved his cross-examination. Michael Isaacs appeared. He too was a formidable witness; calm, self-possessed and having apparently total verbal recall. And after him, Commander Leake's chauffeur, who was perfectly definite as to times, places and faces. Again, the defence stood back pending the next hearing. The Magistrate adjourned the case until the afternoon of 21 February, the following Tuesday.

Norman Birkett, having heard the strong points of the Prosecution's case, had a meeting with Maundy Gregory. He asked him to defend himself on specific matters. Maundy Gregory could not.

Norman Birkett's task was to convince him that in the matter of Billyard-Leake, if he persisted in pleading not guilty, the case would be sent to trial at a higher court – in this case, the Old Bailey. Huffing and puffing about his charitable work and distinguished friends would get him nowhere. This was a court, and the question before judge and jury was, did he do it? On the evidence presented at Bow Street, it would be hard to show otherwise. If he were found guilty he could well get two years in jail and a fine of £500, *pour encourager les autres*. Was he willing to spend two years in jail?

Maundy blustered. He could reveal things . . .

Birkett was dismissive. Patiently he explained it again. Maundy would be tried on the Billyard-Leake case *only*. The opportunity to snitch on the great and famous would not arise. Even if it did, nobody liked a sneak. He was the one in the dock. He had, had he not, managed to convey to Commander Leake – regardless of whether Commander Leake misunderstood him – that he was offering a knighthood in exchange for £10,000? . . . And as Birkett interpreted what he had seen, Billyard-Leake had sought legal advice from the start. The Prosecution would wheel in witnesses to their meetings, copies of the résumé he had presented to Billyard-Leake, somebody who would have heard Billyard-Leake's end of the conversation . . . Did Maundy want to risk public humiliation and two years on Dartmoor plus a whopping great fine? Or would he be a sensible man, plead guilty at Bow Street and walk out with a £50 fine?

He dithered. He had just four clear days between the first and second hearing in which to decide. J.C.C. Davidson noted:

> Nobody knew to what extent Maundy Gregory would betray his past in his desperation and financial stringency. We accordingly organised somebody to go and see him, who told him that he couldn't avoid a term of imprisonment, but that if he kept silent we could bring pressure to bear on the authorities to let him live in France after his sentence had been served.

Who were 'we'? J.C.C. Davidson was the Chairman of the Conservative Party, but as we shall see, the visit was probably made by a friend associated with more shadowy organisations.

On the afternoon of Tuesday 21 February 1933, at Bow Street, Maundy pleaded guilty.

Mr Rollo Graham-Campbell had to decide whether to fine him, or imprison him as well, so Mr Fulton – Sir Thomas Inskip's junior in this case – questioned Chief Inspector Askew as to this man's character. Maundy Gregory had no previous convictions. However,

'Have the police had a number of complaints of a similar character to this one?'
'Yes.'

Mr Fulton murmured to the Magistrate. 'I don't propose to carry it any farther than that.' On the press bench, the *Daily Sketch* man raised an eyebrow. Fulton gathered his gown about him in preparation to sit but Mr Graham-Campbell said sharply

'I don't know exactly what that means.'

Mr Fulton, only fleetingly disconcerted, turned again to Askew. 'A number of people have paid, or have been asked to pay, money to Gregory in connection with the receiving of honours?'

'Similar transactions.'[4]

And there the questions ended. A 'similar transaction' would include the Farrow case, though there is nothing in police files to show that any complaint was ever made to them. Askew had been told a few things, though.

Acting under directions I have endeavoured to interview people from whom Gregory has obtained large sums of money, some of whom have and others who have not succeeded in getting a title, but in no case have I been successful.[5]

Passing on Askew's report to the Assistant Commissioner the following weekend, Superintendent Horwell would draw attention to Askew's reference to J.D. Moffatt as having been a 'tool for Gregory for a very long time and has taken part with the latter in a number of offences against the Act under which the prosecution was framed'. Horwell pointed out that this was based on:

> . . . what Moffatt said which was in effect that on a certain
> occasion he walked out of 10 Downing Street with £50,000
> with instructions to pay back portions of this amount to
> certain persons who had advanced money to Gregory in
> connection with the Honours List. He however declined to
> give dates and details.[6]

A suspicion of systematic and persistent honours touting could be said to
undermine the State apparatus and therefore to come within the remit
of MI5. MI5 documents available to us show that investigations were
mounted, and dropped, by MI5 in 1927, and again in 1931/32.[7] At least
one instance recorded in MI5, not police, files, shows that Sir Thomas
Inskip had backed away from prosecution on a previous occasion and
the files were immediately cleaned up. This does not look as if MI5
despaired of finding enough evidence, but rather as though the interests
of the State would be best served by silence.

In the afternoon of 21 February 1933 Maundy was led away to start
a two-month sentence in the second (relatively lenient) division. He
must also pay a £50 fine and 50 guineas costs. Lawyers leaving the court
included Mr Bensley Wells, instructed by Messrs. Johnson, Jecks, and
Colclough, who had been there to hold a watching brief for interested
parties. These would include his creditors, and should have included
lawyers acting for Mr Farrow, whose civil case would not come up until
1934.

If he behaved himself, Maundy Gregory would have just seven tedious
weeks in which to hum Ray Starita's great hit of last year, *The Flies
Crawled up the Window*. Two months of boredom would not make all his
troubles go away; but he could at least console himself that his capacity
to earn a living from his past had so far been exploited barely at all.

The *Daily Sketch* was suspicious. Commenting after the Bow Street
sentence, it said:

> It would have been more completely reassuring if it had been
> proved that Gregory never had any sort of authority, direct or
> implied, to negotiate, or if he ever had, when so scandalous a
> connection existed and when it ceased.

That put the Conservatives and the Liberals, at least, on notice that the *Sketch* was on the scent of something not altogether honest.

The police thought much the same way, but were keener to unravel the tangled web of Gregory's other activities. Superintendent Horwell must have read DCI Askew's report on the case with interest. It did not end with the result of the court hearing but with a glancing reference to Maundy's pre-war employment, the dodgy nature of the *Whitehall Gazette* and the even more sordid goings-on at the Ambassador Club.

> The Club was managed by one Peter Mazzina. . . said to be an associate of known receivers of stolen property the most notorious of whom is 'Hubby' Distleman CRO#5326/12 and a man named 'Biff' Byfield who are said to have displayed very valuable jewellery at the Club.
>
> Enquiry is in hand by Officers of the Flying Squad in consequence of an anonymous letter on Corres. 230/ROO/80 in respect to the persons referred to as 'receivers.'
>
> I am given to understand that the Ambassador Club was conducted at a great loss and that the Bailiffs are in there; also that Drummonds Bank is involved in the loss to the extend of many thousands of pounds.
>
> Suggestions have been made that Maundy Gregory benefited under a will of a Mrs Rosse who died at his house in 1932, and that the will was forged; this is dealt with by a separate report.

Superintendent Horwell passed this on to the Assistant Commissioner. 'Distleman,' he added grimly, 'is well known to myself and most West End officers as a thief. He will receive close attention.'[8]

As soon as the Honours case was over, Askew's beady eye swivelled back to the Suspicious Death and the allegation of forgery. Motive was certainly present. There was no doubt that last year, Maundy Gregory had been as badly in need of money as he was now. Edith's death could provide it if she left a will in his favour. But he must separate a possible charge of murder from a possible charge of forgery, and this could not be done unless he had more background understanding of Maundy Gregory's personal history, his life at home and his work at 38 Parliament Street. His first appointment, on Thursday 23 February, was with Edith's husband.

Frederick Rosse was a hard-working and sensitive man without much money, whose grasping wife had died. His arrogant solicitors in Lincoln's Inn had told him they were looking after his interests, so he was furious when he discovered that the will had been proven within three weeks of Edith's death. Shamefaced, Mr Betts could only ask Maundy Gregory's solicitors for restitution of taxable income due from the money his client had paid, over eight years, to his late wife.

 Mr Rosse intended to hire new solicitors to get some action. He told the interviewing officer that his wife had been an astute businesswoman, who had owned several properties when he left her,

> …and knowing her thorough business mind I cannot conceive her making such a will as I now know has been admitted to probate…I am convinced that in her normal state of mind my wife would not have used a pencil to make her will and I am not satisfied with the execution of her will which I am given to understand is in the handwriting of Maundy Gregory – in the body of the document.
>
> I certainly think the matter calls for police enquiry…I certainly think the doctor and the housekeeper should be interviewed.[9]

Maybe DCI Askew had not seen that morning's *Daily Sketch* when he began his interview with Mr Rosse, but it was drawn to his attention pretty quickly. For the *Daily Sketch* had printed, under the headline POLICE AND WOMAN'S DEATH SECRET… HER £18,000 WILL, heavy hints about Maundy's involvement in Edith's murder. It pre-empted Askew's enquiry into the death by saying it had officially begun, and gave his own name and those of DS Ruffett and DS Hodge.

He had not yet had permission to devote substantial resources to this and quickly ascertained that the leak had come from Ethel, the garrulous niece. Whether or not he vented his irritation on DS Hodge or DS Ruffett is unknown.

However, Askew put in his report to the Superintendent and initiated background checks on Maundy Gregory's family circumstances. The Head Constable of Winchester later reported back that Mrs Gregory, his mother, was about eighty-four and still comfortably alive at Morley College, and there was a brother, Stephen, in Canada.

Permission for the Suspicious Death enquiry was not forthcoming. It was submitted on 25 February. Ethel Marion Davies had talked to the *Daily Sketch* with intent to spur the Metropolitan Police into action, but publicity had the opposite effect. There was to be *no investigation whatsoever* of the suspicious death between 23 February, the date of the article, and 12 April, the date when – with remission for good conduct – Maundy Gregory would be released. On 25 February Askew wrote a long report to Superintendent Horwell and in conclusion, mentioned that he had given the Davises to understand that they should expect no further police attention.

Somebody powerful enough to postpone a police enquiry made absolutely sure that Maundy Gregory would not be detained on suspicion of murder when he walked out of Wormwood Scrubs. Special Branch, who had his passport number and were put on the alert in February, were given no grounds to renew the order. Nor, oddly, would his creditors file a petition for his Bankruptcy at the High Court until hours after his release, to whereabouts unknown, on that precise date.[10]

At some point, Maundy also became aware of the *Daily Sketch* article. Twelve days before his release, Kenneth Brown, Baker and Baker wrote to the police. They were undertaking a libel action on behalf of their client Mr Gregory against that newspaper and its sister, the *Sunday Graphic*. The *Sketch's* defence was that the allegation was true, and the police were indeed investigating a suspicious death. They requested from the police statements that they were not. On 5 April (7 days before his release) they received permission to interview officers.

Whether or not they did so, the issue remained in abeyance for another five months.

Maundy was in prison throughout March. While the police did nothing, and the commissioners in bankruptcy did nothing, and even Maundy's solicitors did nothing until the last day of March – while they were all supine, Maddin's, a firm of solicitors in Surbiton, was not. Maddin's hired enquiry agents on behalf of their clients Ethel Marion Davies, Frederick W. Davies, and Frederick Rosse.

These agents interviewed Mr Sterling Mackinlay at his home, 41 Portman Mansions. Sterling Mackinlay was a musician, writer and singer from a family that made a living on the stage and by writing and composing. As Malcolm Sterling Mackinlay, a name he sometimes used, he had published a book only last year, oddly enough, called *Enemy Agent*. He described how he and his wife (now on tour) had known Maundy and Edith for many years, having been introduced to them before the War.[11] His wife's letters to Edith late in August had gone unanswered, but she was working in Torquay and did not telephone until her return to London at the end of the month.

Mrs Rosse complained that her eyesight was badly affected and she was not therefore able to write. She then said to my wife 'Oh dear. I cannot say more. I am terribly sick' and my wife heard what appeared to be a telephone receiver drop, and could get no further reply.

She had phoned daily after that, but Maundy told her Edith was too ill to see anyone. On 14 September he rang to tell them she had died and the next day they came to view the body. They attended the funeral, which they had been told would be at Pangbourne but in fact took place at Bisham. So – nothing controversial there.

The men from Maddin's visited Dr Wilson, a Harley Street heart specialist, who had been called in by Mr Levi. They did not succeed in obtaining an interview but Dr Wilson's nurse, going to his diary, said at once 'I remember the case. That was the case where he was called in too late to do anything.'

The next interview is more interesting since it obviously came from a lead obtained elsewhere. This person was the one who preferred to remain anonymous (although he was willing to be subpoenaed if necessary) but who had met Maundy several times during September in connection with 'work on the continent'. Thomson, perhaps? We do not know.

According to the date on Maddin's letter, transcripts of these interviews were sent by Maddin's to Askew on the day of Maundy's release. They refer to other interviews, sent the previous day; but that earlier set of interviews – which might provide a clue to other contacts – is not in the police file.[12]

On 6 April, Maddin's wrote to the Home Office asking for permission to exhume the body.[13]

Early in the morning of 12 April 1933, Maundy Gregory was met out of Wormwood Scrubs by Captain Richard Kelly, whom he knew, in the familiar taxi driven by Bramley. According to Kelly's wife Edith:

> They drove to an address in Kensington where my husband had laid on breakfast. That same evening they drove to Newhaven and boarded the ferry to Dieppe.[14]

According to Edith Kelly, Newhaven was chosen rather than the quicker, more expensive route via Dover so that Gregory could be certain of meeting no-one he knew. In Paris, he registered at the extremely smart Hotel Lotti in the rue de Castiglione, between the rue de Rivoli and the Place Vêndome, where he registered as Peter Michael. He would receive telegrams from Mazzina under that name, and at that address, for at least a year.

J.C.C. Davidson related a similar version of his release:

> When this occurred he was met at the prison gates by a friend of mine who drove him in a motor car to Dover, took him to France, ensconced him in previously arranged accommodation, gave him a sum of money and promised him a quarterly pension, on condition that he never disclosed his identity or made any reference to the past ... Maundy Gregory did keep his word, and as far as we know he never betrayed his identity to the French police or to the public or the people he consorted with in Paris, and we kept him until the end ...[15]

The casual reader might think that 'we' referred to the Conservative Party. Captain Richard Kelly had been Admiral Hall's right-hand man at National Propaganda since 1919. National Propaganda was part of that network of right-wing 'anti-Bolshevik' Diehard Tory organisations that had cemented their relationship with people in the Secret Service during and after the War, the backbone of which in the late 1920s became the Central Economic League – and remained The Economic League until the next millennium. Kelly was now secretary of a similar outfit, the brewery industry's National Publicity Agency, based like other such organisations in the 1930s at 3 and 4, Dean's Yard, Westminster. The NPA is believed to have been the conduit for Maundy's future stipend.

This 7am reception by Captain Kelly indicates where pressure had been coming from. It is believed by some investigators that the aim of these paranoid post Great War diehards had always been to create a 'secret state' – a set of relationships which operated beyond, above and largely unknown to the relatively transparent government machine. In this case, they appear to have succeeded. The extent to which Baldwin and other senior Tories understood this to be their aim is opaque. So is the extent to which people at the British Embassy in Paris protected him. His instructions were 'to install him in an apartment near the British Embassy in Paris, and to look after all of his wants, paying him frequent visits both in Paris and in Dieppe.' After many weeks at the Hotel Lotti, Maundy took a conveniently central apartment and employed a firm of solicitors, Theodore Goddard & Co., well known to British diplomats in Paris and London, to look after his interests in the matter of libel.

CHAPTER SEVENTEEN

Open Verdict

On 12 April 1933 Gregory occupied every corner of the Chief Inspector's well-organised mind. Most annoying was the scoundrel's unimpeded disappearance, with his own passport, within hours of leaving prison and seven weeks after Askew had submitted his report.

Did DCI Askew, one may wonder, never feel that strings were being pulled, somewhere, out of sight? It seems not. He was off on 13 April like a rat out of a trap, instigating enquiries and keeping a watching brief on many fronts at once: Maundy's own libel suit against the *Sketch*; an impending Bankruptcy hearing and associated investigations into the finances of the Deepdene (in liquidation), the Ambassador Club (in liquidation), Peter Mazzina's affairs and Maundy Gregory's affairs; the den of thieves and rascals at the Ambassador Club; the circumstances under which the will had been signed; the financial relationship between Maundy Gregory and Edith Rosse; the possibility of conspiracy to murder, involving Maundy and Dr Plummer; whether or not Edith Rosse had died by foul means; what Maundy had done with the money; whether Edith Rosse had been in her right mind when she signed her will. Add a couple of civil suits which had been simmering when Maundy went to prison, and it was a regular gallimaufry of conflicting arguments and interests.

His men had already obtained copies of Maundy's war record. Dr Plummer had testified at Maundy's request that Edith Rosse's will was perfectly genuine. Were they in cahoots? Had they known each other during the Great War? An officer obtained Plummer's War Office file and it seemed that they had not. Their paths had not crossed at all before 19 August 1933. If Maundy had a co-conspirator, it was unlikely to be Plummer.

On 13 April, DCI Askew and Inspector Nunn interviewed Pengelly, the accountant. It was impossible not to feel sorry for the man. Maundy Gregory had not paid him since November, and he was disabled and out of work. He had a wife and small children and they were being turned out of their home.

Pengelly said some electrifying things. One was that last year – at the time of the furious quarrel between Maundy and Ethel, i.e., in February – Maundy had urged Edith to destroy the (second) will in favour of her niece. He had also tried to borrow money from her and urged her to put some of the money she kept on deposit into more easily realisable War Loan.

Maddin's[1], in their letter to the Home Office, imply that according to Pengelly, the (second) will in favour of Ethel had been torn up in July, 1932. This was a misunderstanding on their part. On 13 April Pengelly said something entirely different and signed it in Askew's presence:

> I did not know that this will [i.e., the one extant in February 1932] had been destroyed until I went to Somerset House after her death and saw the will proved by Mr Gregory.

And – and this was highly suspicious – when, after her death, Pengelly wrote to Maundy asking for Edith's locked diary-cum-cashbook for Inland Revenue purposes, Maundy's confidential secretary Pratley sent the diary to him from Hyde Park Terrace, and Pengelly found that whole chunks were missing:

> I found that pages No 2 to No 14; No 115 to No 132, had been cut out since I had previously seen it about April 1932… About summer time 1932, it was obvious to me that Mr Gregory was getting into financial difficulties.

He had seen those pages, but there is no hint in his statement as to what they might have contained.

Peter Mazzina held Power of Attorney for Maundy in his absence, and Pengelly, who liked to do things by the book, discovered that the Abbey Road Building Society was owed money. A clerk had accidentally paid Maundy, over the counter, a £70 dividend twice. The Abbey Road would like to be repaid.

I took this matter up with his Attorney, who is Peter Mazzina, who told me that once they get money they never return it.

Pengelly was still kept busy working out exactly where the accounts stood.

DS Gillen, meanwhile, was up in Islington taking a statement from Fred Davies's friend William Rombough, who said he had been with Fred when they went together on the bus to Baker Street on 22 August last year to meet Mrs Rosse. He had met Fred's sister before on several occasions, and took the opportunity to go over there to collect some money he was owed by a Mr Gordon, who lived off Baker Street. He was with Fred when Edith turned up at 7.30, looking fine as far as he could see, and when Edith suggested going for a drink at the Globe he made his excuses and left to see Mr Gordon and collect his money.

On the other hand, Mrs Eyres was certain that Mrs Rosse had not left the house that Monday and Dr Plummer said she had not been well enough to go out unaided.

All three housekeepers described the events surrounding the illness, recovery, relapse and death. All mentioned Edith's complaints about her eyesight and her confusion – Mrs Hilda Howard had had a phone conversation with her, ten days after the first collapse, during which Mrs Rosse called her 'Daisy'. Mrs Eyres, who was almost constantly present, was quite specific also about vomiting, restless nights and headaches. She said Mrs Rosse had had eye trouble from the first day of her illness onwards.

The medical men – Mr Levi the surgeon, Dr Parsons-Smith who was called in by Dr Plummer, Dr Plummer himself, and Dr Wilson – placed less emphasis on the symptoms of confusion and poor eyesight which were so evident to Edith Rosse's friends and housekeepers. Dr Parsons-Smith certainly noticed partial paralysis. *Diplopia*, or double vision, is common after a stroke, including the kind of stroke which can take place during sleep; and confusion can result from a number of conditions. Her very high blood pressure was pertinent to all this and again, it seems that Dr Plummer had taken no particular notice of it, if he had even known about it, when he diagnosed sunstroke in August.

Askew was frustrated. To him, the progress of the illness was in doubt, as to some extent was the cause of death.

The police had not searched Maundy Gregory's house. It was only when Ethel Davies, looking around the top two uninhabited floors before the sale of contents, notified Askew of the presence of poisons at 10 Hyde Park Terrace, that he despatched Inspector Nunn to 10 Hyde Park Terrace, whence he removed, on 20 April:

> Twenty-six bottles, mostly labelled with the names of various chemicals including highly toxic substances mercury, nitric acid and lead nitrate. One (copper sulphate) was labelled in German *Kupfersulfat*;
> A couple of jars containing (1) green liquid (2) white substance;
> Three glass holders containing coloured liquid;
> A couple of canisters, one labelled Perhydrol (hydrogen peroxide), and the other Calcium;
> Two retorts, one containing black powder, the other labelled Sand & Mercury;
> Two small cylinders with gas tubing attached;
> Three burners and a quantity of black rubber tubing;
> A tin of Perhydrol;
> A quantity of test tubes, glass jars and bottles;
> A glass methylated lamp;
> A set of metal tubes.[2]

Inspector Nunn took a statement from Mrs Eyres. She knew there was lumber up there, but had never noticed these bottles and jars. Inspector Nunn took the collection to Scotland Yard, where it awaited the attention of someone who knew what it all meant. It would have seemed familiar enough, perhaps, to those such as Korostovetz who were aware of Maundy's fascination with alchemy and the 'gold' made above the Ambassador Club.

To Chief Inspector Askew, the poisons clinched it. The request for an exhumation by Maddin's remained with the Home Office, and now the way forward seemed clear. He wrote a long memo to Superintendent Horwell pointing out the anomalies in the progress of Mrs Rosse's disease, the inadequacy of Dr Plummer's initial diagnosis, Maundy Gregory's motive, his hold over Mrs Rosse, the inadequacy of the way the will was drawn up and signed, the sections cut out of the diary and the despatch with which Maundy Gregory had obtained probate and disposed of the money. All this would go into the balance in favour of an exhumation, and on 27 April, Mr W. Owen C. Stuchberry, Coroner for Berkshire, signed one:

To the Minister and Churchwardens of the Parish of Bisham in the County of Berks
    And to the Constables of the Metropolis and of the said County of Berks.

The body was to be taken up and removed into the jurisdiction of Mr Samuel Ingleby Oddie, Coroner for Central London. It would go to the Paddington mortuary, pending examination and an inquest.

Ingleby Oddie, if he was already aware of the case, may have remembered Maundy Gregory's name. They had both been present at the installation of the Archbishop of York at Christmas, 1922.

On Friday 28 April 1933, Askew and Nunn convened at Bisham graveyard with Dr Roche Lynch the senior Home Office analyst, a Sergeant from Berkshire Constabulary and a representative of Kenyons the Undertakers. The grave was next to the riverside path, surmounted by a white marble cross. In the course of the morning, several representatives of the press trickled in.

Kenyons were sub-contractors for Harrods. Last September they had taken the order from Maundy Gregory, after a preliminary call by Mr Blackmore Beer at 38 Parliament Street, from Maundy Gregory for an expensive lead-lined coffin, into which they had loaded the corpse at 10 Hyde Park Terrace and placed the lid on top – unsealed; when asked about sealing it, Maundy had said 'Oh no, that would seem too final.' He could have been spared that anxiety, had he known that the body would be exposed to prying eyes seven months later.

The gravediggers began work, and a spade struck the coffin within a remarkably short time. Askew had not expected this. To pre-empt seepage of Thames water from the river, only three or four feet down, it had been buried only 18 inches below the surface.

And when the grave was opened, the coffin – after a single winter underground – was not just heavy because of the lead lining, but almost immovable, since it was already waterlogged and lying in sodden ground. Bisham Churchyard can flood, and gravediggers told them that Edith's grave had been underwater that winter. It occurred to Inspector Askew that Maundy knew as much about Thames floods as anyone, having occupied a house on the riverbank every summer for over twenty years.

Today was a damp, chilly spring day and they had to wait for a winch to be set up, by which time there were nine men and a photographer on site. As the coffin's head end was heaved upwards, water poured out. It had engulfed poor Edith over the winter and she remained in her icy, leaden bath when the flood receded. Dr Roche Lynch is said to have muttered a curse. He knew then that the chance of finding any proof of poisoning had floated clean away.

The coffin plate read

> EDITH MARION ROSSE
> Born 22nd March 1873
> Died 14th September 1932
> R.I.P.

Without much hope, Dr Lynch took samples of the water that poured out and of the soil from the grave.

The following morning – a Saturday – Mr Ingleby Oddie opened a Coroner's Court hearing and adjourned it until 25 May, pending the post mortem and pathology reports.

On the same day, Dr Roche Lynch and Sir Bernard Spilsbury saw the coffin opened at Paddington Mortuary. They found the corpse lying in a shallow bath of icy river water.

Frederick Rosse identified his late wife.

Sir Bernard, the most famous, august and prolific pathologist of his day, began the post-mortem. Dr Roche Lynch removed certain organs for testing in his laboratory at St Mary's Hospital.

Maundy's chemistry set was handed over to Dr Roche Lynch on Tuesday 2 May, presumably to give him an idea of what to look for. In the organs, he found nothing. In view of the conditions in which the body had been kept over the winter:

> It is quite possible that certain poisons could have become decomposed, thus rendering their detection impossible.[3]

On the same day Mrs Wells was interviewed again. She had become aware that the chemicals were put upstairs in the summer last year, before Mrs Rosse's illness, and thought that they came from Maundy Gregory's office. But Mr Pratley would know more about that. She had had no occasion to go up to the top two floors.

Publicity surrounding the exhumation and suspicions about Maundy Gregory brought forth Miss Weakley, of Ramsgate, and Hugh Jervoise Donaldson, now a policeman in Malaya. Edith Rosse had placed an advertisement for a companion in the *Morning Post* in 1930 and had exchanged letters with Miss Weakley afterwards, although nothing had come of it; Hugh Donaldson had known Maundy, Edith and Ethel and had been meaning to see Edith at around the time of her illness. Both provided background information, though neither had anything pertinent to say about Mrs Rosse's death.

Askew could do little more but wait, and hope that the Coroner would conclude this was Murder by a Person or Persons Unknown. *Then* he could do something. He heard towards the end of May that Ingleby Oddie had decided to postpone the inquest until 28 June. Frederick Rosse, and other potential witnesses, were informed. Just before the date in June, the Inquest was postponed again until late July.

Frederick Rosse was irritated. Although in his late 60s, he was still – of necessity – working, and needed more advance notice than he was getting of the need to appear. Of Maundy Gregory, there was no sign.

Inspection of A. J. Maundy-Gregory's accounts, under the terms of the Creditors' Petition for Bankruptcy, commenced on Tuesday 2 May. By the time it was complete two weeks later two things were obvious. One was that he had accomplished the con man's favourite trick of building trust, and then suddenly whisking the rug from under his creditors' feet. Some of his debts were so enormous that they could only have been incurred by a man who had often paid similar sums on the nail.

The second obvious deduction was that if the debtor had any money, nobody could find it.

At various banks, he had unsecured overdrafts of £3,150. The National Provincial was owned £1,500 for a loan 'on lease of' 10 Hyde Park Terrace – though it is unclear whether this was secured against the lease. The National Provincial did hold first charge over his launch *Vigilate*.

He owed nearly £300 to the tax man, not counting his personal tax liability which Mr Pengelly had not yet calculated. The Sun Life Assurance company was owed £544; the Paddington Estate was due £87.10s in rent due last Christmas for Number 10 and unpaid rates on the property amounted to £63. Pontifex Pitt & Co., solicitors and agents for 38 Parliament Street, hadn't been paid for the Christmas quarter so they were missing £211. He owed about £6 for electricity at Parliament Street, £29 for the installation of electricity in the bungalows at Thames Ditton, and £25 to the Gas, Light and Coke Company. A firm of electricians in Berners Street was owed £93.

Christmas had been expensive. He was famous for his extravagant gifts, and Edith's death had made no difference. He had run up a bill of £892 at the Goldsmiths' and Silversmiths' Company (this at a time when a working man might take home £2 a week and many families lived on that much.) At Plante, Jewellers, he had incurred a debt of £800, at Cartier, £389, and at L.G. Sloan, £41 for pens. At other shops he had bought cigars to the value of £160, walking sticks for £39, field glasses for £20, and objets d'art worth £7.

When things got tough, the tough went shopping. He owed his wine merchant £107, his optician £46, his shirtmaker £23, his bootmaker £5, and £38 and £25 to two different tailors. His slate at the Carlton Hotel Restaurant amounted to £95.

There were unpaid business expenses: for *Burke's Landed Gentry* the design of arms (£15); 'disbursements' £3; and £50 in unpaid salary to Harry Pirie-Gordon. At the *Whitehall Gazette* he owed £10 to Dr Whymant for translations (Dr Neville Whymant was an eminent Sinologist and writer on Mandarin and Mongolian, and the Sino-Japanese war was going on at the time); and £21 to Professor O'Connor for 'literary contributions'. Various blockmakers, printers, and stationers together were owed £832.

His lifestyle choices had meant keeping up appearances. The Victory Garage was owed £550 for car hire. Then came the maintenance of the various properties: gardeners and a decorator, an agent for the Thames Ditton bungalows, a plumber – adding another £10 or so. There was an outstanding phone bill of £20. A picture framer had not been paid £47; Harts, Boatbuilders, were due £155. Booksellers and newsagents were due about £85, of which £80 was owed to Dulau the booksellers.

Maundy owed £500 to each of three firms of solicitors: Kenneth Brown, Baker & Baker, Leach Sims, and Woolf & Woolf. He had prevailed upon Henry Merckel, of Kenneth Brown, to make him a personal loan of £250, never repaid. There was also a 'final call' for £250 from Technical Investigations Ltd. There were other debts. Ethel claimed against the estate, as did Frederick Rosse, of course, and the executors of Daniel Radcliffe. Over twenty years before Radcliffe, a businessman well known at Cardiff docks, had been a valuable supporter of Scott's Antarctic expedition, and a correspondent of Scott's on his voyage. How he had the misfortune to meet Maundy remains a mystery.

Dr Plummer had not received his £10 attendance fee and Harrods had not had the £82 for Edith's funeral. And the tax man was still waiting for £1,750 outstanding in Legacy Duty.[4]

Creditors (like Pengelly) were still adding their names to the list when their first meeting took place at Carey Street on 16 May 1933. They resolved, unsurprisingly, to have A.J.M. Gregory declared bankrupt. Mr F.S. Salaman was to be appointed Trustee in Bankruptcy, at a fee to be decided by a Committee of Inspection. This committee would consist of Mr Moses, from Langton's, Military and Naval

Tailors (had Maundy been re-outfitting the staff at Number 38?), Mr Marsh from the Goldsmiths & Silversmiths Company, and Mr H. Allen Pratt, an executor of the will of Daniel Radcliffe. The order of bankruptcy was obtained a week later; the following Monday, the Committee and the Trustee met to decide their next move.

They were pretty bullish at this stage. They were going to instruct Goldman's, lawyers, to petition for extradition. In the presence of a person from Goldman's the Trustee would formally interview Pratley, Mazzina and Pengelly, as well as Mr Blackmore Beer and Mr Bissett who had both worked at 38 Parliament Street. And if they couldn't get Gregory extradited, Mr Salaman would go over to Paris in person and confront him.

On 9 June 1933 they met again. The plot had thickened. Mr Salaman had an idea that some money might be owing which, if they could get their hands on it, would fill up the bankrupt coffers. They now proposed to interview a Mr George Ansley 'to ascertain the circumstances with regard to the payment to the latter of £12,000 on 20 January 1933.' This would be a formal interview carried out by a barrister.

The order for bankruptcy was granted. The Debtor failed to appear at a public examination so it was postponed indefinitely. The summer rolled by and further hopes of money sprang up here and there; there might be something due under the will of a Mr Holland; Mr Farrow owed £500 on a bill of exchange. Mr Farrow's solicitors were evidently as dozy as Mr Betts had been, or they would have made his position clear by now.

The executors of Daniel Radcliffe got £2,000, and the outstanding assets would realise at least £5,000. Mr George Ansley paid £2,000 and their costs. At the end of 1933 the Committee had collected some debts, but decided to spend a bit of money in pursuance of some more.

They thought about trying to get something back from Sir George Watson's executors. They were claiming money which had been both paid and demanded by someone who had commissioned a service illegally, which service had never been delivered. The legal arguments were like looking into a hall of mirrors.

On that cold April day when Edith's corpse was loaded off the back of a truck at Paddington Mortuary, matters had seemed relatively straightforward; to Sir Bernard Spilsbury at least. He examined 150 murdered corpses between 1926 and 1939, having begun his glittering career with the very dead Mrs Crippen. Edith was almost too decomposed to come to a decision about. Anything indicative of poisoning – the forensic pathology on her organs – was up to Dr Roche Lynch in his laboratory at St Mary's.

The two men did their work. The body was re-interred. Dr Roche Lynch had the opportunity to revisit his results as the inquest was postponed from May to June, then from June to July. Ethel, whose indignant appearance at Scotland Yard in February had prompted the whole thing, must have been on tenterhooks. Maundy Gregory, in Paris, is said to have role-played, with friends, rehearsals for his appearance at the Old Bailey on a murder charge.

On Wednesday 19 July, Ingleby Oddie at last opened the proceedings. Sir Bernard Spilsbury testified that he could not ascertain the cause of death. The Coroner asked:

> 'Could you say whether there had been any haemorrhage of the brain?'
> 'There had not.'
> 'Were there any signs of Bright's disease?'
> 'No.'
> 'Is it a fact that the death certificate is quite wrong?'
> 'Yes.'

Spilsbury was adamant.

Dr Roche Lynch said he had found no trace of poison, although he qualified this with gruesome remarks about the body's advanced state of decomposition. He pointed out – in so many words – that seven months underground, several of them spent underwater, would have made a lot of poisons disappear or decompose, too.

So that was that. Ingleby Oddie concluded:

All I will say is that no poison has been found, and no poison will ever be found in this body. Therefore no possible charge could arise out of this enquiry.[5]

He pronounced an Open Verdict, the newspapermen rushed off to file their copy, and in Paris, Maundy gave an interview to a reporter from the *Daily Express*. There were no inconsistencies in his story, nothing that did not fit with what other observers had said. Motive was of course missing, although those who knew the state of his finances would have seen it clearly enough. And it would have been pretty stupid for a poisoner to leave his poisons kit lying about. But people believed he was a villain.

In July 1933, Mr Cocks, a Labour MP, smelled a conspiracy. He asked questions in the House. Why had Scotland Yard abandoned the case? He did not get a satisfactory answer, and nor did DCI Askew, who remained convinced to the end of his days that Maundy Gregory was a murderer.

Did Maundy like Edith? Yes. He may have been furiously angry at her ingratitude when she refused to give him money, but this is different from wishing she was dead and a million miles from being willing to commit murder. In 1932 murder was a capital offence. He could surely never have risked a cold early-morning walk to the gallows at Pentonville.

In order to gain a definitive appraisal of Mrs Rosse's final illness and cause of death, Professor Derrick Pounder, Head of Forensic Medicine at Dundee University and a senior government pathologist, was asked by this author to undertake a review of the original Autopsy Report and forensic evidence. Professor Pounder is one of the country's leading forensic pathologists and is regularly called upon to give expert testimony in major criminal cases which have included the trial of mass murderer Dr Harold Shipman. In Mrs Rosse's case, he has seen the statements of all the medical personnel, the housekeepers and others who testified to the progress of the illness; and also the reports of Spilsbury and Roche Lynch that were placed before the Coroner's Court. As he points out:

The diagnosis and approach to this case has to be viewed in
the light of the fact that it occurred seventy-five years ago . . .
Her doctors would have recognised she was suffering from a
condition which was inevitably going to kill her but they would
have had little understanding of the disease process and would
have had no effective treatment available to offer.[6]

Askew failed to nail down the medical diagnosis in his mind, then,
because the doctors themselves only vaguely understood what they
found. In support of this is Maundy's own fuzzy impression of what
he had been told: he wrote about a 'heart-stroke' to Frederick Rosse
– a term which even a layman would query nowadays.

Professor Pounder seized immediately on the statement of Dr
Parsons-Smith 'which is a treasure-trove of factual information of
considerable medical importance.' Parsons-Smith (unlike Plummer)
looked at Edith's medical history of high blood pressure. It was
184/124 – which places her 'in the modern category of severe
hypertension and and just below the threshold for a diagnosis of
malignant hypertension (the threshold being 130 diastolic).' Her
headaches, difficulties with vision and vomiting are all associated with
this level of hypertension.

She also had kidney disease, as shown by albumen in the urine.
Professor Pounder's explanation of this, summarised, is as follows. A
patient can have severe hypertension, period; or she can have severe
hypertension as a consequence of something else, including kidney
disease – and Edith Rosse had had recurrent, sometimes severe,
cystitis, which often leads to kidney infection. or, conversely, she can
have kidney disease as a consequence of severe hypertension. Today a
doctor would be more specific, but in 1932 to name kidney disease
generally as 'chronic Bright's disease' on a death certificate was 'not
unreasonable' in Professor Pounder's view.

Dr Plummer's definition of cause of death as a stroke was equally
reasonable, though as Askew suspected, not definitive. Plummer
would not have been able to tell, from his simple visual examination,
whether she had had a cerebral haemorrhage (bleeding into the brain)
or a cerebral infarction (lack of blood to part of the brain.)

Spilsbury, at the court, was absolutely certain that there had *not* been a cerebral haemorrhage. In Professor Pounder's view, while Spilsbury could have excluded cerebral haemorrhage he 'would not have been able to exclude cerebral infarction as a cause of stroke.' Nor would he, given the state of the organs after seven months, have been able to exclude all kinds of kidney disease.

I therefore harbour a strong suspicion that the brief dogmatic assertions of Spilsbury were not as firmly founded in scientific fact as a casual reader might think. . . I should add that Spilsbury has not been well thought of for some decades by forensic pathologists. He was a formidable witness and it was said of him that he could readily convince a jury of a wrong theory. He had a habit of making statements supportive of the prosecution which were unsustainable from a scientific point of view.

He draws attention to two articles. One is in the American Heart Journal (August, 2001) and contrasts current with past practice in treating hypertension. In 1928, a group of American researchers 'used the term malignant hypertension for the first time in the English literature,' dividing their patients into four groups, of whom the worst sufferers (Group IV) had 'cotton-wool exudates, haemorrhages, oedema of the optic discs' and a 90 per cent mortality at 1.5 years.[7] This would seem to me, as a layman, to have a lot in common with Edith's symptoms, although we may question whether, in 1932, any London specialist – and Dr Parsons-Smith was a heart specialist – would have seen the American research.

The other article, from the Journal of the American College of Cardiology in 2000, points out that not only did doctors at that time not take hypertension particularly seriously, but systolic hypertension, in particular, was not understood as a risk factor for cardio-vascular disease. There was a vague perception that people with high diastolic pressure died young but high systolic pressure was thought to be a consequence of ageing. Edith had always claimed to suffer from heart problems yet the cardiac specialist, Dr Parsons-Smith, could not pronounce a definite link between heart disease and blood pressure.

Professor Pounder adds that today the police would routinely have obtained an independent assessment of the medical diagnosis, and that 'most of the chemicals which are described as being found in the residence contain heavy metals which would have been readily detectable at autopsy had they been present.'

I have given only the substance of Professor Pounder's thorough and pellucid explanation. He concludes:

This is a death from natural causes and not a poisoning.

For the rest of his life, Maundy Gregory was reputed to have got away with murder. In the 1960s Gerald Hamilton wrote confidently about Maundy Gregory's reputation as a man who had murdered 'his wife'. Gerald Macmillan, in his 1954 book *Honours for Sale,* was uncertain either way but wouldn't have put it past him. A lady interviewed by Tom Cullen early in the 1970s remembered how he had told her he had some curare, and was fascinated by the idea of the perfect murder; he explained, further, that curare was soluble in water so no trace would ever be found. This made even Tom Cullen, an otherwise level-headed researcher, look a second time at Mrs Eyres' account of the bottle and two glasses she cleared away the morning after Edith's second seizure. But curare must be injected to work.[8]

Maundy did not murder Edith, but it is quite likely that when she fell ill, he took the opportunity not to get mad, but to get even. She was confused, and he could have double-crossed her over the will. He was, as we know, the sort of passive-aggressive thief who takes from the trusting, and never gives back.

The fact is, at the start of 1932 there was a will in Ethel's favour, and in September 1932, there was a pencilled menu card leaving everything to Maundy Gregory. It was not forged, but it seems that Maundy Gregory lodged it at Somerset House and did not mention it again until he knew she was safely dead. He then realised Mrs Rosse's assets (some of which may have been his own in all but name anyway) extremely fast and kept all the money.

Where was it now? Money other than the quarterly stipend from the National Publicity Agency may have reached the fugitive in Paris. Askew noted that Peter Mazzina had taken £250 to Paris for him in the summer.

Maundy began to frequent the bar of the Hotel Meurice. He engaged Theodore Goddard & Co to continue his case against the *Daily Sketch* and it was settled out of court in November, 1933; none of the lawyers would tell Askew's men how much the settlement was.[9]

Towards the end of the year the Trustee in Bankruptcy sold *Burke's Landed Gentry* for £250. Georgian terraces, Early and Late, were being demolished all over central London at the time, and the Paddington Estate decided to sell numbers 9 and 10 to property developers. Dr Roche Lynch and Sir Bernard Spilsbury put their invoices in, and were paid. The Home Office forked out for Edith's funeral, which had Maundy known, would have made him chuckle.

The newspapers moved on, over the Christmas period, to other things.

At 10 Downing Street, Ramsay Macdonald had been Prime Minister for nearly five years. He kept copious diaries and the following, from the last weeks of 1933, is of particular interest to followers of the Maundy Gregory 'Honours Scandal':

13 December.
This entry is especially private but in my own interest I must make the record. Baldwin came into Cabinet Room in the morning, sat down and straight away asked what I had against Julian Cahn. I said he was one of those Honours hunters whom I detested, and his friends and agents had beset me for a long time for a baronetcy for him, that he was not a commendable person, that he had put money into *Everyman* stating that it was in my interests – in short just the man whom I should not dream of honouring. I had let it be known that do what he might no recommendation for an honour to him would be put up by me. B replied that I must yield and when I asked why he said that Maundy Gregory's papers and Maundy Gregory's presence here would stir up such a filthy sewer as would poison public life, that many innocent persons had become indirectly involved; that all parties were involved

(I corrected him at once and said 'Not ours.' He smiled and said that unfortunately friends of mine were. I replied that if they were I knew nothing about it. Then I remembered that Clynes and Henderson were mentioned at an earlier stage); that people like Winston Churchill, Austen Chamberlain, Birkenhead were involved; that Gregory had been used by Ll.G and Bonar Law; that his subscription lists for the rebuilding of St George's Chapel Windsor were involved; and several other things. Gregory, as indeed I knew, was a blackguard who netted innocent people who did nothing that was irregular or bad, but worse associations with those who had surrounded [?] them in a cloud. The dunghill had to be cleared away without delay and £30,000 were required to do it. So I *had* to give him the honour. I pointed out that if I did so, the many people who know of Cahn's baits to me would say at once that he had made one tempting enough and I had taken it, and that in order to do what he wanted I should have to accept odium and be quite unable to explain it away. I asked him to consider the matter for a day and see me again.

15 December.
Saw Baldwin as above and he agreed to postpone till next list (May).[10]

Sir Julian Cahn had provided the £30,000 required by the National Publicity Agency for its £2,000 p.a. payments to Maundy Gregory.

CHAPTER EIGHTEEN

Sanctuary

Paris was not altogether comfortable for the first year or so, because Maundy was lying low to dodge his creditors and there was a warrant out for his arrest.[1] Although he seems never to have left the Hotel Lotti, he was not to be found, and early in 1934, the Trustee's solicitors took Foreign Office advice on how to engage an agent in France who would bring him before a *commission rogatoire*.[2]

Mr Salaman, Mr Moses, Mr Pratt and Mr Marsh worked doggedly to advance the interests of the banks, tradesmen and others to whom Maundy owed money by re-possessing everything he had paid for, and not received, including things he might have paid for illegally. Mr Salaman went to France (the expenses of the trip having been fixed at 25 guineas) and bearded the monster in his lair. Much joy it got him. He returned with more questions for the executors of Sir George Watson, Drummonds Bank, Mr Pengelly and Mr Korostovetz.

They settled on an agreement with the executors of Mr H.R.H. Holland; they had got some pictures back from Peter Mazzina; they had paid a few guineas to Mr Pengelly and Mr Beer, for their time; and they slowly prepared to pay a dividend.

The Patriarch of Jerusalem had received money from Maundy in 1932, in connection with the Order of the Holy Sepulchre – but Pengelly got to him before the Trustee. Pengelly had hung onto Maundy's crossed cheques when they came back from the bank, and – desperate for money at Christmas 1933 – had written to His Beatitude to say that:

Certain members of the Press have asked me to have these cheques in order to photograph them for publication in the newspapers. I should be glad to know if you have any objection to my doing this.[3]

The Patriarch's secretary, the Rev. Alexander Kirby, gave as good as he got in reply:

> We think it would not be wise to publish these cheques, since it might oblige us to publish also letters signed by prominent persons referring to money paid to Mr Maundy Gregory for the Order. The cheques sent to Mr Maundy Gregory appear to be personal gifts, according to letters we have in our possession.

Pengelly was not deterred. Sensationally (in his letter of 9 January 1934, read out in court later) he said he was sorry to insist, but so far as the cheques were concerned,

> I am compelled by force of circumstances to make use of them for the following reasons. Maundy Gregory owes me several hundreds of pounds for fees and emoluments, of which I cannot obtain one penny. In consequence my home is sold up, my family are in great poverty and distress, we are suffering hunger, cold, and degradation through the evil brought on us by Maundy Gregory. My two-year-old son is continually crying for food, but I am without the means of purchasing any. Therefore I have decided on advice to publish a book describing my experiences covering 12 years with Maundy Gregory, giving the inside story of his dealings with honours and titles, British and foreign. In order to verify my statements I am having the cheques photographed and reproduced in the book. Arrangements have been made with the publishers, because I must obtain sums for my family ... If you are prepared to assist me financially I will withold publication of the matter so far as the Order of the Holy Sepulchre is concerned, and stop reproduction of the cheques.[4]

DCI Askew arrested him. Thirty-nine cheques were found, among which were two, for £500 each, to the Patriarch of Jerusalem, signed J. Maundy Gregory.

In court in March, 1934, the Rev Kirby utterly denied the defence's contention that these sums had been paid for Knighthoods of the Order of the Holy Sepulchre. The Recorder was not satisfied and dug deeper, but in the end, dropped it. Pengelly testified that he had dealt with Mr Gregory's business affairs for twelve years, including the Order of the Holy Sepulchre and the auditing of the accounts of the Ambassador Club. He had been approached by newspapers around the time of the trial in February, just over a year ago. He had not had any intention whatever of 'menacing' the Patriarch. He felt his state of mind had been such that his judgement was clouded at the time he wrote the letter.

The Recorder was sympathetic, but the jury did not even leave the box to confer, and he had to say:

> I hoped the jury would have recommended you to mercy. They have not done so, but I will pass a merciful sentence. You will go to prison for six months in the second division.[5]

So much for blackmail. The Trustee, on the other hand, pursued the Patriarch of Jerusalem's profits through the courts. He obtained an order that a notice be served, in Palestine, upon His Beatitude Luigi Barlassina in relation to payments made by Maundy Gregory in March, June and July, 1932 'for which, it was alleged, there was no consideration' so the Trustee wanted them back 'under section 42 of the Act of 1914.' Signor Barlassina never appeared.

The executors of Sir George Watson also faced the wrath of the Trustee. Their barrister protested that ' . . . there can be no claim by the trustee to have any part of the £30,000 repaid. The trustee has no better title than the bankrupt would have had, and it is quite clear that the bankrupt himself could not in any circumstances recover this money or any part of it.' Justice Clauson ruled that Mr Norton, the representative executor, had questions to answer. And on 6 July he did. He agreed that the whole sum had been repaid.

It was further alleged that Mr Norton had found notes pencilled by Sir George Watson – from 1923 onwards and after – indicating that Sir George had paid Maundy Gregory in hopes of obtaining an honour. Mr Norton refused to answer any questions about that. According to legal precedent, sums advanced in an illegal transaction could be recovered by the Trustee in bankruptcy; but in this case, certain conditions were unmet, and the action failed.[6]

At the end of July, 1934, the Trustee agreed to pay 10s in the £1.

On 1 August, 1934, Superintendent Arthur Askew – he had been promoted – wrote to the Assistant Commissioner, bringing to his notice a letter, just arrived, from Miss E. Marion Davies of 76 Upper Gloucester Place, W1. Ethel had at one time claimed as a creditor, but had been induced to desist. She now informed interested parties that Maundy Gregory was still living at the Hotel Lotti as 'Peter Michael' and Peter Mazzina sent telegrams to him under that name. She continued:

> From Mr Byford of 5j, Hyde Park Mansions, W1, information has reached me this weekend that just before December a £30,000 transaction was passed through to Paris for MG by Peter Mazzina – and he is living in the lap of luxury. This business was done through a man in Hove.

Supt. Askew pointed out to the Assistant Commissioner that:

> After receipt of the letter I had a telephone message from Mr Compton, Assistant Official Receiver in Bankruptcy, who had received a similar letter from Miss Davies. Mr Compton informed me that so far as the Bankruptcy Court is concerned the position of Maundy Gregory's affairs remains unchanged and the latter's return to England is still awaited.

The man Byford (known as 'Biff') is a suspected receiver and was believed to have been engaged at one time with Peter Mazzina at the Ambassador Club in deals with stolen jewellery. Having this in mind it is interesting to note that Miss Davies mentions a man at Hove which is the town at which John William Bell resides.[7]

'Biff' Byfield we must assume was a fence; interestingly, living in a flat once owned by Edith (or Maundy). As for the £30,000, would he lie to Ethel? Of course he would. She would believe anything about Maundy. She still believed he had murdered her aunt. If this new £30,000 ever existed, it effected no difference in Maundy Gregory's lifestyle. £30,000 would have been enough to buy an elegant house in Paris at that time. He moved to a nice apartment, which he rented. Of John William Bell, whose existence was such anathema to Arthur Askew, we know nothing.

In fact nothing much came of any of it; the shouting and fighting, the bulging files and indignant letters, the expenses claims and mortifying revelations, the resentments and the celebrations of Maundy's career as an honours tout, gradually died away. Maundy stayed in his modestly opulent flat in Paris, Ethel in discontented obscurity in London. The last note in the Bankruptcy file is from early 1935. Mr Farrow had reached an agreement with the Committee of Inspection. There would be a settlement with him, on the understanding that that the Trustee would pay Mr Farrow's costs.

Mr Farrow in 1936 married Miss Maureen O'Sullivan and had seven children, among them Maria de Lourdes Villiers (Mia) Farrow, whose deep faith in Our Lady of Perpetua would be no bar to her marrying and divorcing Frank Sinatra, André Previn, and Woody Allen in turn.

Maundy had just one other remarkable connection with Hollywood. In 1941, a classic film had appeared: *The Maltese Falcon*, from a novel by Dashiell Hammett. Hammett had been working for Pinkerton's in 1922, when William Pinkerton himself – he knew the eponymous boss – came to London, and spoke at the Savoy in the presence of senior policemen such as Basil Thomson. When the film was released in England, many remarked upon the similarities between the preoccupations, preferences and mannerisms of Gutman, The Fat Man, as played by Sidney Greenstreet, and Maundy Gregory. Gutman was mysterious, somehow threatening, telling long conspiratorial stories about magical powers and the Knights Templar; in the plot, he is a con man who engages others to pursue a McGuffin – a solid gold falcon encrusted with precious jewels which proves (like Maundy's gold leaf at Westminster Abbey) to be faked. Greenstreet, oddly enough, had been – in younger, slimmer years – in Ben Greet's company and on the London stage where he had crossed paths with Maundy. He worked in both England and America, and appears to have spent the war years in England, as well as a great deal of time between 1927 and 1933.

The old rogue Maundy, or 'Peter Michael', having been hunted down by the Trustee in 1934 and yet remained safe, felt he could move on. He reinvented himself as Sir Arthur Gregory and resurfaced at an elegant apartment at 8 rue d'Anjou. This was the old *hôtel privé* where the Marquis de Lafayette died in 1834.

An apparently genuine letter to Donald McCormick, mentioned previously in chapter six, gives some background here. McCormick's researcher Frank Dorsey of the *International Herald Tribune*, living at Yvelines, reported in 1969:

> I had an interesting half-hour talk with Maître Jean-Jacques Grumbach, the lawyer who knew Gregory. Here is what he told me:
>
> Grumbach's parents had an antique shop in the courtyard of the building . . . and an apartment on the third floor. They set their son up, when he began to practise law at the age of twenty-four, in a small, luxurious apartment across the hall from theirs. But clients were slow in coming, so the young lawyer needed to sell off the expensive furniture and find cheaper quarters. He ran an ad, and Gregory answered it. This was in 1935 or 1936.
>
> Gregory, who seemed very much in funds, bought the furniture and took over the lease. He got to be on friendly terms with the Grumbach parents. When young Grumbach was in the building he occasionally had a drink with Gregory.

He liked someone to talk English with. Young Grumbach was glad of a chance to practise his English. (Incidentally, he speaks it almost perfectly today. He said he spent a lot of time working on it while he was a prisoner of war.)

Grumbach saw Gregory as a very kindly old gentleman, a little crotchety and set in his ways, a typical old bachelor. Very fond of whisky. He spoke little of his past except to tell stories of his travels in the Far East. The Grumbachs assumed he was a superior civil servant on a pension. He spoke of knowing important people.

Grumbach senior once told his son he thought there was some kind of mystery about Gregory because he disclosed so little about himself, and speculated that Gregory might have been in the Secret service.

Gregory spoke of writings he had published, but Grumbach does not remember if it was books, or magazines, or newspaper articles.[8]

Apart from whisky, conversation, the company of his beloved dog and frequent visits to the Eglise de la Madeleine around the corner from his flat, Gregory was bored. The English newspapers, out of date anyway, contained no good news. Peter Mazzina was declared bankrupt and was sent to jail for non-payment of debt. So was the Vicar of Stiffkey. Then the Vicar of Stiffkey was exhibited in a barrel at Blackpool . . . had slept on a bed of nails... Suddenly, the Vicar of Stiffkey had been eaten by a lion at Skegness . . . How *awful*. Poor Jumbo, putting his head in the lion's mouth in order to raise a few more pounds for the Fighting Fund against the Bishop of Norwich, had it almost torn off.

Otherwise, like Lloyd George in his own retirement, Maundy needed to be at the centre of power and intrigue and without either, he felt rather lost. He harked back to the old days and never learned French. It was apparently Captain Kelly who had spotted the advertisement for 8 rue d'Anjou. It was a bachelor flat: an entrance hall and one big room, with kitchen and bathroom attached, high ceilings, smart furniture and a grand piano which he played for visitors. He had friends, but because of his hopeless French and his secrets (he was ever mindful of the arrest warrant) he remained a rather lonely figure.

Like the First World War, the second caught him unprepared. He could have escaped, with a little effort, at the start. Early in 1939 he and Monsieur le Beau took up semi-permanent residence in Dieppe, to be near to some friends, the d'Roubaix family. It was conveniently close to England and he went home for a visit; in May, MI5 got his Paris address and phone number from Mr Blackmore Beer.[9] The war began, the blackout started, and Maundy and a disreputable Irish crony of his took to drinking in Dieppe's bars and tottering home hilariously through pitch darkness. He made friends with some English officers in the town and some reported him as a suspected German spy. MI5 asked the French police to intercept his mail for scrutiny. Maundy Gregory was not a spy.[10] He had nothing good to say of the Germans. A rather lost figure, he took consolation in whisky, religion and the happy family life he found with the d'Roubaix household. He stayed in their clifftop home when his lodgings were bombed out. Cullen has a marvellous description of him in those days:

> The man in the fur coat tugging at the little brown Pomeranian as they made their way haltingly along the promenade became a familiar sight to the Dieppois in that twilight period known as the *drôle de guerre*. The fur coat was of a long-haired variety and reached down nearly to his ankles, giving Maundy Gregory the appearance of an ambulatory caterpillar.[11]

He had gout in one leg, had lost a lot of weight, and had aged in every way. It is difficult to remember that when he arrived in France he was fifty-six, an age when men nowadays run marathons and cycle to work. During the phoney war of 1939-40, he was sixty-two, but seemed ten years older. People loved him for his generosity; he was kind and made extravagant gifts. Back in Paris, all anyone knew of his income was the arrival of a monthly brown-paper parcel of cash, sent by registered mail from England. With the start of war, they stopped coming.

With a German invasion imminent, Captain Kelly offered him the chance to spend the war at his family home in East Sussex – but the outstanding warrant for his arrest dissuaded him. He was going to join Ronnie Russell, the barman, in Paris and decide what to do from there. While he prevaricated, trains to Paris stopped running. The last sighting of him, on 26 May 1940 as the Germans rolled in and people closed their doors or fled, was by Peter Taylor at the British Consulate:

> Maundy managed to get hold of a bicycle from somewhere, and had it fitted up with a basket on the handlebars for his dog, Monsieur le Beau. I saw them start out on that Sunday morning on the road to Rouen, Maundy with his fur coat flapping around him, wobbling uncertainly as he tried to get his balance, the dog yapping furiously at the unaccustomed indignity of the basket...I wondered if they would get beyond the outskirts of Dieppe.[12]

Somehow Gregory and his dog appear to have come across a Parisian dentist and his family. Maybe he simply could not face another minute on the bike; maybe they told him Paris was too dangerous; but he accepted their offer of transport to the wilds of Britanny. Alighting – apparently at random – at Mme Yvinec's Hôtel Belle-Vue in Châteauneuf-du-Faou, an unremarkable inland town far to the west, he and M le Beau became non-paying guests. This was *la France profonde*, where local women still wore coifs and some of the old people spoke Breton. Sir Arthur was very good company and Mme Yvinec was most impressed by the tone he lent to her establishment, though money was always about to arrive. He registered as M. de Grégoire.

He turned up at the very beginning of June, just before the Occupation began. Within weeks, the German customs service arrived in force to set up a checkpoint in the town, which was on a contraband route from Quimper and Brest to the rest of France. German customs men were billeted in thirteen of the hotel's rooms, the other four being left to the family and M. de Grégoire. Then began months of concealment. Maundy's French would not have convinced even a German. He could not risk running into one of these people. He hid in his room, where the maid brought his meals; to go to the bathroom he wore a bandage around his face, as though he had toothache and could not speak. When the troops periodically changed at the garrison in the town, all billets were inspected, so he then concealed himself in the attics. Sometimes he had to remain there for days on end.

After many months of this, very warily, as winter came on and the evenings grew dark, Maundy began making quick trips out into the town with M le Beau. Early in November a local shopkeeper, a collaborator, finally remarked upon his existence to one of the German customs men. They really had thought he was French. But of course the whole town knew he was not. He was arrested the following morning. They were going to take him away and he pleaded to be allowed to keep his little dog.

Dogs were not acceptable. Maundy Gregory was loaded onto the back of a lorry going east; to his enormous relief Mme Yvinec promised to look after M le Beau. Sir Arthur, visibly upset, promised that his pet would be his security for his unpaid bill.

Drancy camp, a complex of hideous blocks in north-east Paris, became notorious from August 1941 as a point of departure for French prisoners on their way to the labour camps and gas chambers. In these early stages of the Occupation it was an internment camp from which some, although not of course the British contingent, were allowed to leave. Gregory's fur coat and fur sabots made him the envy of everyone; that winter was freezing. But he was seriously ill, and early in 1941 he was admitted to the prison hospital. After a few months he was transferred to the St Denis internment camp.

Ronnie Russell, the barman from the Meurice, was a prisoner at St Denis camp when he saw the name 'Arthur Gregory' on a list of newcomers. St Denis was slightly less regimented than Drancy and Maundy was able to get little bottles of whisky smuggled in. A prisoner later testified that he was 'a very sick man, fussy, erratic and secretive.' He lasted through the summer, but in August 1941, he collapsed and was taken to the Val de Grâce military hospital, on the left bank.

The hospital records state that he was 'in a very bad general condition, absolutely fleshless with notable dwindling of the muscles and a swollen liver.' There on Saturday 21 September he made his will. A typed copy is all that remains:

> I leave everything I possess in England, France and any other else place to Marcel d'Roubaix Bulger, my dearest friend. This will cancels all other wills codicils and documents.

> AMG

> Arthur John Maundy Gregory (Sir Arthur)
>   It is witnessed by Benzion Samuel Homesky of 74 Avenue des Champs Elysées.

On the reverse was written

> Marcel d'Roubaix Bulger
> Resident in Dieppe many years

> A J Maundy Gregory

In French there is a note to say 'Sir Maundy Gregory was in possession of all his faculties at the moment when this document was signed.' Lieutenant Dr Le Bayon signed below, the following Tuesday; 12 March, 1942, the document was countersigned by a senior doctor whose name is illegible.

Maundy's form of words demonstrates the lasting effect of his experience. Unlike Edith, he was careful to specify that this will cancelled all previous ones. Also, he got a medical witness to state, as soon as possible after he made the will, that he was in his right mind.

On 28 September, the Saturday after he wrote his will, he died. He was buried at Ivry and remained underground rather longer than Edith. When the plot's unpaid bills had mounted over five years, his remains were disinterred and placed in an ossuary.

'Sir Arthury Gregory's' flat at the rue d'Anjou had been emptied as early as June 1940 by a man who presented the card of M. Février, a Parisian dentist from 106 Avenue Kléber. This man had a key to the property, which Maundy presumably must have given to him as he drove his family to safety in Britanny.

M le Beau lived out his remaining doggy years at Mme Yvinec's expense.

Michel d'Roubaix was executed by lethal injection in 1944 as a member of a Resistance group.

Benzion Homesky, who had Maundy's watch and chain after his death, was accused of stealing it by the Germans. He protested 'claiming that they had been bequeathed to him verbally, but the Germans had different views, stealing and looting being a German prerogative.'[13] His fate is unknown, but not hard to imagine.

The Ambassador Club closed its doors in 1936 and Deepdene in the same year. Peter Mazzina remained at liberty during the war as a naturalised British subject. He was pursued by debtors for the rest of his life, which ended in 1943 when he hanged himself by the silken cord of his dressing-gown in the bathroom of his flat in Welbeck Street.

After the war, Maundy's trail of financial destruction looked like being investigated yet again. There was a flurry of publicity in the early 1950s before his death was finally confirmed, and when the will was discovered Michel d'Roubaix's son Micky was at first convinced that he must be the heir to millions. Mme Yvinec, remembering her unpaid bill, got on a train and stomped up to the concierge's office at 8 rue d'Anjou. There was nothing. The Cheerful Giver had given his last.

As Micky d'Roubaix later said 'The cupboard is and always has been bare.'[14]

APPENDIX 1

Enquiry Agent

Gregory's work for Special Branch, and the information he volunteered to them, essentially flowed from his 'hotel network' of informants that had evolved from *Mayfair*'s 'At the Hotels' feature. According to Gregory's records[1], the hotels network comprised the following:

Anderson's Hotel, 162 Fleet Street, E.C – Francis H. Clemow
Arundel Hotel, 8 Arundel Street, Stand – Patrick Caldon
Baldwins Hotel, 19 Dover Street – B. Poletti
Belgrave Mansions Hotel, Victoria – Emilie Bonvin
Bucklands Hotel, 41 Brook Street, Grosvenor Square W1 – Mrs Jane
    Chaplin
Cannon Street Hotel, Cannon Street E.C – John Aptommas
Carlton Hotel, Haymarket SW – Jacques Kraemer
Carter's Hotel, 14 Albermarle Street, W1 – Mrs Julia Pakerman
Cavendish Hotel, 81 Jermyn Street, SW – Mrs Rosa Lewis
Charing Cross Hotel, Strand SW – R. Neuschwander
Claridge's Hotel, Brook Street W1 – John Cochrane
Coburg Hotel, Carlos Place, Grosvenor Square W – Alfred King
De Vere Hotel, 50 Hyde Park Gate W – R.C. Vaugbarr
Euston Hotel, Euston Station – Robert Glasspool
Fleming's Hotel, Half Moon Street, W – Percy Sanford
Goring Hotel, 15/21 Ebury Street SW – O.R. Goring
Great Eastern Hotel, Liverpool Street EC – Henry Thomas
Great Northern Hotel, Kings Cross Station – William Trask
Great Western Hotel, Praed Street W- Joseph Bonn
Hotel Cecil, Strand SW – William Elderkin
Hotel Curzon, Curzon Street W – Simon Harwath

Hotel Great Central, Marylebone Road NW – George Pollard

Hyde Park Hotel, 66 Knightsbridge SW – Charles Ward

Langham Hotel, Portland Place – George Cox

Metropole Hotel, Northumberland Avenue – Henry Lodge

Midland Grand Hotel, St Pancras Station – Walter Towle

Norfolk Hotel, Surrey Street, Strand WC – Arthur Harris

Piccadilly Hotel, 21 Piccadilly W – Frederick Heim

Prince's Hotel, 190 Piccadilly W – Edward Colegrave

Queen's Hotel, Leicester Square – George Smith

Ritz Hotel, Piccadilly W – Theodore Kroell

St Ermins Hotel, Caxton Street W – Percy Gutteridge

St James' Palace Hotel, 15 Bury Street, St James' SW – Romeo
  Sartori

Savoy Hotel, Strand W – James Dudley

Waldorf Hotel, Aldwich WC – Lionel Cornut

Westminster Palace Hotel, 4 Victoria Street SW – John Brinkworth

German Suspects

Among the names volunteered by Gregory to Sir Basil Thomson
during 1917 were the following: [2]

Gustav Stoecker

Karl Liebermann

Ernst Schonherr

Max Uhl

Friedrich Blucher

Georg Eberlain

Johann Foerster

Otto Gerhardt

Wilhelm Heinze

Fritz Hodel

Alfred Leuthold

Ludwig Mohr

Heinrich Schultz [3]

Rudolf Weiss

Albert Voigt

A Brief History of the Honours System 1485–2007[1]

The present assumption that there has always been something disreputable or discreditable about the buying and selling of honours seems somewhat misplaced in light of past history. Most titles bestowed prior to the mid nineteenth century had clearly been given in return for a consideration of either money or favour, a practice that was neither frowned upon nor seriously questioned as the historical record amply testifies.

The Tudor monarchs, for example, with memories of civil war and the discord nobles could cause, were understandably reluctant to further increase the peerage from the minimal level it had reached by 1485. Elizabeth, during her forty-five year reign, for example, created only eight new titles [2]. The Stuarts, by contrast, had no such apprehensions. Their frequent disputes with parliament and the consequent difficulties in raising money led to an abrupt change in outlook. Between 1603 and 1629 the House of Lords doubled in size. Almost overnight, obtaining a title suddenly became easy for those who could afford it.

Records from the reign of James I make no attempt to conceal the free flow of cash from the pockets of the wealthy into the coffers of the King, often via Court favourites such as the Duke of Buckingham, who acted as brokers. In 1616, for example, Sir John Roper and Sir John Holles paid £10,000 each to be elevated to the peerage. [3]

Despite the pressures of inflation, the price of a peerage seems to have remained static throughout James's reign, for seven years later in 1623 records indicate that Sir Philip Stanhope became Baron Stanhope of Shelford, again for the sum of £10,000. [4] Shortly before James's death in 1625 Sir Richard Robartes too became Baron Robartes of Truro for a consideration of £10,000. [5] Under Charles I, who, with a civil war to contend with, was even more in need of hard cash, the price of ennoblement began to climb, rising to £15,000 by 1642. [6]

However, the principal method of raising funds during the Stuart period was the selling of baronetcies. The existence of such titles can be traced back to the reign of Edward III, who conferred one on William de la Pole and his heirs in return for the payment of money needed by the King for himself and his army. Other baronetcies were created by later kings, but were hereditary only in very few cases, and in any case such creations had fallen from use well before the reign of James I. The existing hereditary title of baronet dates specifically from 1611, for it was in this year that James I revived the title for the sole purpose of raising money for the settlement of Ulster. [7]

In 1619 [8] the Baronetage of Ireland was created, initially with a limited membership of 100. Five years later in 1624 James created the Baronetage of Scotland, limited to 150 members, and earmarked income from this source appropriately for the settlement of Nova Scotia. [9] Demand failed to materialise and due to insufficient applicants James allowed English and Irish gentlemen to apply for a Scottish baronetcy. Even this desperate measure failed to produce many more applicants and so James, reluctantly, had little choice but to cut the price of baronetcies. By the following reign they were down to £400 with at least one on record as having been obtained for a paltry £350. The laws of supply and demand in time led to an upturn in the baronetcy market to such an extent that Charles I soon disregarded the original limitation on numbers.

Following the defeat and death of Charles I at the hands of Parliament, the House of Lords was abolished and a republic declared. The House of Lords was later revived by Oliver Cromwell, who created a limited number of new peerages. [10] On the Restoration of 1660, normal business was resumed as both Charles II and James II found themselves financially embarrassed. Not only were they short of money, but had an additional need to reward their supporters. During his exile Charles II had created nineteen peerages in order to keep the Stuart cause alive. In the early years of his reign expansion of the peerage appeared to be almost boundless, even going so far as to create twenty-nine new dukedoms.

Charles II also followed his father's example of creating baronets at bargain basement prices. Charles was also responsible for the innovative step of openly employing agents to hawk baronetcies for him. They travelled the country armed with blank patents which they were empowered to fill in and emboss whenever they found any one willing and able to pay the asking price.

On the accession of George I in 1714 the vast majority of peerages and titles began to be conferred on the recommendation of the Prime Minister. Although George III successfully regained control of patronage for a while, his periods of illness allowed the politicians to regain the upper hand on a permanent basis. [11] A further watershed landmark, reached during George III's reign, occurred in 1783 when William Pitt became Prime Minister and proceeded, with the King's full consent and connivance, to create 141 new peers in order to establish a permanent Tory majority in the Upper House. This had the undeniable effect of sweeping away all restraint and circumspection in terms of bestowing honours. When, in the following century, Earl Grey feared the House of Lords might reject the 1832 Reform Bill, he had little problem in securing an undertaking from William IV to consent to the creation of some 80 new peerages should resistance present itself. As it turned out, the mere threat had the desired effect. Although Asquith experienced a little more reluctance on the part of George V, there was little doubt that the monarch would, in due course, consent to the creation of as many as 400 new peers in order to facilitate the passage of the 1911 Parliament Act. Again, the mere rattling of the patronage sabre was sufficient to concentrate the minds of the Upper House.

Of course, not everyone was happy with the outcome. Asquith's Chief Whip Alick Murray already had a list of potential new peers at the ready for submission to the king should the Lords not back down. A good many of these worthies were apparently ready and waiting with open cheque books for word from Murray that the mass ennoblement was to proceed. Disappointed donors would not have to wait too long, however, before providence would provide a further opportunity for large scale ennoblements. In 1916 Lloyd George found himself in the unenviable position of being a Prime Minister without a party. Having burnt his bridges with Asquith and the mainstream Liberal Party, he would sooner or later have to create a new, more permanent, political grouping if he was to have a long term political future. Without party members or institutional backers he would equally need to find other ways to secure the vast funds necessary to create and sustain a new political force. Honours sales were seen as the most practical solution. While Lloyd George ultimately failed to create this new political force, the negative publicity surrounding the 1922 Honours List led directly to the Honours (Prevention of Abuses) Act 1925.

It would take another four decades, however, before Parliament had the time or inclination to consider reform of the House of Lords itself. In February 1958, Prime Minister Harold Macmillan introduced his controversial Life Peerage Bill. It was an unashamed compromise. The hereditary principle was to be safeguarded, but it would be progressively watered down over the passage of time by the extension of the House of Lords to include nominated life peers, with no hereditary rights.

The fact that few if any new hereditary peers would henceforth be created to counteract those that became extinct would ultimately lead to a withering on the vine. Life peers could now be created apace without fear of expanding the overall size of the House. When Harold Wilson became Prime Minister in 1964 he further underscored this principle by declaring that he would henceforth recommend no new hereditary peerages or indeed any new hereditary baronetcies. [12] This in no way restrained his granting of new life peerages. At a rate of some thirty-three new peers a year he became the biggest enobler since Charles II. [13]

No significant constitutional developments took place until 1984 when Margaret Thatcher resolved to recommend Harold Macmillan for a hereditary earldom, the first for twenty-three years. Although William Whitelaw and former Speaker George Thomas were similarly ennobled with hereditary titles by Mrs Thatcher, there were to be no further hereditary peerages created. Under John Major there was, however, to be one hereditary baronetcy created in favour of Denis Thatcher in 1991 shortly after his wife's resignation.

With the return to power of a Labour Government in 1997, major reform was undertaken, resulting in the House of Lords Act 1999. This excluded the main body of hereditary peers, leaving a small core of ninety (excepting any hereditary peer holding the office of Earl Marshall or Lord Great Chamberlain) who would be elected by the hereditary peers as a whole. In March 2007 the House of Commons voted in favour of an entirely elected House of Lords, although it is far from clear at the present time the precise form this will take and the timetable for implementing such a reform.

APPENDIX 3

The Asquith Peerage List 1911

In 1911 Prime Minister H.H. Asquith and his Chief Whip Alick Murray compiled an interim list of nominees should it be necessary to swamp the House of Lords with Liberal peers in the event of the rejection of the Parliament Bill.[1] The list is reproduced below:

Sir John T. Brunner, Bart
James Stuart
Robert Farquharson, M.D., LL.D
Sir Algernon West, G.C.B
Frederick Huth Jackson
Arnold Morley
Sir John Rhys
Sir Edgar Speyar, Bart
Sir George O. Trevelyan, Bart
Arthur H. Dyke Acland
Eugene Wason, M.P
John W. Mellor K.C
Sir William Mather
Sir Henry E. Roscoe, F.R.S., Ph.D., LL.D
George W.E Russell
Thomas W. Russell
John F. Cheetham
Robert G. Glendinning
James Caldwell
Arthur Cohen K.C

Alfred Emmott, M.P [2]

Sir T.Vezey Strong

H. J.Tennant, Esq., M.P

Sir J. Herbert Roberts, Bart., M.P

Sir Archibald Williamson, Bart [3]

Sir John A. Dewar, Bart., M.P

John S. Ainsworth, Esq., M.P

William Phipson Beale K.C., M.P

The Earl of Clonmel [4]

Sir Thomas Courtenay T.Warner Bart., C. B., M.P

Sir Edward Strachey, Bart., M.P [5]

Charles Norris Nicholson M.P

Sir Thomas Borthwick, Bart [6]

Sir Francis Layland-Barratt, Bart

David Erskine

Sir William H. Lever, Bart [7]

Sir A.Thomas [8]

J. Crombie

Sir Frederick Pollock, Bart

Sir James Low, Bart

Sir George H. Lewis, Bart [9]

Sir Edward Donner, Bart

The Hon. Arthur L. Stanley

Major Gen. J. F. Brocklehurst, C.B., C.V.O [10]

Col.Arthur Collins

Col. Sir Arthur Davidson, K.C.B., K.C.V.O

The Hon. O. S. B. Brett

Sir Francis D. Blake, Bart

Sir John Barker, Bart

R. Farrer, Esq

The Hon.W. Pember Reeves

Sir H. Harmsworth, Bart [11]

Seymour Allen, Esq

William Caird, Esq. (Dundee)

A. Chamberlain, Esq

Sir K. Muir Mackenzie, G.C.B., K.C

George Fuller, Esq
H. Holloway, Esq
Captain A. F. Luttrell
Sir Walter Runciman, Bart
Sir E. Russell [12]
Sir H. Primrose, K.C.B
Sir A. R. Simpson
Professor Henry Jones, LL.D
Anthony Hope Hawkins, Esq
Henry Neville Gladstone, Esq
H. Beaumout, Esq
J. A. Bright, Esq
Hugh E. Hoare, Esq
Sir Edward T. Holden
Emslie J. Horniman, Esq
Oswald Partington, Esq
Sir T. T. Scarisbrick, Bart
F. Verney, Esq
Capt. The Hon. Clive Bigham
The Hon. A. J. Davey
Sir Murland de Grasse Evans, Bart
The Lord Haddo [13]
The Hon. W. J. James
Sir Harry H. Johnston, G.C.M.G., K.C.B
The Hon. H. A. Scudamore Stanhope, R.N
R. C. Phillimore, Esq
Sir Robert H. Hobart, K.C.V.O., C.B
The Hon. John Wallop
Sir Albert E. H. Naylor-Leyland, Bart
The Hon. H. W. Blyth
Sir Kenelm E. Digby, G.C.B
Sir Philip Burne-Jones, Bart
The Hon. L. U. K. Shuttleworth
Major A. L. Langman
The Hon. Sir Edward Chandos Leigh, K.C., K.C.B
The Hon. Bertrand Russell

Sir Edgar Vincent, K.C.M.G [14]
Sir Alfred E. Turner, K.C.B [15]
Sir T.D. Gibson-Carmichael Bart., K.C.M.G [16]
Principal J Roberts
R. Collins, Esq
G. Freeman Barbour, Esq
Admiral Sir Cyprian Bridge, G.C.B
Sir Fowell Buxton
The Hon. Geoffrey Coleridge
Sir W. Dunbar, Bart
Principal G Donaldson
W.S. Haldane, Esq
Victor Horsley, Esq
Sir John F. F. Horner, K.C.V.O
Gwynne Hughes, Esq
Sir T.W. Nussey, Bart
General Sir R. S. Baden-Powell, K.C.B., K.C.V.O
Frank Lloyd, Esq
Joseph Rowntree, Esq
F. Thomasson, Esq
Sir Ernest Soares, LL.D
Sir Charles E. Tritton, Bart
Sir James Woodhouse [17]
Donald Crawford, Esq., K.C
W Tangye, Esq
R Bowing Esq
T. H. Amory, Esq
Lord Ernest St. Maur [18]
Sir T. Barlow, Bart
The Hon. R. Cavendish
John Cowan, Esq
A. H. Crosfield, Esq
Laurence Currie, Esq
Sir Andrew Fraser, K.C.S.I
Sir Walter Gilbey, Bart
G. P. Gooch, Esq

The Rt. Hon. Sir J. Gorst, LL.D., F.R.S., K.C
Cecil Grenfell, Esq [19]
General Sir Ian S. M. Hamilton, G.C.B., D.S.O
F. Harrison, Esq
R. H. Harrison, Esq
Norman Lamont, Esq
R. C. Lehmann, Esq
Sir H. S. Leon
K McKenna Esq
J.P. Maclay, Esq [20]
John Massie, Esq [21]
Gilbert Murray, Esq
Sir William Robertson Nicol
Sir Owen Philipps, K.C.M.G
The Hon. Rollo Russell
Arthur Sedgwick, Esq
Captain C.W. Norton, M.P [22]
Sir David Brynmor Jones, K.C., M.P
T. R. Ferens, Esq., M.P
Sir Edwin Cornwall, M.P
Sir Leonard Lyell, Bart
Austin Taylor, Esq
Sir William L.Younger, Bart
Sir William J. Crossley, Bart
Sir William J. Collins
Sir E. Evans
J.A. Spender, Esq
Sir William E. Garstin, G.C.M.G
Sir Francis A. Channing, Bart [23]
Major Edward M. Dunne
The Hon. M. Napier
Ernest A.Villiers, Esq
Sir William Wedderburn, Bart
Sir Henry Ballantyne
Sir Samuel Chisholm, Bart
Sir Jeremiah Colman, Bart

Sir Frank Crisp
Robert Wallace, Esq., K.C
Sir T. Roberts
Sir Abe Bailey [24]
Sir Alexander D. Kleinwort, Bart
Alexander Cross, Esq
Harold Ellis, Esq
Thomas Hardy, Esq., O.M
Sir Hubert H. Longman, Bart
W. H. Dickinson, Esq., M.P
James Brian, Esq
John Churchill, Esq
C. H. Corbett, Esq
Sir George J. E. Dashwood, Bart
Alfred Edison Hutton, Esq
Sir Clarendon Golding Hyde
Sir Benjamin Sands Johnson
Algernon Marshall S. Methuen, Esq
Sir Swire Smith
Sir William James Ingram, Bart
Harry Sturgis, Esq
H Leedam, Esq
Sir Robert Buckle
The Hon. Charles Lawrence
Sir Francis Flint Belsey
Charles Edward Mallet, Esq
The Hon. Geoffrey R. C. Fiennes
David Davies, Esq., M.P
Sir Robert A. Hadfield
Sir William E. Clegg
Sir William Angus
J.M. Barrie, Esq
Sir Robert Andrew Allison
Charles R. Buxton, Esq
Sir Joseph F. Leese, Bart
William Fuller-Maitland, Esq

Sir Frank Hillyard Newnes, Bart

H. J. Glanville, Esq., M.P

Sir E. J. Boyle, Bart

J.H. Brodie, Esq

Col. Henry Platt, C.B

Percy Barlow, Esq.

Stanley George Barwick, Esq

Sir Edward Nelson, K.C.M.G [25]

Herbert Neumann

Sir J. Briscoe, Bart

Sir Charles Cameron, Bart

Chatfield Clarke, Esq

Frank Debenham, Esq

E.O. Fordham, Esq

Sir John Fleming

St. George Lane Fox Pitt, Esq

Capt. The Hon. Fitzroy Hemphill

A. Holland, Esq

Sir Jonathan Hutchinson

Sir Thomas J. Lipton, Bart

Wilson Marriage, Esq

Sir H. Marshall

Sir Edward L. O'Malley

Sir C. Parry, Bart

Sir David Paulin

Sir George Riddell [26]

J Dunean, Esq

Sir William Robertson

Sir C. Shaw

J. Seligman, Esq

Sir George H. Sutherland

David S. Waterlow, Esq

Sir Frederick W. Wilson

Lord Wodehouse [27]

G Muspratt, Esq

R. Hunter Craig, Esq

Sir Charles Gold
Sir A. P. Gould
B. F. Hawksley, Esq
Sir Frank Hollins, Bart
Sir Alexander Waldemar Law-Rence, Bart
Sir Wilfrid Lawson, Bart, M.P
Sir H. Munro
Henry Oppenheim, Esq
F. St. Quintin, Esq
F.H. Smith, Esq
J. Weston Stevens, Esq
Halley Stewart, Esq
James Thornton, Esq

Lloyd George Peerages

Over the past eight decades a variety of statements have been made concerning the number of new peerages allegedly created by David Lloyd George. The numbers given in press articles and books have varied enormously, many as high as 120.

Many such calculations have been based on erroneous statistics. Some titles, for example, were granted to individuals who were already peers and members of the House of Lords. These cannot, therefore, be considered to be *new creations*. F.E. Smith, for example, was made a Baron in 1919, a Viscount in 1921 and an Earl in 1922. He has often been counted three times by some reckonings.

Some peers who took their seats in January 1917 had, in fact, received their peerages in Asquith's resignation honours list, but have often been counted into the Lloyd George total because of the year they took their seats. There were also peerages created during Lloyd George's period of office that were Royal peerages, ie created by the King who is able to bestow peerages on members of the royal family by Warrant under the Royal Sign Manual. A number of these were created by George V in 1917 when the royal family changed their name from Saxe-Coburg-Gotha to Windsor and decreed that all German titles should be dispensed with. In compensation, George V created new English titles for those family members who had lost their German titles.[1] Such peerages are created without any reference to the Prime Minister, and again should not be counted as new Lloyd George creations.

In order to discover the correct number of *new creations*, original sources from 1917–1922, including the *London Gazette* (the official publication of the Government in which titles are initially announced), The House of Lords Record Office, The College of Arms, Burke's Peerage and Debrett's Peerage were utlised. As a result, the sum total of new Lloyd George creations was calculated to be eighty-two. A dossier on every peer who took his seat during this period was also created and the reason for each peerage being granted was investigated. Much of this research was conducted with the co-operation of the heirs and descendents of those ennobled during this period. This information was then cross-referenced with Maundy Gregory's own records.

It must also be appreciated that during this period of coalition government, the Honours List was actually drawn up jointly by Lloyd George and the leader of the Unionist Party (Bonar Law up until March 1921 and Austen Chamberlain from then until November 1922). The Unionist leader would therefore present a list of nominees to the Prime Minister, who would also have his own list. They would then endorse one joint and collective list.

Of the eighty-two new peerages created between 1917 and 1922, no more than fourteen involved any monetary consideration. Of these fourteen, eight were actually nominated by Andrew Bonar Law and Austen Chamberlain, not by Lloyd George.

Contrary to popular belief, peerages comprised a small percentage of titles sold during this period. Even among the typically 'nouveaux-riches' clientele of the honours broker, only a very limited number could afford a peerage. Most of Maundy Gregory's customers, for example, bought knighthoods or baronetcies.

The following is a summary of the backgrounds to the eighty-two new peerages createed between 1917 and 1922:

1   Hugh Graham – Baron Atholstan
     Created 5 May 1917
     Nominated by David Lloyd George
     Publisher
     Title: Extinct

2   Amelius Lockwood – Baron Lambourne
      Created 19 June 1917
      Nominated by Andrew Bonar Law
      Unionist MP
      Title: Extinct

3   Sir Ivor Herbert – Baron Treowen
      Created 20 June 1917
      Nominated by David Lloyd George
      Major-General
      Title: Extinct

4   Sir Frederick Smith – Baron Colwyn [2]
      Created 21 June 1917
      Nominated by David Lloyd George
      India Rubber & Cotton Manufacturer
      Title: Current

5   Sir William Leaver – Baron Leaverhulme
      Created 21 June 1917
      Nominated by David Lloyd George
      Soap Manufacturer
      Title: Extinct

6   Richard Chaloner – Baron Gisborough
      Created 23 June 1917
      Nominated by Andrew Bonar Law
      Unionist MP
      Title: Current

7   Sir Francis Hopwood – Baron Southwood
      Created 1 November 1917
      Nominated by David Lloyd George
      Civil Lord of the Admiralty
      Title: Extinct

8   Sir John Jellicoe – Viscount Jellicoe
     Created 15 January 1918
     Nominated David Lloyd George
     Admiral of the Fleet
     Title: Current

9   Sir Edward Morris – Baron Morris
     Created 15 January 1918
     Nominated by David Lloyd George
     Prime Minister of Newfoundland
     Title: Current

10   Frederick Cawley – Baron Cawley
     Created 16 January 1918
     Nominated by David Lloyd George
     Chancellor of the Duchy of Lancaster
     Title: Current

11   Sir John Lonsdale – Baron Armaghdale
     Created 17 January 1918
     Nominated by Andrew Bonar Law
     Chairman of the Unionist Party
     Title: Extinct

12   Almeric Paget – Baron Queensborough
     Created 18 January 1918
     Nominated by Andrew Bonar Law
     Unionist MP
     Title: Extinct

13   Sir James Woodhouse – Baron Terrington
     Created 19 January 1918
     Nominated by David Lloyd George
     HM Railway Commissioner
     Title: Current

14   Sir William Weir – Baron Weir
      Created 26 June 1918
      Nominated by David Lloyd George
      Secretary of State for Air
      Title: Current

15   Sir Matthew Arthur – Baron Glenarthur [3]
      Created 27 June 1918
      Nominated by Andrew Bonar Law
      Iron & Coal
      Title: Current

16   Sir William Tatem – Baron Glanely [4]
      Created 28th June 1918
      Nominated by Andrew Bonar Law
      Ship Owner
      Title: Extinct

17   George Faber – Baron Wittenham
      Created 29 June 1918
      Nominated by Andrew Bonar Law
      Unionist MP
      Title: Extinct

18   Sir Ignatius O'Brien – Baron Shandon
      Created 1 July 1918
      Nominated by David Lloyd George
      Lord Chancellor of Ireland
      Title: Extinct

19   Sir Walter Phillimore – Baron Phillimore
      Created 2 July 1918
      Nominated by David Lloyd George
      Lord of Appeal
      Title: Current

20   Sir Arthur Lee – Viscount Lee
     Created 9 July 1918
     Nominated by David Lloyd George
     President of the Board of Agriculture
     Title: Extinct

21   Sir Charles Bathhurst – Baron Bledisloe
     Created 15 October 1918
     Nominated by Andrew Bonar Law
     Unionist MP
     Title: Current

22   Sir William Pickford – Baron Sterndale
     Created 14 November 1918
     Nominated by David Lloyd George
     Lord Justice of Appeal
     Title: Extinct

23   George Cave – Viscount Cave
     Created 14 November 1918
     Nominated by Andrew Bonar Law
     Home Secretary
     Title: Extinct

24   William Fisher – Baron Downham
     Created 16 November 1918
     Nominated by David Lloyd George
     President of Local Government Board
     Title: Extinct

25   Sir Frederick Smith – Baron Birkenhead
     Created 3 February 1919
     Nominated by Andrew Bonar Law
     Attorney-General
     Title: Extinct

26 Rowland Prothero – Baron Ernle
    Created 4 February 1919
    Nominated by Andrew Bonar Law
    President Board of Agriculture
    Title: Extinct

27 Sir George Askwith – Baron Askwith
    Created 24 March 1919
    Nominated by David Lloyd George
    Chairman Government Arbitration Committee
    Title: Extinct

28 Robert Chalmers – Baron Chalmers
    Created 24 April 1919
    Nominated By David Lloyd George
    Permanent Secretary of HM Treasury, Governor of Ceylon
    Title: Extinct

29 Thomas Cochrane – Baron Cochrane
    Created 16 May 1919
    Nominated by Andrew Bonar Law
    Home Office Minister
    Title: Current

30 Sir Robert Hodge – Baron Wyfold
    Created 17 May 1919
    Nominated by Andrew Bonar Law
    Conservative MP
    Title: Extinct

31 Sir John Roberts – Baron Clwyd
    Created 19 May 1919
    Nominated by David Lloyd George
    Liberal MP
    Title: Current

32   Sir Thomas Dewar – Baron Dewar 5
     Created 20 May 1919
     Nominated by Andrew Bonar Law
     Distiller
     Title: Extinct

33   Sir Satyendra Sinha – Baron Sinha
     Created 22 June 1919
     Nominated by David Lloyd George
     Member of the Imperial War Cabinet, and Under Secretary
     of State of India
     Title: Current

34   Andrew Weir – Baron Inverforth
     Created 26 June 1919
     Nominated by Andrew Bonar Law
     Minister of Munitions
     Title: Current

35   Sir David Beatty – Earl Beatty
     Created 27 September 1919
     Nominated by David Lloyd George
     Admiral of the Fleet
     Title: Current

36   Douglas Haig – Earl Haig
     Created 29 September 1919
     Nominated by David Lloyd George
     Field Marshall
     Title: Current

37   Sir Herbert Plumer – Baron Plumer
     Created 4 October 1919
     Nominated by
     Field Marshall
     Title: Extinct

38   Sir Edmund Allenby – Viscount Allenby
     Created 7 October 1919
     Nominated by David Lloyd George
     General
     Title: Current

39   Henry Rawlinson – Baron Rawlinson
     Created 7 October 1919
     Nominated by David Lloyd George
     General
     Title: Extinct

40   Sir Julian Byng – Baron Byng
     Created 7 October 1919
     Nominated by David Lloyd George
     Field Marshall
     Title: Extinct

41   Sir Edward Russell – Baron Russell
     Created 7 October 1919
     Nominated by David Lloyd George
     Newspaper Editor
     Title: Current

42   William Walker – Baron Wavertree
     Created 27 October 1919
     Nominated by Andrew Bonar Law
     Conservative MP
     Title: Extinct

43   Charles Eady – Baron Swinfen
     Created 1 November 1919
     Nominated by David Lloyd George
     Lord Justice of Appeal
     Title: Current

44   Henry Sinclair – Baron Horne
     Created 8 November 1919
     Nominated by David Lloyd George
     General, ADC to King George V
     Title: Extinct

45   Sir Rosslyn Wemyss – Baron Wester Wemyss
     Created 18 November 1919
     Nominated by David Lloyd George
     Admiral of the Fleet
     Title: Extinct

46   Sir James Meston – Baron Meston
     Created 20 November 1919
     Nominated by David Lloyd George
     Member of War Cabinet, Representative of India
     Title: Current

47   Sir Henry Foster – Baron Foster
     Created 12 December 1919
     Nominated by Andrew Bonar Law
     Conservative MP and Governor General of Australia
     Title: Extinct

48   Albert Stanley – Baron Ashfield
     Created 9 January 1920
     Nominated by Andrew Bonar Law
     President of the Board of Trade
     Title: Extinct

49   St John Brodrick – Earl Midleton
     Created 2 February 1920
     Nominated by Andrew Bonar Law
     Secretary of State for War, Secretary of State for India
     Title: Extinct

50 Sir Bertrand Dawson – Baron Dawson
    Created 9 February 1920
    Nominated by David Lloyd George
    Royal Physician
    Title: Extinct

51 Sir George Riddell – Baron Riddell
    Created 28 February 1920
    Nominated by David Lloyd George
    Newspaper Proprietor
    Title: Extinct

52 Sir Brien Cokayne – Baron Cullen
    Created 21 April 1920
    Nominated by David Lloyd George
    Governor of the Bank of England
    Title: Current

53 Ronald Munro-Ferguson – Viscount Novar
    Created 6 December 1920
    Nominated by David Lloyd George
    Governor General of Australia
    Title: Extinct

54 William Beardmore – Baron Invernairn [6]
    Created 15 January 1921
    Nominated by Andrew Bonar Law
    Steel Manufacturer and Shipbuilder
    Title: Extinct

55 Sir Horace Marshall – Baron Marshall
    Created 14 January 1921
    Nominated by David Lloyd George
    HM Lieutenant of City of London and Lord Mayor of
    London
    Title: Extinct

56   Sir Ernest Cable – Baron Cable
     Created 17 January 1921
     Nominated by David Lloyd George
     British-Indian Civil Servant
     Title: Extinct

57   Mathew Vaughn Davies – Baron Ystwyth
     Created 18 January 1921
     Nominated by David Lloyd George
     Liberal MP
     Title: Extinct

58   Sir Edmund Howard – Viscount Fitz Alan
     Created 28 April 1921
     Nominated by David Lloyd George
     Viceroy of Ireland
     Title: Current

59   Sir Edward Carson – Baron Carson
     Created 1 June 1921
     Nominated by David Lloyd George
     Member of the War Cabinet without Portfolio, Lord of
     Appeal
     Title: Extinct

60   Sir Francis Napier – Viscount Chelmsford
     Created 3 June 1921
     Nominated by David Lloyd George
     Viceroy of India
     Title: Current

61   Albert Illingworth – Baron Illingworth
     Created 4 June 1921
     Nominated by David Lloyd George
     Postmaster-General
     Title: Extinct

62   Walter Long – Viscount Long
     Created 4 June 1921
     Nominated by Austen Chamberlain
     First Lord of the Admiralty, Chief Secretary for Ireland
     Title: Current

63   James Mackenzie – Baron Seaforth
     Created 19 June 1921
     Nominated by Austen Chamberlain
     Land Owner
     Title: Extinct

64   Sir James Dalziel – Baron Dalziel
     Created 28 June 1921
     Nominated by David Lloyd George
     Newspaper Proprietor
     Title: Extinct

65   Sir Ailwyn Fellowes – Baron Ailwyn
     Created 1 July 1921
     Nominated by Austen Chamberlain
     Vice Chamberlain of Royal Household, Chairman of
     Norfolk County Council
     Title: Extinct

66   Sir James Lowther – Viscount Ullswater
     Created 1st July 1921
     Nominated by Austen Chamberlain
     Speaker of the House of Commons
     Title: Current

67   James Campbell – Baron Glenavy
     Created 26 July 1921
     Nominated by Austen Chamberlain
     Lord Chancellor of Ireland
     Title: Extinct

68   Sir Alfred Lawrence – Baron Trevethin
       Created 24 August 1921
       Nominated by David Lloyd George
       Lord Chief Justice of England
       Title: Current

69   Sir Robert Nivison – Baron Glendyne [7]
       Created 23 January 1922
       Nominated by Austen Chamberlain
       Stockbroker
       Title: Current

70   Sir James Buchanan – Baron Woolavington [8]
       Created 24 January 1922
       Nominated by David Lloyd George
       Distiller
       Title: Extinct

71   Joseph Watson – Baron Manton [9]
       Created 25 January 1922
       Nominated by David Lloyd George
       Soap Manufacturer
       Title: Extinct

72   Francis Willey – Baron Barnby [10]
       Created 26 January 1922
       Nominated by Austen Chamberlain
       Wool Merchant
       Title: Extinct

73   Sir Gordon Hewart – Baron Hewart
       Created 24 March 1922
       Nominated by David Lloyd George
       Attorney General
       Title: Extinct

74   Sir Arthur Balfour – Earl Balfour
     Created 5 May 1922
     Nominated by Austen Chamberlain
     Former Prime Minister and Foreign Secretary
     Title: Current

75   Samuel Waring – Baron Waring [11]
     Created 18 June 1922
     Nominated by Austen Chamberlain
     Aeroplane Component Manufacturer and Retail
     Distributor
     Title: Current

76   Sir Archibald Williamson – Baron Forres [12]
     Created 19 June 1922
     Nominated by David Lloyd George
     Oil Industrialist
     Title: Current

77   Sir William Vestey [13]
     Created 20 June 1922
     Nominated by David Lloyd George
     Cold Storage and Shipping Line Owner
     Title: Current

78   Sir Robert Borwick – Baron Borwick [14]
     Created 17 July 1922
     Nominated by Austen Chamberlain
     Custard and Baking Powder Manufacturer
     Title: Current

79   Francis Mildmay – Baron Mildmay
     Created 20 November 1922
     Nominated by Austen Chamberlain
     Deputy Speaker of the House of Commons
     Title: Extinct

80   Sir Joseph Maclay – Baron Maclay [15]
      Created 21 November 1922
      Nominated by David Lloyd George
      Ship Owner
      Title: Current

81   Sir Edward Goulding – Baron Wargrave
      Created 22 November 1922
      Nominated by Austen Chamberlain
      Conservative MP and Financier
      Title: Extinct

82   Sir John Bethell – Baron Bethell
      Created 23 November 1922
      Nominated by David Lloyd George
      Liberal MP and Banker
      Title: Current

Baronetcies

Purchased peerages comprised but a small proportion of honours sold during the early decades of the twentieth century. Knighthoods were comparatively more affordable and were created in profusion. Asquith, Bonar Law, Lloyd George and Chamberlain between them were responsible for over two thousand such creations. Being non-hereditary, they were not however such an attractive investment as a baronetcy, which could be passed from father to son down subsequent generations. Obtaining a hereditary title seems to have been one of the key objectives so far as potential purchasers during this period were concerned. From written and anecdotal family sources, the desire to purchase a permanent ticket (as opposed to one lasting a single lifetime) into the respectability of the aristocracy for the subsequent generations of their family seems to have been a very powerful motivator. Baronetcies, while being more expensive than knighthoods, were more affordable than peerages and met this desire. The following represents a list of purchased baronetcies created between 1917 and 1924:

Sir William Gray (1917) – Gray of Tunstall
Chairman, William Gray & Co Ltd, South Durham Steel
    & Iron Co
Title: Current

Sir Thomas Watson (1918) [1] – Watson of Newport
Director, Pyman, Watson & Co, Shipowners
Title: Extinct

Sir Abraham Bailey (1919) – Bailey of South Africa [2]
Financier
Title: Current

Sir Ernest Jardine (1919) – Jardine of Nottingham
Chairman, John Jardine Ltd, Trent Navigation Co Ltd,
Title: Extinct

Sir Fredrick John Jones (1919) – Jones of Treeton
President, South Yorkshire Coal Trade Association
Title: Current

Sir John Holden (1919) – Holden of Leigh
Managing Director, Tunnicliffe and Hampson (Ltd); Mayor of
    Leigh
Title: Current

Sir William Ernest Cain (1920) – Cain of Wargrave
Managing Director, Peter Walker (Warrington); Robert Cain &
    Sons Ltd, Brewers
Title: Extinct

Sir Erik Olof Ohlson (1920) – Ohlson of Scarborough
Coal and Timber Merchant
Title: Current

Sir William Aykroyd (1920) – Aykroyd of Lightcliffe
Chairman, T.F. Firth & Sons Ltd, Carpet manufacturers
Title: Current

Sir Milton Sheridan Sharp (1920) – Sharp of Heckmondwike
Chairman, Bradford Dyers Association.Ltd
Title: Current

Sir George Sleight (1920) – Sleight of Weelsby
Grimsby trawler fleet owner
Title: Current

Sir William Reardon-Smith (1920) – Reardon-Smith of
    Appledore
Shipowner, Coal Exporter; Director, St Just Steamship Ltd; Leeds
    Shipping Co Ltd
Title: Current

Sir John Stewart (1920) – Stewart of Fingask
Chairman, Sheffield Steel Products
Title: Current

Sir George Holcroft (1921) – Holcroft of Eaton Mascott
Chairman of Littleton Colleries Ltd
Title: Current

Sir August Cayzer (1921) Cayzer of Roffey Park
Chairman, Clan Line Steamships Ltd
Title: Extinct

Sir Henry Samman (1921) – Samman of Routh
Chairman, Henry Samman & Co, Steamship owners and brokers
Title: Extinct

Sir Sven Wohlford Hansen (1921) – Hansen of Bideford
Colliery proprietor, Shipowner and Shipbuilder
Title: Extinct

Sir Rowland Hodge (1921) [3] – Hodge of Chipstead
Chairman, Eltringham's Ltd, Shipbuilders
Title: Current

Sir Frederick Mills (1921) [4] – Mills of Ebbw Vale
Chairman, Ebbw Vale Steel and Iron Co Ltd
Title: Current

Sir John Drughorn (1922) [5] – Drughorn of Ifield
Director, F Drughorn Ltd, and Anglo-Brazilian Line Ltd
Title: Extinct

Sir David Richard Llewellyn (1922) – Llewellyn of Bwllfa
Chairman, Bwllfa and Merthyr Dare Steam Colleries Ltd
Title: Current

Sir Edmund Keith Nuttall (1922) – Nuttall of Chasefield
Director, Edmund Nuttall Co Ltd; Chairman, Winters Brewery
    Ltd
Title: Current

Sir James Readhead (1922) – Readhead of Westoe
Chairman, John Readhead & Sons Ltd, Shipbuilders of South
    Shields
Title: Extinct

Sir John Noble (1923) – Noble of Ardkinglas
Vice Chairman of W. G Whitworth& Co Ltd, | Shipbuilders
Title: Current

Sir Alexander Grant (1924) [6] – Grant of Forres
Chairman, McVitie & Price, Biscuit Manufactuers
Title: Extinct

Fees on Account

Between 1921 and 1926 Maundy Gregory received sums of money from the following individuals. In none of these cases were honours ever forthcoming.

James C. Calder
J. Conway Davies
Joseph Silvers Williams-Thomas OBE, JP
Lawrence Gunn Sloan JP
John Maddocks JP
Daniel Radcliffe JP
Walter Lee JP
Walter Kent [1]
Sir George Watson
J.A. Milne CBE, JP
James Luddlington
Henry Astley-Bell JP
John F. Bodinnar
William Williamson
William Tomlinson JP
Sidney Boulton
Gerald Howard
William Whitelaw JP

Notes

Abbreviations used in the notes and Bibliography

BL	British Library
BT	Board of Trade
CID	Criminal Investigation Department
CUL	Cambridge University Library
DPP	Director Public Prosecutions
FO	Foreign Office
HO	Home Office
MI1c	Military Intelligence 1c – the former name for MI6
MI5	Military Intelligence 5 – the Security Service
MI6	Military Intelligence 6 – the Secret Intelligence Service
MEPO	Metropolitan Police
NID	Naval Intelligence Department
NYSC	New York Supreme Court
PRO	Public Record Office (now TNA)
SSB	Secret Service Bureau
TNA	The National Archive
TS	Treasury Solicitor
WO	War Office

CHAPTER ONE

The Visitors

1   Philip, George, ed., *Philips' Atlas of the British Empire*, Liverpool, George
    Philip & Son 1924; also Robertson & Bartholomew, *Historical and
    Modern Atlas of the British Empire*, London, Methuen & Co 1924.

2   The uniforms worn by Gregory's attendants intentionally bore a very
    close resemblance to those worn by parliamentary messengers. It is
    unlikely, however, that they were completely identical. Superintendent
    Arthur Askew, who visited the offices during his 1933 investigation
    into Gregory's affairs, later recalled they were designed to deceive and
    were very similar to the real thing (Memorandum dated 24 August
    1954 ,entitled 'The Man Who Frightened Whitehall' *The Askew
    Papers*).

3   Greater London Council Department of Architecture and Civic
    Design, Case #64277: 9–10 Hyde Park Terrace, Bayswater Road,
    Paddington; Application under Building Act, 4 June 1929, with
    plans, and Application to demolish and rebuild, 27 June 1934, with
    plans (London Metropolitan Archive). Also TNA/MEPO 2/9147
    Suspicious death of Mrs E.M.Rosse. Statement of Kate Wells, 2 May
    1933.

CHAPTER TWO

A False Start

1   Rev Francis Maundy Gregory (ref D/Pitt 2/xii), Southampton City
    Archive.

2   Indexes of baptisms, marriage & burials, St Michaels Parish;
    Southampton City Archive. Further material on the Gregory family;
    The Elsie Sandell Collection (ref D/S 16/73), Southampton City
    Archive and material supplied by the Gregory family to the author.

3   Entry 441, Register of Deaths in Kensington in the sub-district of
    Brompton in the County of Middlesex, Stafford Michael Gregory,
    12 March 1882.

4 Cullen, Tom, *The Prostitutes' Padre: the story of the notorious Rector of Stiffkey*, London, The Bodley Head, 1975.

5 Oxford University matriculation records; The Bodleian Library, Oxford.

6 City of Oxford Directory, 1896.

7 Theatre and performance collections, The Theatre Museum, Covent Garden, London.

8 Cullen, Tom, *Maundy Gregory, Purveyor of Honours*, London, The Bodley Head, 1974, p73

9 TNA BT 31/12588/100532. File of Combine Attractions Syndicate Ltd, Registration No 189767.

10 Theatre Museum, ibid.

11 *The Stage*, November 1908 – March 1909.

CHAPTER THREE

The Phoenix Arising

1 Entry 9, Register of Marriages, Registration District of Paddington in the County of London, 8 December 1908, Moritz Frederick William Lichtenstein and Edith Marion Sheppard; London Telephone Book 1909.

2 Frank Dorsey, letter from Yvelines of 13 July 1969 to Donald McCormick in Beckenham (copy in author's possession) Linton, William James. Memories, London, Lawrence and Bullen 1895.

3 Linton, ibid.

4 TNA KV2/340 #264520. MI5 file on the Gregory and the Keen-Hargreaves brothers. J C Keen-Hargreaves 'is understood to have been received by HM the King of Italy.'

5 TNA/MEPO 2/9147. Suspicious Death of Mrs E. M. Rosse. Statement of Ethel Marion Davies. When Ethel Marion Davies first stayed with the Rosses, in August 1916, they were living at Thamesways, The Dittons, Long Ditton. Other evidence suggests that they were still resident at Hyde Park Mansions in 1916, so it is quite probable that they only stayed in Thames Ditton in the summer.

To the best of Ethel's knowledge, Edith Rosse still owned Thamesways when she died.

6   Cook, Andrew, *Prince Eddy: The King Britain Never Had*, Stroud, Tempus Publishing Ltd 2006, p147ff, 283ff.

7   Cook, ibid., p. 285.

8   Cook, ibid., p. 287.

9   Symons, Julian, *Horatio Bottomley*, London, The Cresset Press, 1955.

10   Symons, ibid.

11   Symons, ibid.

12   Hamilton, Gerald, *The Way it Was With Me*, London, Leslie Frewin Publishers Ltd 1969.

13   Macmillan, Gerald, *Honours for Sale: the strange story of Maundy Gregory*, London, The Richards Press, 1954, p. 216

14   TNA KV2/340 #264520. MI5 file on the Gregory and the Keen-Hargreaves brothers; File on Maundy Gregory, Segr. Stato An. 1932 Rubr. 6 fasc. 6, Prot. 118.265, ff. 246r–253r, Vatican Secret Archive, Rome.

15   Rose, Kenneth, *King George V*, New York, Alfred A. Knopf, Inc 1984, p. 245.

16   Letter from Lord Selborne to Lord Lansdowne, 11 May 1912, forwarded by Lansdowne to Bonar Law 15 May 1912, BL/26/3/21, Bonar Law Papers, Parliamentary Archive, London; Letter from Arthur Steel-Maitland to Bonar Law, 6 December 1911, BL/24/4/113, Bonar Law Papers, Parliamentary Archive, London.

17   Percy Illingworth (1869–1915) was MP for Shipley 1906–1915 and a Liberal Whip from February 1910. He succeeded Alick Murray as Chief Whip in 1912 and was one of Gregory's early 'Man of the Day' clients. Assisted Murray in compiling the peerage list for implementation in the event that the Parliament Bill's rejection. Five known Gregory clients appear on the list; Cecil A Grenfell, Sir George Lewis, John Massie, Sir Edward Nelson and Sir Alfred Turner. Illingworth died of food poisoning in January 1915.

CHAPTER FOUR

Not a 'Sahib'

1   TNA BT/31 22577/138192, File on Albermarle Investments Ltd.
2   TNA KV2/340 #264520. MI5 file on Maundy Gregory and the Keen-Hargreaves brothers.
3   New York State Supreme Court/1916/Keen-Hargreaves H v Lauten C E, File #34152.
4   TNA KV2/340 #264520, MI5 File on Maundy Gregory, note of 22 March 1926 from Major Holt-Wilson to Sir Maurice Hankey.
5   TNA/HO144/590/380368, 'Steps to be taken on the establishment of a Directorate of Home Intelligence' explains the background to his role.
6   TNA HO/144/1590/380368, ibid.
7   Stevenson, Frances, *Lloyd George*, A. J. P. Taylor, ed., New York, Harper & Row 1971. Entry of 10 February 1916.
8   TNA KV2/340 #264520, MI5 File on Maundy Gregory, letter of 22 June 1916 from Sir Basil Thomson to Vernon Kell.
9   Ibid.
10   Ibid.
11   Ibid.
12   McCormick, ibid., p. 19.
13   Inglis, Brian, *Roger Casement*, London, Penguin Books Ltd 2002
14   Inglis cites for the Casement/Christensen story TNA files FO 95/776 (Findlay affair) 1914; FO337/105 (Findlay affair) 1914; 366/778 (Pension); and at the National Library of Ireland file 14,914 (Copies of correspondence relating to Casement in the German archives).
15   Inglis, ibid. p. 277.
16   Inglis, ibid. p. 285.
17   Inglis, ibid.
18   Inglis, ibid.
19   Singleton-Gates, Peter, and Girodias, Maurice, *The Black Diaries, an account of Roger Casement's life and times with a collection of his diaries and public writings*, Paris, Olympia Press 1959. Introduction, p. 21.

20   TNA MEPO 2/10672. Sheet marked 'Special Branch 8296' is a list
     dated July, 1916 following the execution, being a list of 'Property
     taken possession of by Inspector Parker and other officers'. The list
     is headed 'brought to New Scotland Yard by Mr Germain, 50 Ebury
     Street, on 25 April 1916, Trunk No 1 containing . . . (and) Trunk No 2
     containing. . . ' Contents include the diaries.

21   Singleton-Gates, ibid.

22   Sir Basil Thomson's wartime diary is reproduced in his 1937 book
     The Scene Changes. I am indebted to the Thomson family for access
     to the original handwritten diaries, from which it is clear that the
     diary in The Scene Changes is an edited version of events recorded in
     the original six volumes.

23   Inglis, *Roger Casement*, p. 358.

24   The story of Craig, Phyllis Barnes and the meeting with Maundy
     Gregory is found in Cullen, Tom, *Maundy Gregory: Purveyor of Honours*,
     London, The Bodley Head 1974, pp. 89-90.

25   TNA KV2/340 #264520, MI5 File on Maundy Gregory, this and
     ensuing correspondence.

26   TNA FO 371/2020, The Tilinsky Case, 7 October 1914.

27   TNA KV2/340 #264520. MI5 File on Maundy Gregory, report by
     Inspector Herbert Fitch, dated 16 July 1917.

28   Coincidentally his old friend Harold Davidson had been curate at
     Combermere Barracks in 1905, before St Martin-in-the-Fields.

29   TNA/WO339/124709, War Office Service File on A. J. Maundy
     Gregory.

30   TNA KV2/340 #264520, MI5 File on Maundy Gregory, Major Holt
     Wilson to Sir Maurice Hankey, 23 March 1926.

31   TNA/MEPO 2/9147 Askew to Superintendent Horwell,
     25 February 1933, Metropolitan Police File on Maundy Gregory
     and the Suspicious Death of Mrs Edith Rosse.

CHAPTER FIVE

Breakthrough

 1   Shannon, Richard, *The Crisis of Imperialism, 1865–1915*, St Albans,
     Paladin, 1976.

2   *The Times,* 8 June 1917, p. 9 col. f

3   Asquith, in the course of his affair with Venetia Stanley which lasted from 1910 until May, 1916, wrote entirely in confidence. Discussing her opposition to Neil Primrose as Chief Whip he wrote, in the second of two notes to her on Wednesday 20 January 1915: 'I had a long talk with Ll George who, failing Neil, was inclined to agree that the Gulland-Benn arrangement was best – tho it is not an exhilarating one (observe the h!)' Prejudices like these were never relinquished. Brook, Michael & Eleanor, eds., *H H Asquith: Letters to Venetia Stanley.* Oxford University Press, Oxford, 1982, Letter 268.

4   On 12 November 1918 Bonar Law told a meeting of Unionist MPs; 'Our party on the old lines will have no future in the life of this country . . . remember this, that at this moment Mr Lloyd George commands an amount of influence in every constituency as great as has ever been exercised by any Prime Minister in our political history.' A week later, at a meeting of the Unionist Parliamentary Party, candidates and the Unionist Central Council at the Connaught Rooms in London, he formally recommended the Coalition's continuation under Lloyd George and outlined its manifesto. Both were agreed unanimously. National Union Archives, 2/1/35, pp. 14–15; Andrew Taylor, *Bonar Law*, London, Haus Publishing, 2006, pp. 96-97.

5   Rhodes James, Robert. ed., *Memoirs of a Conservative: J. C. C. Davidson's Memoirs and Papers 1910-37*, London, Macmillan 1970 p. 265.

6   Royal Commission on Honours, 1922, Templewood Papers, Part 1, Box 2, File 11, Paper 32: copy of statement of evidence furnished by the Duke of Northumberland, Cambridge University Library.

7   Upon his death in August, 1919, the American steel magnate Andrew Carnegie would leave Lloyd George an annuity of £2,000.

8   McEwen, J.M. 'Lloyd George's Acquisition of the Daily Chronicle', *Journal of British Studies*, 1982, Vol 22, Part 1, p. 127ff.

9   *Daily Chronicle*, Monday 25 November 1918, p. 1.

10   Lloyd George Papers, F/11/9/25, undated, no provenance other than 10 Downing Street, Parliamentary Archive, London.

11   'Marconi' had been a case of insider trading from which Lloyd George and Rufus Isaacs, later Marquis of Reading (Attorney General, and brother of Marconi's Chairman at a time when Marconi was about to receive a fat contract) appear to have benefited; as did Alick Murray

who bought Marconi shares for Liberal Party funds. His employment in 1912 by Lord Cowdray, for whom he had obtained a peerage in 1910, facilitated his convenient disappearance to Bogota. Jeers of 'BogoTA!' followed him at public meetings ever after.

12   Entry 303, Register of Births in the District of Morpeth in the County of Northumberland, 10 February 1874, Thomas Henry Shaw; I am particularly grateful for the co-operation of Harry Shaw's family during the writing of this book.

13   While Shaw's main function was to identify potential donors through his social connections, particularly in the racing world, and steer them towards the Unionist Whips Office, he was very much a Coalition Unionist. He could count as friends several members of Lloyd George's cabinet, both Unionist and Liberal. His public exposure as an honours tout in 1922 was almost certainly the work of the anti-coalition 'die-hard' faction of the Unionist Party, seeking to discredit the pro-coalition leadership by drawing them into the honours scandal mire.

CHAPTER SIX

A Vanishing

1   TNA/WO 339/24709, Maundy Gregory's War Office Service File; Maundy Gregory's post-war address details were written 24a High Street. Ethel Marion Rosse later testified that her aunt owned 5 flats at 34a, Hinde Street (TNA/MEPO 2/9147 Statement, 15 February 1933).

2   www.parliament.the-stationery-office.com/pa/ld/ldresource/4411. htm.

3   Cullen, Tom, *Maundy Gregory,* p. 90.

4   Coote, Colin R. *The Other Club*, London, Sidgwick & Jackson 1971.

5   Coote, ibid.

6   Coote, ibid.

7   TNA/MEPO 2/9147. Suspicious Death of Mrs E.M. Rosse. Statement of Ethel Marion Davies, 15 February 1933.

8   TNA HO 283/40/22 The 1944 statement of Neil Francis-Hawkins, interned 1940 as member of BUF and formerly of BF.

9   TNA KV2/340 #264520, MI5 File on Maundy Gregory, Note of 22 March 1926 from Major Holt-Wilson to Sir Maurice Hankey.

10   Grayson was not an official Labour Party candidate. The Labour Party in fact refused to endorse him as a parliamentary candidate. He was selected by the Colne Valley Labour League, an alliance of Labour, Social Democratic Federation, Socialist Party and Independent Labour Party members. It was affiliated to the ILP, who did retrospectively endorse Grayson's candidature. On election he was offered the Labour Party Whip in the House of Commons but refused it.

11   Clark, David, *Victor Grayson: Labour's Lost Leader*, London, Quartet Books, 1985, pp. 92-3, 154-5, 160.

12   http://www.1in12.go-legend.net/publications/library/spies/spies. htm. Hughes, Mike, *Spies at Work*, Bradford, 1 in 12 Publications, 1994, Chapter 3.

13   Letter (copy in author's possession) dated 18.12.1970 to Donald McCormick from H.P. Smallwood, who had in 1950 as an investigator working at Mount Pleasant 'in co-operation with the GPO-SIB' who made friends with a fat, rather derelict and disabled street character called Victor Garston. 'I do not claim Victor Garston was Victor Grayson. All that I can say is . . . I have never come across so many coincidental facts without there being more to it than meets the eye!' I believe Mr Smallwood's letter to be genuine. The orators in the picture, Garston said, included himself.

14   Hilda Porter's testimony is not given verbatim although David Clark did meet her. Some of her reported testimony may have originated in newspapers of the 1920s.

15   The late Melvin Harris, author of several books on Jack the Ripper, must take a great deal of the credit for exposing Donald McCormick's *modus operandi*. McCormick had two books published in 1959 – *The Mysterious Death of Lord Kitchener* and *The Identity of Jack the Ripper*. Harris first came to suspect McCormick of fabrication shortly after their publication. While working for BBC Radio he was assigned to look into the possibility of a programme based on the claim that the Admiralty were hiding the truth about Kitchener's death. He concluded 'that the only new evidence (ie first person revelations)

was simply manufactured'. For a detailed account of the fabrications unearthed by Harris in respect to McCormick books see www. casebook.org/dissertations/maybrick_diary/mb-mc.html.

16 Letter from Eileen W. McCormick, of 8 December 2000, referring to meeting with the author of 5 November 2000, in author's possession.

17 Daily Weather Report of the Meteorological Office, British Section, 1919 No 27DB, Sunday 28 September, Met Office Archive, Exeter.

18 Interview between the author and Eileen McCormick, 5 November 2000.

CHAPTER SEVEN

Ups and Downs

1 TNA/MEPO 2/9147. Suspicious Death of Mrs E.M. Rosse. CID Chief Inspector Askew to Superintendent Horwell, 25 February 1933.

2 Cullen, 1974, ibid., interview with Miss Leila Sterling Mackinlay, p.129.

3 TNA/MEPO 2/9147. Suspicious Death of Mrs E.M. Rosse. Fred Davies, in his Statement to the police of 14.2.1933, put this date as July, 1914. Ethel's recollection is different, and since she was only twelve at the time and could remember her subsequent schooling, and also since the likelihood of Fred's having let a child go when he was called up (as a married man, in 1916) is greater, I have chosen to favour Ethel's version.

4 Lloyd George Papers, F/21/3/23, letter of 16 May 1919 from F.E. Guest to Lloyd George, Parliamentary Archive, London.

5 Stevenson, *Lloyd George*, Diary entry of 23.5.1919.

6 Lloyd George Papers, F/21/3/24, letter of 30 May 1919 from F.E. Guest to Lloyd George, Parliamentary Archive, London

7 *The Times*, 19 May 1920.

8 Lloyd George Papers, F/9/2/9, a shortlist of names for the new centre party to be created by the fusion of the Coalition Liberals and Unionists, Parliamentary Archive, London.

9   Lloyd George Papers, F/22/1/38, letter of 17 May 1920 from F.E. Guest to Lloyd George, Parliamentary Archive, London.

10   Beaverbrook, Lord, *Decline and Fall of Lloyd George*, London, Collins 1963. Introduction, note 1, p. 9.

11   Lloyd George Papers, F/29/4/34, letter of 19 January 1921 from Lord Stamfordham to Lloyd George's Private Secretary J.T. Davies. Hodge was charged under the Defence of the Realm Act and found guilty of food hoarding at Gosforth Assizes on 18 April 1918. The court was told that when police visited his home they found 1,148 lbs of flour; 333lbs of sugar; 148lbs 6oz of bacon and ham; 29lbs of sago; 19lbs 7oz of split peas; 32lbs of lentils; 31lbs of rice; 25 tins of sardines; 10 jars of ox tongue; 19 tins of salmon; 85 lbs of jam and marmalade and 61 tins of preserved fruit.

12   Lloyd George Papers, F/8/2/44, letter of 8 December 1918 from Churchill's Private Secretary Sir Edward Marsh to Lloyd George's Private Secretary J.T. Davies, Parliamentary Archive, London.

13   Campbell, John, *F.E. Smith, First Earl of Birkenhead*, London, Jonathan Cape, 1983, p. 696.

14   *The Times*, 1 November 1921 and numerous reports throughout this month and the next; see *The Times* Digital Archive.

15   *The Times*, 7 November 1921, p. 11 col. g.

16   *The Times*, 2 December 1921.

17   *The Times*, 2 March 1934. Payments by cheque to Sir Basil Thomson in the 1920s after his retirement from the police, recorded among papers of Mr Pengelly and mentioned during Pengelly's court appearance.

CHAPTER EIGHT

Gathering Storm

1   Coote, Colin R. *Editorial, the Memoirs of Colin R Coote*, London, Eyre & Spottiswoode, 1965, p. 112.

2   Lord Beaverbrook, *The Decline and Fall of Lloyd George*, p. 39.

3   Morgan, Kenneth O. *Consensus and Disunity: The Lloyd George Coalition Government 1918-22*, Oxford, Clarendon Press 1979 p. 32.

4   Hope, John, 'Fascism, the Security Service and the Curious Careers of

Maxwell Knight and James McGuirk Hughes', in *Lobster: The Journal of Parapolitics* number 22, November 1991.

5   Bonar Law Papers, BL/100/1/2, letter of 2 January 1921 from Sir George Younger to Bonar Law, Parliamentary Archive, London.

6   Rhodes James, Robert, ed., *Memoirs of a Conservative*, p. 265.

7   Royal Commission on Honours, Templewood Papers, Part 1, Box 2, File 11, Paper 32, p. 11, Cambridge University Library.

8   Austen Chamberlain Papers, AC 26/4/37. Letter of 24 November 1921 from 'Bal', (David Lindsay, 27th Earl of Crawford and 10th Earl of Balcarres) at 7 Audley Square, University of Birmingham.

9   Austen Chamberlain Papers, AC/26/4/39. Letter of 28 November 1921 from Austen Chamberlain to 'Bal', University of Birmingham.

10   Austen Chamberlain Papers, AC/32/2/25. Letter of 10 January 1922 from Lloyd George at Villa Valetta, Cannes to Austen Chamberlain, University of Birmingham.

11   Lloyd George Papers, F/29/4/103, Letter of 3 July 1922 from HM King George V to Lloyd George, Parliamentary Archive, London.

12   Templewood Papers, Part 1, Box 2, File 11, Sir Clive Wigram on HM Victoria & Albert, 4 July 1922, Cambridge University Library.

13   Knightley, Phillip, *The Vestey Affair*, London, Macdonald Futura Publishers, 1981.

14   Knightley, ibid.

15   Cullen, Tom, *Maundy Gregory*, p. 112.

16   Lloyd George Papers, F/252/2, Memorandum of 29 June 1922 from A.J. Sylvester to Lloyd George; Letter of 23 June 1922 from Sir J.B. Robinson to Lloyd George appended.

17   *The Times*, 20 July 1922, p. 10.

18   Ibid.

19   *The Times*, 19 July 1922, p. 10.

20   *Hansard*, House of Lords, 5th Series, v. i, col. 507.

21   *The Times*, 29 December 1921, p. 5. Stowe School is today one of the country's leading public schools and a member of the Headmasters & Headmistresses Conference.

CHAPTER NINE

New Opportunities

1   Stevenson, *Lloyd George*, Diary entry of 14 February 1915.

2   Royal Commission on Honours, Templewood Papers, Part 1, Box 2, File 2, Paper 32, pp. 1-2, University of Cambridge.

3   Lord Beaverbrook, *The Decline and Fall of Lloyd George*, p184ff.

4   The Newport by-election was held on 18 October 1922. Lloyd George and Chamberlain hoped that the predicted Labour victory would convince Unionist MPs of the merits of the coalition as the only way of keeping Labour out of power. J.W. Bowen, General Secretary of the Postal Workers Union was the Labour candidate and favourite to win. R.G. Clarry, the Conservative candidate was anti-coalition as indeed was the Liberal William Moore. The result was Clarry 13,515, Bowen 11,425 and Moore 8,841. Although retrospectively interpreted by history as an anti-coalition vote, (for example, see Beaverbrook, *The Decline and Fall of Lloyd George*, p 190) the reality was that the coalition was not an issue in the election. The biggest issue was undoubtedly alcohol. Clarry came out strongly against the Licensing Bill whereas the Liberal and Labour campaigns backed it and received support from prominent temperance campaigners. If, as expected, Bowen had won the seat it may well have strengthened Chamberlain's hand at the Carlton Club meeting. However, in an election where all three candidates declared themselves anti-coalition, Moore's poor performance can hardly be portrayed as a decisive rejection of the coalition. For daily reports on the by-election campaign, see *South Wales Argus*, in particular, editions of 15, 16, 17, 18, 19 October 1922.

5   Lord Beaverbrook, ibid. p. 190.

6   These included Sir Robert Horne (Chancellor of the Exchequer); Austen Chamberlain (Lord Privy Seal); Sir Laming Worthington-Evans (War); and Sir Arthur Lee (First Lord of the Admiralty).

7   Campbell, John, *F.E. Smith*, p. 598.

8   Campbell, ibid, p. 601.

9   The Baldwin Papers, 162/24. Letter of 29 September 1927 from Stanley Baldwin to A.J. Bennett, on his appointment as Assistant

Treasurer 'for the purpose of collecting funds. This work you will carry
out in co-operation with the Principal Agent, and under the direction
of the Chairman of the Party.', Cambridge University Library.

10   Walter Kent was Chairman and Managing Director of the hydraulic
instrument firm George Kent Ltd of Luton. In 1918 he was awarded
the CBE in connection with the war time government contracts
undertaken by the firm. In February 1923 he met with Maundy
Gregory in pursuit of a higher honour. As a result, money changed
hands and as a precursor, Kent was given the same high profile
treatment in the *Whitehall Gazette* (June 1923 edition, p. 2-23) as had
been given to the likes of Rowland Hodge, Joseph Robinson and
other title seeking clients. In a gushing editorial Gregory referred to
Kent as holding a 'prominent place in the engineering world' and
his firm 'as everyone knows is famous for its domestic labour-saving
appliances such as the knife-cleaning machine'. As this edition of
the *Gazette* was at the printers, Bonar Law, with whom Gregory had
a longstanding association, resigned due to ill health. His successor,
Baldwin, was resolved to dispense with the use of touts and Kent's
name was effectively blackballed. In 1927 it was suggested to a number
of individuals who had paid sums to Gregory that if they could
retrieve their money they might then find favour on a future Baldwin
Honours List. Kent's name finally appeared on the 1929 Birthday
Honours List. His Knighthood was gazetted for 'political services',
although he had been chairman of his local association for some four
years at the time. Furthermore, as the Luton News pointed out (June
6, 1929), he had only been an active member of the Conservative
Party since shortly before the December 1923 General Election. On
this account, virtually every constituency association chairman in the
land would have been entitled to a knighthood.

11   Campbell, *F.E. Smith*, p. 172.

12   *The Times*, 27 December 1922.

13   Rose, Kenneth, *King George V*, p. 253.

14   The 'quarterly emoluments' described in Maundy's own c.v. See
Chapter 15.

15   Campbell, *F.E. Smith*.

16   Brook, Michael & Eleanor, eds, *H H Asquith*, Letter 337, Note 4. Author's

inference – the 'MP and shipowner' concerned is not named.

17 Wentworth Day, J. , *Lucy Houston*, London, Wingate, 1958.

18 The most concrete reference – its source is unknown – is in the Vatican's file on Maundy Gregory; Archivio Segreto Vaticano, Segr. Stato An. 1932 Rubr. 6 fasc. 6 246r-253r.

19 *The Times*, 20 March 1929 p. 5 col. f, (Pavlos) Smikitis vs Nigeradze (*sic*) in the High Court.

20 See *The Times*, Friday 20 March 1921, p. 5, col. a. 'Hammersley, Kennedy & Co. Ltd vs Nigeradse'; also Surrey Record Office Acc. 1358, Dorking Rate book April 1921.

21 See Mercer, Doris, and Jackson, Alan A. *Deepdene, Dorking and District Preservation Society*, 1996. Title deeds shown by Mrs Grimaldi, formerly Mazzina, to Doris Mercer; also Deepdene Estate, financial papers and correspondence 1891–1962, 25870/2226; Deepdene sale particulars 1932, 6003/54-65; Deepdene sale particulars 1921, CC99/40/1, Surrey County Council Archive Centre, Woking.

22 Serkov, A.I., *Encyclopedia of Russian Masons*, Moscow, 2001, p. 45;

23 Svitkov, N., *Masonstvck Russkoi emigratsii*, Paris, 1932, p. 56.

24 Mercer and Jackson, ibid.

25 *The Times*, 29 April 1925, p. 23 col. c.

26 Cook, A., *Ace of Spies, the True Story of Sidney Reilly*, Stroud, Tempus, 2003, p. 107.

27 Russian *laisser-passer* attached to Sidney Reilly's letter to Colonel Byron, War Office, dated 19 January 1918 (Sidney Reilly's MI5 file PF 864103).

28 Cook, *Ace of Spies*, p. 195ff.

29 Copy in author's possession.

30 Mercer and Jackson, ibid. Local accounts of a flamboyant foreign princess in residence.

31 Bennett, Gill, 'A most extraordinary and mysterious business': the Zinoviev Letter of 1924, London, Foreign and Commonwealth Office, General Services Command, 1999; and Bennett, Gill, *Churchill's Man of Mystery*, London, Routledge, pp. 79-85.

32 TNA/MEPO 2/9147. Suspicious Death of Mrs E.M. Rosse. Statement of Frederick Rosse to Chief Inspector Agnew, 23 February 1933, recorded in Agnew's own Suspicious Death report.

33   British Library VOC/1923/ROSSE (awaiting full cataloguing) TNA/
      MEPO 2/9147. Suspicious death of Mrs E. M. Rosse. Letter of Edith
      Marion Rosse to Janet Weakley, 15 April 1930, and Statement of Mrs
      Eyres her housekeeper, 15 April 1933.

CHAPTER TEN

The Rot Sets in

1   Singleton-Gates, Peter, and Girodias, Maurice, *The Black Diaries*. Ensuing
     extracts are from his Introduction.
2   Singleton-Gates, ibid.
3   Singleton-Gates, ibid. Strictly speaking he was right. Thomson had left
     the police when Sir Wyndham Childs took his job.
4   *The Times*, 17 December 1925, p. 5 col. f, and hearing shortly afterwards.
5   TNA KV2/340 #264520, MI5 File on Maundy Gregory, Major Holt
     Wilson to Sir Maurice Hankey, 23 March 1926.
6   TNA KV2/340 #264520, MI5 File on Maundy Gregory.
7   Campbell, John, *F E Smith, First Earl of Birkenhead*.
8   Stevenson, *Lloyd George*, Diary entry of 18 June 1921.
9   TNA/BT 226/4757, outline of Gregory's financial affairs in connection
     with bankruptcy, 1933.
10   Cullen, *Maundy Gregory*, p. 121.
11   Rhodes James, Robert, ed., *Memoirs of a Conservative*, pp. 276-7.
12   George II (2007), www.britannica.com/eb/article-9036489.
13   Vatican reference, with enclosure, number 118.265. Report to Monsignor
     Luigi Barlassina, Patriarch of Jerusalem, from the Secretary of State to
     His Holiness at the Vatican, 10 April 1933.
14   *The Times*, Wednesday 20 March, 1929, p. 5 col. f. Smikitis vs Nigeradze
     (*sic*) in the High Court.
15   TNA/MEPO 2/9147. ibid. Mrs Howard's statement says Edith had been
     ill and asked Ethel to come back; Ethel's statement says she returned
     at her own suggestion, the reason being that her aunt had disposed of
     properties (though cause and effect are unclear).

16 Stevenson, *Lloyd George*, 18 June 1921. Lloyd George was wrong about Beaverbrook's motive.

17 Lloyd George Papers, G/4/3/4. Letter of 3 December 1927 from Austen Chamberlain to Lloyd George, Parliamentary Archive, London.

18 Lloyd George Papers, G/4/3/6. First draft of letter from Lloyd George at 25 Old Queen Street 14 December 1927, Parliamentary Archive, London.

19 Lloyd George Papers, G/4/3/6. This is Lloyd George's short, restrained final draft of 14 December 1927. The two un-named Unionist nominated individuals, whose honours attracted great controversy in 1922, and to whom Lloyd George refers in both draft and final version, were Samuel Waring and John Drughorn.

20 TNA KV2/340 #264520, MI5 File on Maundy Gregory, initialled note of 1 December 1928.

21 TNA KV2/340 #264520, MI5 File on Maundy Gregory, letter of 5 December 1928 from J.C.C. Davidson at 12 Palace Chambers to Vernon Kell.

22 Rhodes, ed., *Memoirs of a Conservative*, p. 280.

23 *The Times*, 7 July 1934, p. 4, col. a. Law Report, July 6, Court of Appeal, J. Maundy Gregory ex parte W.T. Norton v. The Trustee.

24 The Baldwin Papers, 162/22. Letter of 26 August 1927 to Viscount Younger of Leckie from Stanley Baldwin, Cambridge University Library.

25 A.J.P. Taylor is rightly sceptical of claims by Baldwin and Davidson to have 'clean hands' concerning cash and honours. In his 1972 biography Beaverbrook, he refers to the example of Andrew Holt, who had paid Davidson £10,000 via Beaverbrook in December 1928 for a knighthood. Davidson acknowledged the money although he indicated to Beaverbrook that there might be some delay in putting the honour through due to the limited number available. Five months later the Conservatives lost power in the 1929 General Election and Davidson returned the money to Beaverbrook as, 'I have had no occasion to make use of the money'. Taylor concludes that, 'Money was paid. A knighthood was promised. Baldwin's claim to clean hands is hardly redeemed by the fact that the promise was not kept'.

CHAPTER ELEVEN

The Dangerous Mr K

1   As related to Tom Cullen (1974, p. 50). John Baker White's own *True Blue, An Autobiography 1902–1939*, London, Frederick Muller Ltd 1970, makes no mention of Maundy Gregory.

2   Meyrick, Kate, *Secrets of the 43*, London, John Long, 1933.

3   Mackenzie, Arthur Compton, *My Life and Times*, Octave Three, 1900-7, London, Chatto & Windus, 1907. Quoted in Cullen, 1975.

4   Symons, A.J.A., *The Quest for Corvo*, London, Penguin Books Ltd, 1940.

5   Glasgow University Special Collections, Manuscripts Catalogue GB 0247 MS MacColl B458.

6   TNA KV2/340 #264520, MI5 File on Maundy Gregory, MI5 interview with Sir Arthur Willert.

7   TNA/KV2/340 #264520, MI5 File on Maundy Gregory. Note to 'B' stating that telephone checks on Maundy Gregory ceased in June, 1932.

8   TNA KV 2/2574, MI5 File on Vladimir Korostovetz, report dated 18 February 1926 to Major Ball at MI5 from Lt Col G S at MI1c.

9   Korostovetz, Vladimir, *Seed and Harvest*, translated from the German by Dorothy Lumby, London, Faber & Faber Ltd, 1931, pp. 343-350.

10 TNA KV 2/2574, MI5 File on Vladimir Korostovetz, report concerning his activities in Berlin during 1926.

11 TNA KV2/2574, MI5 File on Vladimir Korostovetz, report to Capt Harker dated 15 September 1930 on Korostovetz' visit to England on behalf of General Von Schleicher.

12 TNA KV2/340 #264520, MI5 File on Maundy Gregory, 8 March 1932, Anglo-Ukrainian Committee, headed 9A, crossed out, then 13A.

13 TNA KV2/2574, MI5 File on Vladimir Korostovetz, report dated 9 March 1932 on Korostovetz' interview with Capt Harker and Capt Miller.

14 TNA KV2/340 #264520, MI5 File on Maundy Gregory, report dated 8 March 1932 on information volunteered by Vladimir Korostovetz.

CHAPTER TWELVE

Keeping up Appearances

1 Cullen, Tom, *Maundy Gregory,* p. 178. Tom Cullen's information – from Dr Abshagen who was there (p. 178) is that Maundy Gregory went also to a Herrenklub meeting, where he revealed himself as a fraud which is why the Hetman dropped him. This may have been a contributory factor but is not the reason stated in the MI5 file.

2 Cullen, *Maundy Gregory*, p. 179.

3 From an MI5 report quoted in a *Guardian* article by Ben Whitford, 26 June 2003. MI5 used the phrase, and Archibald Maule Ramsay's Right Club membership list of 740 Fascists, in support of moves for their imprisonment in 1940.

4 Baker White, John, *True Blue.*

5 Hamilton, Gerald, *The Way it Was with Me.*

6 Vatican File #118.265 sent to His Most Reverend Excellency, Mons. Luigi Barlassina, Patriarch of Jerusalem, on 10 January 1933, Segr. Stato An. 1932 Rubr. 6 fasc. 6 246r – 253r, Archivio Segreto Vaticano, Rome.

7 Chilcott, Sir Warden, *Political Salvation, 1930–32*, London, Ernest Benn Ltd.

8 Chilcott, ibid.

9 Chilcott, ibid.

10 TNA KV2/340 #264520, MI5 File on Maundy Gregory, memo of 8 March 1932, p. 11.

11 *The Times*, 12 Jan 1932, p. 4 col. f. Settlement, at High Court, of action for breach of contract brought in 1930.

12 *The Times*, Wednesday 20 March 1929, p. 5 col. f. She had to pay about £155 for wrongful dismissal and false imprisonment (by the police at her instigation) plus £10 salary owed.

13 As with a number of Gregory ventures, the hotel was owned by Gregory but fronted by others in whose name the business was run and registered.

CHAPTER THIRTEEN

Uncle Jim

1   TNA/MEPO 2/9147, letter from Head Constable of Winchester to Norman Kendal, Assistant Commissioner, CID, New Scotland Yard, 2 March 1933. A family photograph shows eighty-four year old Mrs Gregory sitting outside the College, where was listed in the local directory in 1933 with seven other clergy widows in receipt of pensions and residence under Bishop Morley's endowment.
2   TNA/MEPO 2/9147. Suspicious Death of Mrs E. M. Rosse. CID Chief Inspector Askew to Superintendent Horwell, 25 February 1933.
3   TNA/MEPO 2/9147. Askew, 25 February 1933, ibid.
4   TNA/MEPO 2/9147. Suspicious Death of Mrs E. M. Rosse. Letter from Hugh Jervoise Donaldson of 8 Hinde Street, Police Inspector of the Federated Malay States, to Chief Inspector Askew, 18 May 1933.
5   TNA/MEPO 2/9147. The Suspicious Death report of 21 April 1933 written by Askew puts this tearing-up of the first will in 1928 and his interview with Dr Blair confirmed that Dr Blair became Mrs Rosse's doctor in the winter of 1928/9.
6   TNA/MEPO 2/9147, Askew, 25 February 1933, ibid.
7   TNA/MEPO 2/9147. Statement of Benjamin George Pengelly, 13 April 1933.
8   TNA/MEPO 2/9147. Letter from B.G. Pengelly to Chief Inspector Askew, 14 April 1933.
9   TNA/MEPO 2/9147. Askew's Suspicious Death report of 21 April 1933 says the sums stopped coming in August, 1931; Ethel Davies said the money was paid until January, 1932. Askew visited the succeeding solicitor and may have seen copy letters.
10 TNA/MEPO 2/9147, Askew, 25 February 1933, ibid.
11 TNA/MEPO 2/9147. Mrs Eyres' testimony (14 April 1933) here contradicts the statement of Ethel Marion Rosse, placing the Eyres' arrival in 1931. Various other statements indicate that this is wrong and the couple came to 10 Hyde Park Terrace in 1932.

12 TNA/MEPO 2/9147, ibid. Pengelly 13 April 1933. In his statement to the police he is clear on this point and also on the date of the telephone call and its co-incidence with the row between Gregory and Ethel, back in February. Maddin's, Solicitors, in their request for exhumation to the Secretary of State, placed Maundy's outright (apparently renewed) request for a loan and the alleged tearing up of the second will together in July. Pengelly is absolutely clear in this statement that he had never been told that the second will had been destroyed.

13 TNA/MEPO 2/9147. Letter from Mrs Frederick Rosse to Janet Weakley, 15 April 1930.

14 TNA/MEPO 2/9147 Statement of Kate Wells, 2 May 1933, p. 2.

15 TNA/MEPO 2/9147, Pengelly, 13 April 1933, ibid.

16 TNA/MEPO 2/9147, Statements of Hugh Jervoise Donaldson, ibid, and Frederick Davies.

17 TNA/MEPO 2/9147. Letter to Miss Janet Weakley, of 136b, Grange Road, Ramsgate, from Edith Rosse, 15 April 1930.

18 TNA/MEPO 2/9147. Mrs Eyres, 15 April 1933, ibid.

19 TNA/MEPO 2/9147. Statement of Ethel Marion Davies, 15 February 1933.

20 Kelly's Directory for 1927 and 1932. Alfred J. Harmsworth lived next door to Zebulon Mennell at number 7.

21 TNA/MEPO 2/9147. Suspicious Death report by Chief Inspector Askew, 21 April 1933, p. 15.

22 TNA/MEPO 2/9147. Mrs Eyres, 15 April 1933, ibid. Dr Plummer says it was he who prompted Maundy Gregory to get a pencil (as opposed to a pen). Maundy Gregory's account in the press the following year mentions her request for a pen.

23 TNA/MEPO 2/9147. Statement of Dr Edgar Curnow Plummer, 15 April 1933 'At my suggestion Mr Gregory got paper and pencil and made the Will at her dictation.'

24 TNA/MEPO 2/9147. Mrs Eyres, 15 April 1933, ibid.

25 TNA/MEPO 2/9147. Statements of Dr Edgar Curnow Plummer, 15 April 1933 and of Mrs Eyres, 15 April 1933, ibid.

26 TNA/MEPO 2/9147, copy Will of Edith Marion Rosse, and Affidavit

of Edgar Curnow Plummer, sworn before a Commissioner for Oaths for Probate purposes on 26 September 1932.

27 TNA/MEPO 2/9147. Dr Edgar Curnow Plummer, 15 April 1933, ibid.

28 TNA/MEPO 2/9147. Statement of William Earl Rombough of Islington, 13 April 1933.

29 TNA/MEPO 2/9147. Mrs Eyres, 15 April 1933, ibid.

30 TNA/MEPO 2/9147. Statement of Mrs Hilda Howard, 19 April 1933.

31 TNA/MEPO 2/9147. Request for exhumation dated 6 April 1933 and addressed to the Secretary of State at the Home Office from C.A.Maddin & Co., Solicitors, Surbiton.

32 TNA/MEPO 2/9147. Statement of Dr Basil Thomas Parsons-Smith, 15 April 1933.

33 TNA/MEPO 2/9147. Statement of David Levi, 18 April 1933.

34 TNA/MEPO 2/9147. Dr Edgar Curnow Plummer, 15 April 1933.

35 Entry No 305, Death in the Registration District of Paddington, Sub-District of Paddington South in the County of London, 14 September 1932, Edith Marion Rosse.

CHAPTER FOURTEEN

Acting Fast

1 TNA/MEPO 2/9147. Statement of Benjamin George Pengelly, 13 April 1933.

2 TNA/MEPO 2/9147. Statement of Ethel Marion Davies, 15 February 1933.

3 TNA/MEPO 2/9147. Statement of Ethel Marion Davies, ibid. Ethel's statement about these events makes no sense, and one might blame the effects of shock for the way events are compressed in her mind, but that her father is more credible on dates. Ethel's version is as follows: having visited Hyde Park Terrace on Saturday 17 September 1932 when the funeral was taking place elsewhere, and having spoken to Maundy on the phone that Saturday evening, she went to see her father in Islington and show him the newspaper. He went out to get

a death certificate. He returned with it 'several hours later' and the following day, a Sunday, she went to see Dr Plummer at his address. Not only could Fred Davies not have obtained the death certificate on a Saturday night, but in fact he did not get it until 19 October 1932. The statement of Frederick Davies, her father, on 14 February 1933 (also in TNA/MEPO 2/9147) makes better sense, being anchored to 19 October when collection of the certificate was officially recorded, and to 21 September 1932, the date of Maundy Gregory's letter to him which is copied in the file.

4   TNA/MEPO 2/9147. Copy letter supplied to Scotland Yard by Fred Davies.

5   TNA/MEPO 2/9147. Copy letter supplied to Scotland Yard by Fred Davies.

6   TNA/MEPO 2/9147. Copy letter supplied to Scotland Yard by Fred Davies.

7   TNA/MEPO 2/9147. Statement of Ethel Marion Davies, 15 February 1933.

8   TNA/MEPO 2/9147. Letter from Frederick Rosse to Fred Davies, 11 November 1932.

9   TNA/MEPO 2/9147 Letter to DCI Askew from Maddin's, Solicitors, 12 April 1933.

10 TNA/KV2/340 # 264520, MI5 File on Maundy Gregory, cover note dated 6 January 1933 with attached copy telegram from Sir Basil Thomson to Maundy Gregory dated 29 December 1932.

CHAPTER FIFTEEN

Downfall

1   The Baldwin Papers, 58/123-158. Sherburn case correspondence, Cambridge University Library.

2   TNA/T527/432. Statement by Edward Billyard-Leake enclosed with letter from Sir Maurice Gwyer, Treasury Secretary, to DPP, 4 February 1933.

3   TNA/T527/432, Statement of Edward Billyard-Leake, ibid.

4   The house was Harefield Park, the hospital which grew to become the world-famous Harefield Hospital, Middlesex.

5   TNA/T527/432 Statement of Edward Billyard-Leake, ibid.

6   This appears to be a Turkish Order. Franz Liszt's letter to Countess Marie d'Agoult, dated 17 July 1847, is quoted in Adrian Williams, *Portrait of Liszt*, Oxford 1990, where he tells her that on meeting the Sultan of Turkey, His Majesty had honoured Liszt's talent with gifts of money and a present, and conferred upon him 'the Order of Nichan-Iftikar in diamonds.' Its scrolled Diploma is in the Liszt Museum, Weimar, Germany.

7   Since Sir Lionel Halsey, one-time Third Sea Lord, had commanded the Australian Navy after the War, and since Billyard-Leake's parents were Australians and he himself was a naval officer, he might have been expected to know something of him. Sir Sidney Fremantle was also an Admiral. In this statement Billyard-Leake refers to a Lady Rathbone being present at the Carlton Hotel, who Gregory pointed out as someone whose husband he had obtained a title for. Billyard-Leake must either have been mistaken about her name or Gregory had been bluffing him. There was no such person as Lady Rathbone.

8   TNA/T527/432 Statement of Edward Billyard-Leake, ibid.

9   TNA/MEPO 2/9147 The police insisted that 'This is the first charge that has been made against the defendant' although they had received several complaints.

10   Cullen, *Maundy Gregory*, p. 51ff.

11   Among Gregory's records for 1932 was found a typed list of six names; James Burrows, Harold Sanderson, Clifford Sherburn, Godfrey Law, Edward Billyard-Leake and Norman Harrington. It would appear that this had been sent to him although there is now no trace of any covering letter or any indication of the sender's identity. It is known that Sherburn's father had apparently been promised a baronetcy prior to his death and that Billyard-Leake's father had been offered a knighthood, which had been rejected as he felt it should be a baronetcy or nothing. Norman Harrington was possibly the son of Sir John Harrington Kt. The fact that Gregory had Billyard-Leake's name on a list prior to the approach that had been made to him by Moffat would strongly suggest that Billyard-Leake did not come into Gregory's orbit by pure chance or by some

misjudgement of Moffat's. Were the names forwarded to Gregory as persons who might be susceptible to an approach? Billyard-Leake was clearly being cultivated well before Moffat's letter in December 1932. In his Treasury Solicitor's statement (TNA/TS 27/432) he referred to having received an invitation to join the Ambassador Club some months prior to receiving Moffat's letter and that (Gregory's friend) Lord Southborough had apparently offered to propose him. This he described as 'curious' as he had never met the peer.

12 TNA/MEPO 2/9147 Copy letter provided by Edward Billyard-Leake.

13 TNA/MEPO 2/9147. Statement by Edward Billyard-Leake.

14 Ibid.

CHAPTER SIXTEEN

Nemesis

1 TNA KV2/340 #264520; quotations in following passage from documents marked 15a, 16a and 17a and initialled on 6, 7 and 9 February 1933.

2 Birkett was knighted later.

3 TNA/MEPO 2/9147 Suspicious death, CID Central Officer's Special Report, Askew to Superintendent Horwell, 21 April 1933.

4 *The Times*, 22 February 1933, p. 11, col. c.

5 TNA/MEPO 2/9147 Askew to Superintendent Horwell, 25 February 1933, with note at end from Horwell to Assistant Commissioner.

6 TNA/MEPO 2/9147 Superintendent Horwell to Assistant Commissioner as above, 25 February 1933.

7 See for instance Captain Salter's clearance of a file (Chapter 10) and the cessation of telephone checks (Chapter 11).

8 TNA/MEPO 2/9147 Superintendent Horwell to Assistant Commissioner as above, 25 February 1933. In 1941, Harry Distleman was murdered in a snooker hall by Antonio Mancini, who was hanged.

9 TNA/MEPO 2/9147. Statement of Frederick Rosse, 23 February 1933.

10 TNA/BT 226/4757. Handwritten High Court summary of events in case #386 of 1933.

11 TNA/MEPO 2/9147. Statement of Fredereick Rosse, 23 February 1933.

12 TNA/MEPO 2/9147. C Maddin, Maddin's Solicitors, Surbiton, to DCI Askew, 12 April 1933. 'Further to our letter of 11th instant, accompanying, we send you *further* reports [my italics] on interviews herein as hereunder: [Sterling Mackinlay, Dr Wilson, Anonymous.]'

13 TNA/MEPO 2/9147 Request for exhumation dated 6 April 1933 and addressed to the Secretary of State at the Home Office from C.A. Maddin & Co., Solicitors, Surbiton.

14 TNA/KV2/340 #264520, MI5 File on Maundy Gregory. Statement of Edith Kelly, 19 December 1946.

15 Davidson, J.C.C. *Memoirs of a Conservative*, p. 288.

CHAPTER SEVENTEEN

Open Verdict

1 TNA/MEPO 2/9147 Copy Request for Exhumation by Maddin's, Solicitors, 6 April 1933.

2 TNA/MEPO 2/9147 Copy 2-page list, New Scotland Yard, 2 May 1933, signed on first page by G. Roche Lynch.

3 TNA/MEPO 2/9147 2-page report from Dr Roche Lynch at the Department of Chemical Pathology, St Mary's Hospital, Paddington, W2, 17 July 1933.

4 TNA/BT 226/4757 re. J. Maundy Gregory.

5 TNA MEPO 2/9147 contains post mortem report of 17 July 1933 and Askew's report 22 July 1933 of the inquest.

6 Report commissioned by the author, dated 5 January 2007, from Professor Derrick J. Pounder at the Centre for Forensic and Legal Medicine, University of Dundee.

7 I have anglicised the spelling. The research was by Keith N.M., Wagener H.P., and Kernohan J.W., 'The syndrome of malignant hypertension', *Arch Intern Med* 1928; 41:141-88. The article, by doctors Ventura, Mehra & Messerli, is in *The American Heart Journal*, August 2001: 'Desperate diseases, desperate measures: Tackling Malignant hypertension in the 1950s'.

8   Cullen, *Maundy Gregory.*, p. 175. Maundy told Mrs Maisie Saunders that he had obtained crude curare from South America. Given Basil Thomson's apparent willingness to make free with material gathered during the Casement case, Thomson may have been its source. Casement had apparently tried to kill himself with curare while in custody: see Inglis, p 320.

9   TNA MEPO 2/9147 Sergeant Ruffett to DCI Askew, 23 December 1933: he has been unable to find out the terms of the out of court settlement made on 4 November 1933.

10 TNA/69/1753 Diary entry of James Ramsay Macdonald, 13 December 1933.

CHAPTER EIGHTEEN

Sanctuary

1   Warrant signed by Official Receiver, issued at High Court of Justice in Bankruptcy and addressed to the Commissioner, Metropolitan Police.

2   The Hotel Lotti in 2007 is a luxurious, centrally placed five-star hotel with high room rates, and in 1933/4 it was similarly prestigious. Gerald Macmillan, who seems to have no information at all about the Hotel Lotti, places Maundy at the Hotel Vendôme immediately before he found the flat in the rue d'Anjou.

3   *The Times*, 2 March 1934.

4   *The Times*, 24 February 1934, p. 9, col. c, 'Blackmail Charge'.

5   *The Times*, 2 March 1934, 'Demanding Money with Menaces'.

6   *The Times*, 12 June 1934, p. 5, col. e (Watson case and Barlassina case); and 7 July 1934, p. 4, col. a (Watson case).

7   TNA/MEPO 2/9147 Ethel Marion Davies' letter of 31 July 1934 is appended to a memo of 1 August 1933 from Askew to the Assistant Commissioner.

8   Frank Dorsey, letter from Yvelines 13 July 1969 to Donald McCormick in Beckenham. I have tried without success to trace Mr Dorsey, whose letter seems entirely genuine. McCormick could, of course, have invented both him and his intriguing letter. I rather hope that my inclusion of such a long section of his own text may flush him out if he ever existed.

9   TNA KV2/340 #264520, MI5 File on Maundy Gregory, note of 18 May 1939.
10 TNA KV2/340 #264520, MI5 File on Maundy Gregory, notes of 24 February 1940 and 20 March 1940.
11 Cullen, 1974 ibid., p. 233.
12 Cullen, 1974 ibid., pp. 235/6.
13 TNA KV2/340 #264520 Note to HM Chief Inspector from an ex-MI5 man arriving at Immigration, Gatwick. The note was on behalf of Mr Percy Eade, immigration officer at Gatwick, to Major Guy Liddell at MI5 on 19 December 1946. (Gatwick did not at that time receive commercial flights.).
14 Cullen, 1974 ibid., p. 246.

APPENDIX 1

Enquiry Agent

1   The two lists date from 1915/16.
2   The list of German names appears to have come from Harry Keen-Hargreaves in New York. Many of the names correspond with names of passenger lists of ships sailing from New York to English ports during this period.
3   TNA KV2/340 #264520, MI5 File of Maundy Gregory. This name appears on the cross reference section of the introductory page of Gregory's file.

APPENDIX 2

A Brief History of the Honours System 1485-2007

1   An edited version of this article, 'Hawking Peerages', by Andrew Cook, appeared in *History Today*, November 2006, p. 36ff.
2   Black, J. B., *The Reign of Elizabeth, 1558–1603*, Oxford, OUP, 1936.
3   TNA/SP14, 1616, State Papers of James I.

4   TNA/SP14, 1623, State Papers of James I.

5   TNA/SP14, 1625, State Papers of James I.

6   TNA/SP16, 1642, State Papers of Charles I.

7   TNA/SP14, 1611, State Papers of James I.

8   TNA/SP14, 1619, State Papers of James I.

9   TNA/SP14, 1624, State Papers of James I.

10 Noble, M., *Memoirs of the Protectoral House of Cromwell*, 2 Vols, Birmingham, 1787, pp. 439-42; Sherwood, R. *Oliver Cromwell: King in All But Name*, Stroud, Sutton Publishing, 1997, p. 105ff.

11 Namier, L. *The Structure of Politics at the Accession of George III*, London, Macmillan, 1959.

12 Pimlott, B. *Harold Wilson*, London, Harper Collins, p. 686.

13 Ibid.

APPENDIX 3

The Asquith Peerage List 1911

1   For Asquith's records concerning honours and honours lists see MS Asquith 2, 46, 82 and 83, Bodleian Library, Oxford.

2   Given a peerage by Asquith in November 1911.

3   Given a peerage by Lloyd George on the controvercial 1922 Birthday Honours List.

4   An Irish peer therefore not already a member of the House of Lords.

5   Given a peerage by Asquith in November 1911.

6   Given a peerage by Asquith in December 1912.

7   Given a peerage by Lloyd George in June 1917.

8   Given a peerage by Asquith in February 1912.

9   A Maundy Gregory client.

10 Given a peerage by Asquith in July 1914.

11 Given a peerage by Asquith in January 1914.

12 Given a peerage by Lloyd George in October 1919.

13 A coutesy title, not therefore already a member of the House of Lords.

14 Given peerage by Asquith in July 1914.

15 A Maundy Gregory client.

16 Given a peerage by Asquith in February 1912.

17 Given a peerage by Lloyd George in January 1918.

18 A courtesy title, not therefore already a member of the House of Lords.

19 A courtesy title, not therefore already a member of the House of Lords.

20 Given a peerage by Lloyd George in November1922.

21 A Maundy Gregory client.

22 Given a peerage by Asquith in January 1916.

23 Given a peerage by Asquith in July 1912.

24 Given a baronetcy by Lloyd George 1919.

25 A Maundy Gregory client.

26 Given a peerage by Lloyd George in January 1920.

27 A courtesy title, not therefore already a member of the House of Lords.

APPENDIX 4

Lloyd George Peerages

1 Prince Alexander of Battenburg, for example, was created Marquess of Carisbrooke on 18 July 1917, while his brother Prince Louis of Battenburg was created Marquess of Milford Haven on 17 July 1917.

2 Although Sir Frederick Smith's peerage was secured by money changing hands, Gregory had no involvement, as his role did not commence until January 1919. A note written by Chief Whip F.E. Guest to J.T. Davies, Lloyd George's Private Secretary, on 11 June 1919 reads; 'Bonar has made a tidy pile for his party coffers with peerages for Sir Matthew Arthur, Sir Thomas Dewar and Sir William Tatem – we have only Sir Frederick Smith to date' (Lloyd George Papers, F/21/3/24).

3 Sir Matthew Arthur (see note 2) was Chairman of Arthur & Co Ltd (company accounts at Scottish Companies House, # SCO44211).

4 Sir William Tatem (see note 2) was an associate of Sir Archibald Williamson (see note 12); they had in common directorships in several companies including Lobitos Oilfields Ltd and Anglo-Ecuadorian Oilfields Ltd (company accounts at Companies House, # 00154228).

5 Sir Thomas Dewar (see note 2).

6 Sir William Beardmore, like fellow iron and steel magnate Sir Frederick

Mills, was a Unionist supporter, but was 'poached' by Gregory much to the chagrin of Unionst Chief Whip Sir George Younger (see his letter of 2 January 1921 to Bonar Law, BL 100/1/2).

7 Maundy Gregory had no involvement in Sir Robert Nivison's peerage. It would appear that Nivison had dealings with Harry Shaw, whom he initially met through a mutual interest in horse racing.

8 Sir James Buchanan had known Maundy Gregory from the early days of *Mayfair* magazine, in which Buchanan's whisky was regularly advertised. Although a Unionist supporter, his peerage was arranged via the Coalition Liberal Whip's office for a consideration of £50,000.

9 Joseph Watson was a rival of fellow soap magnate Sir William Lever of Lever Brothers. When Lever was ennobled in 1917 Watson was determind to match him. Watson made Maundy Gregory's acquaintance through A.H. Crosfield, of soap manufactuers Joseph Crosfield & Sons Ltd, who had been one of Gregory's Mayfair clients.

10 Maundy Gregory had no connection with wool merchant Francis Willey's ennoblement which was granted for a consideration of £40,000.

11 In December 1927 Lloyd George noted that in 1922 a substantial cheque had passed to the managers of the Unionist Party Fund in respect to Waring's peerage. He further stated that he had grave misgivings about granting the peerage and would have vetoed it if certain facts known to him now had been known to him at the time (Lloyd George Papers, G/4/3/6).

12 Sir Archibald Williamson had originally been on Asquith's 1911 peerage list (see Appendix 3) to be actioned in the event of the Lord's rejection of the 1911 Parliament Bill. During the war his firm Williamson, Balfour & Co had been accused of trading with the enemy. After the war it was felt that it was best to delay his peerage a while in light of the sensitivity surrounding this issue (see letter of 17 May 1920 from F.E. Guest to Lloyd George, Lloyd George Papers, F/22/1/38). The peerage was eventually granted in the Birthday Honours List 1922.

13 It is no coincidence that that majority of sold peerages occurred during 1922. Both Lloyd George and Chamberlain knew that a general election in the later part of that year was more than likely and both therefore strove to accumulate as much money as possible for their campaign coffers.

Sir William Vestey's cheque was destined for the Liberal Coalition Whip's office. He remained a generous benefactor during the early 1920s (Blue Star Line Ltd, company accounts at Companies House, # 00165678).

14 Sir Robert Borwick, a baking and custard powder manufacturer obtained his peerage via Unionist Chief Whip Lesley Wilson. He had made a number of large payments to Unionist funds (George Borwick & Sons Ltd, company accounts at Companies House, # 00074959).

15 Sir Joseph Maclay was another veteran from Asquith's 1911 list. On 9 September 1922 The King's Private Secretary, Lord Stamfordham, wrote to J.T. Davies, Lloyd George's Private Secretary, expressing the King's view that Maclay's nomination should be delayed. He apparently feared this would 'elicit public criticism' and revelations about the 'large fortune' Maclay had apparently made out of the war. With a planned general election approaching, Lloyd George felt unable to forgo Maclay's money and would not back down. The King therefore reluctantly agreed to sanction the peerage.

APPENDIX 5

Baronetcies

1 When, in March 1922, Harry Shaw approached Walter Pyman, of Pyman, Watson & Co, offering a baronetcy, he was rejected. Pyman was a Unionist die-hard and wrote to the Duke of Northumberland about the incident. On 14 July 1922, Northumberland read Pyman's letter in the House of Lords exposing Harry Shaw but omiting Pyman's name (*Hansard*, House of Lords, 5th Series, v. i, col. 507, 14 July 1922). The die-hard *Morning Post* published an article about Shaw the following day and Lloyd George issued a statement in response: 'I do not know Mr Shaw. I have never heard of him before. I never authorised anyone on my behalf to instruct Mr Shaw'. Although this was met with some scepticism, Lloyd George was in fact telling the truth – Shaw was a Coalition-Unionist tout.

2 The critical meeting of 3 December 1916 which led to Lloyd George succeeding Asquith was held at Bailey's home, 38 Bryanston Square, London.

3   A Maundy Gregory client from *Mayfair* magazine.

4   Sir George Younger wrote to Bonar Law on 2 January 1921 complaining
     that Mills, a Unionist supporter, had been 'poached' by Gregory and F.E.
     Guest, who had provided his baronetcy. Younger regretfully mused that
     if he had got to Mills first he would no doubt have 'proven generous' to
     the Unionist Party fund (Bonar Law Papers BL 100/1/2)

5   Drughorn had been convicted in 1915 for trading with the enemy.

6   Although he received his title from Ramsay Macdonald it is clear from
     his own correspondence and diaries that Grant had been a Coalition
     supporter and that his title had been arranged during the Coaltion period
     of office. Grant, however, knew Macdonald personally and loaned him
     a Daimler car and £40,000 of securites (see diaries, National Library
     of Scotland, MS 15978; NA Scotland, GD 3813/1-3; correspondence
     with Ramsy Macdonald, TNA 30/69/1/94 and 30/69/1/34). Grant
     was also an associate of Walter Kent (see notes, chapter 9, #10), a fellow
     member of the Industrial Welfare Society.

APPENDIX 6

Fees on Account

1   Kent was knighted in 1929, but only after obtaining a refund from
     Gregory (see Notes, Chapter 9, #10)

Bibliography

Adams, R.J. Q. *Bonar Law,* London, John Murray, 1999

Aldington, R. *Frauds* London, Heinemann, 1957

Andrew, C. *Secret Service*, London, Heinemann, 1985

Aronson, T. *Prince Eddy and the Homosexual Underworld,* London, John Murray, 1994

Balfour, P. *Society Racket*, London, John Long, 1933

Beaverbrook, Lord, *Men and Power*, London, Hutchinson, 1956

Beaverbrook, Lord, *The Decline and Fall of Lloyd George*, London, Collins, 1963

Bennett, G. *Churchill's Man of Mystery*, London, Routledge, 2007

Birkenhead, Earl, *The Life of F E Smith,* London, Eyre & Spottiswoode, 1965

Black, J. *The Reign of Elizabeth 1558–1603*, Oxford, Clarendon Press, 1936

Blake, Lord, *The Unknown Prime Minister: The Life and Times of Andrew Bonar Law,* London, Eyre & Spottiswood, 1955

Blake, Lord, *The Conservative Party from Peel to Thatcher*, London, Fontana, 1985

Blythe, R. *The Age of Illusion: England in the Twenties and Thirties*, London, Hamish Hamilton, 1963

Boghardt, T. *Spies of the Kaiser*, Basingstoke, Palgrave Macmillan, 2004

Bradford, S. *The Reluctant King*, London, Weidenfield & Nicolson, 1989

Brook, M & E, eds. *H H Asquith: Letters to Venetia Stanley*, Oxford, OUP, 1982

Brust, H.I. *Guarded Kings*, London, Stanley Paul & Co, 1936

Brust, H. *In Plain Clothes*, London, Stanley Paul & Co, 1937

Campbell, J. *F E Smith, First Earl Birkenhead*, London, Jonathan Cape, 1983

Chilcott, Sir W. *Political Salvation*, London, Ernest Benn, 1932

Churchill, W. *My Early Life, 1874–1908*, London, Collins, 1930

Clark, D. *Victor Grayson: Labour's Lost Leader*, London, Quartet, 1985

Cook, A. *On His Majesty's Secret Service*, Stroud, Tempus, 2002

Cook, A. *Ace of Spies, The True Story of Sidney Reilly*, Stroud, Tempus, 2003

Cook, A. *M: MI5's First Spymaster*, Stroud, Tempus, 2004

Cook, A. *Prince Eddy*, Stroud, Tempus, 2006

Coote, C. *Editorial, the Memoirs of Colin Coote*, London, Eyre & Spottiswoode, 1965

Coote, C. *The Other Club*, London, Sidgwick & Jackson, 1971

Cowling, M. *The Impact of Labour 1920–1924*, Cambridge, CUP, 1971

Cullen, T. *Maundy Gregory, Purveyor of Honours*, London, The Bodley Head, 1974

Cullen, T. *The Prostitutes' Padre*, London, The Bodley Head, 1975

Curry, J. *The Security Service 1908–1945: The Official History*, London, PRO, 1999

Deacon, R. *A History of the British Secret Service*, London, Frederick Muller, 1969

Dilnot, G. *Great Detectives and their Methods*, London, Houghton, 1928

Donaldson, F. *Evelyn Waugh*, London, Weidenfeld & Nicolson, 1967

Dutton, D. *Austen Chamberlain: Gentleman in Politics*, Bolton, Ross Anderson, 1985

Dutton, D. *His Majesty's Loyal Opposition, The Unionist Party in Opposition 1905–1915*, Liverpool, Liverpool University Press, 1992

Fitch, H. *Traitors Within*, New York, Doubleday, 1933

George, P. ed; *Philips' Atlas of the British Empire*, Liverpool, George Philip & Son, 1924

Graves, R. and Hodge, A. *The Long Weekend*, London, Faber & Faber, 1940

Grigg, J. *Lloyd George: The People's Champion, 1902–1911*, London, Eyre Methuen, 1978

Grigg, J. *Lloyd George: From Peace to War, 1912–1916*, London, Eyre Methuen, 1985

Grigg, J. *Lloyd George: War Leader, 1916–1918*, London, Allen Lane, 2002

Groves, R. *The Strange Case of Victor Grayson*, London, Pluto, 1975

Hamilton, G. *The Way It Was With Me*, London, Leslie Frewin, 1969

Harrison, M. *Clarence*, London, W H Allen, 1972

Hazlehurst, C. *Politicians at War*, London, Jonathan Cape, 1971

Horne, A. *Macmillan 1894–1956*, London, Macmillan, 1988

Hoare, Sir S. *The Fourth Seal*, London, Heineman, 1930

Inglis, B. *Roger Casement*, London, Penguin, 2002

Jenkins, R. *Asquith*, London, Collins, 1964

Jones, T. *Lloyd George*, London, OUP, 1951

Jones, T. *Whitehall Diary: 1916–1930, London*, London, OUP, 1969

Judd, A. *The Quest for C: Mansfield Cumming and the founding of the Secret Service*, London, Harper Collins, 1999

Kettle, M. *Salome's Last Veil*, London, Granada, 1977

Korostovetz, V. *Seed and Harvest*, London, Faber & Faber, 1931

Knightley, P. *The Vestey Affair*, London, Macdonald Futura, 1981

Linton, W. *Memoirs*, London, Lawrence & Bullen, 1895

Lloyd George D. *War Memoirs*, 2 vols, London, Odhams, 1938

Lloyd George, R. *David & Winston*, London, John Murray, 2005

McCormick, D. *The Identity of Jack the Ripper*, London, Putman, 1959

McCormick, D. *The Mystery of Lord Kitchener's Death*, London, Putman, 1959

McCormick, D. *Murder by Perfection*, London, John Long, 1970

Mackenzie, A. *My Life and Times*, London, Chatto & Windus, 1907

Macmillan, G. *Honours for Sale*, London, Richards Press, 1954

McKinstry, L. *Rosebery*, London, John Murray, 2005

Mackie, J. *The Earlier Tudors 1485–1558*, Oxford, Clarendon Press, 1952

Magnus, P. *King Edward VII*, London, Dutton, 1964

Marquand, D. *Ramsey MacDonald*, London, Jonathan Cape, 1977

Meyrick, K. *Secrets of the 43*, London, John Long, 1933

Mosley, N. *Rules of the Game*, London, Martin Secker & Warburg, 1982

Mosley, N. *Beyond the Pale*, London, Martin Secker & Warburg, 1983

Morgan, K.O. *Consensus and Disunity: The Lloyd George Coalition Government*, Oxford, Clarendon Press, 1979

Mowat, C. *Britain Between the Wars: 1918–1940*, London, Methuen & Co, 1955

Namier, L. *The Structure of Politics at the Accession of George III*, London, Macmillan, 1959

Nicolson, H. *King George V*, London, Constable & Co, 1952

Owen, F. *Tempestuous Journey: Lloyd George, His Life & Times*, London, Hutchinson, 1954

Petrie, Sir C. *The Life and Letters of Rt Hon Sir Austen Chamberlain*, London, Cassell & Co Ltd, 1939

Pimlott, B. *Harold Wilson*, London, Harper Collins, 1992

Porter, B. *Plots and Paranoia 1790–1988*, London, Unwin Hyman, 1989

Porter, B. *The Origins of the Vigilant State*, Weidenfeld & Nicolson, 1987

Ramsden, J. *An Appetite for Power: A History of the Conservative Party since 1830*, London, Harper Collins, 1998

Ramsden, J. *The Age of Balfour and Baldwin 1902–1940*, London, Longmans, 1978

Rhodes James, R. ed. *Memoirs of a Conservative: J C C Davidson's Memoirs and Papers, 1910–1937*, London, Macmillan, 1970

Richardson, M. *Coronets for Sale*, London, Lilliput, 1950

Roberts, A. *Salisbury*, London, Weidenfeld & Nicolson, 1999

Rose, K. *King George V*, London, Weidenfeld & Nicolson, 1983

Service, R. *Lenin*, London, Macmillan, 2000

Shannon, R. *The Crisis of Imperialism*, St Albans, Paladin, 1976

Singleton-Gates, P. *The Black Diaries*, Paris, Olympia Press, 1959

Sherwood, R. *Oliver Cromwell: King in all but name*, Stroud, Sutton Publishing, 1997

Skidelsky, R. *Mosley*, London, Macmillan, 1975

Smith, M. *New Cloak, Old Dagger*, London, Gollancz, 1996

Smith, M. *The Spying Game*, London, Politico's, 2003

Sparrow, G. *The Great Swindlers*, London, John Long, 1959

Spence, R. *Trust No One*, Los Angeles, Feral House, 2002

Stevenson, F. *Lloyd George*, A J P Taylor, ed, New York, Harper & Row, 1971

Sylvester, A.J. *My Life with Lloyd George*, London, Macmillan, 1975

Symons, J. *Horatio Bottomley*, London, Cresset Press, 1955

Symons, J. *The Quest for Corvo*, London, Penguin, 1940

Taylor, A. *Bonar Law*, London, Haus Publishing, 2006

Taylor, A.J.P. *Beaverbrook*, London, Hamish Hamilton, 1972

Toye, R. *Lloyd George & Churchill*, London, Macmillan, 2007

Thompson, W. *The Life of Victor Grayson*, Sheffield, Bennett, 1910

Thomson, B. *Queer People*, London, Hodder & Stoughton, 1922

Thomson, B. *The Story of Scotland Yard*, London, Grayson & Grayson, 1935

Thomson, B. *The Scene Changes*, London, Gollancz, 1937

Thomson, M. *David Lloyd George: The Official Biography*, London, Hutchinson, 1954

Thorpe, D. *Alec Douglas Home*, London, Sinclair Stevenson, 1997

Tuberville, A. *The House of Lords in the Reign of William III*, Westport, Greenwood Press, 1970

Wentworth Day, J. *Lucy Houston*, London, Wingate, 1958

West, N. *MI5*, London, The Bodley Head, 1981

White, J. *True Blue: An Autobiography, 1902–1939*, London, Frederick Muller, 1970

Windsor, D. *A King's Story*, London, The Reprint Society, 1953

Wood, A. *Great Britain 1900–1965*, London, Longman, 1978

Zeigler, P. *King Edward VIII*, London, Collins, 1990

Index